EUL VERLAG

PLANUNG, ORGANISATION UND UNTERNEHMUNGSFÜHRUNG

Herausgegeben von Prof. Dr. Dr. h. c. Norbert Szyperski, Köln, Prof. Dr. Udo Winand, Kassel, Prof. (em.) Dr. Joachim Griese, Bern, Prof. Dr. Harald F. O. von Kortzfleisch, Koblenz, Prof. Dr. Ludwig Theuvsen, Göttingen, und Prof. Dr. Jan Marco Leimeister, Kassel

Band 131
Andreas Palm
Post Merger Integration von Unternehmenskulturen – Interkulturelles Integrationskonzept unter besonderer Berücksichtigung einer ganzheitlichen Kommunikationsstrategie
Lohmar – Köln 2012 ◆ 192 S. ◆ € 49,- (D) ◆ ISBN 978-3-8441-0137-9

Band 132
Katja Theuerkorn
Corporate Social Responsibility als Erfolgsfaktor bei M&A-Transaktionen
Lohmar – Köln 2013 ◆ 360 S. ◆ € 64,- (D) ◆ ISBN 978-3-8441-0233-8

Band 133
Christian Zuber
Kulturelle Veränderungen bei international handelnden Unternehmen – Der Bedarf eines kulturellen Managements im internationalen Wertschöpfungsverbund
Lohmar – Köln 2013 ◆ 340 S. ◆ € 63,- (D) ◆ ISBN 978-3-8441-0254-3

Band 134
J. Ruben Dost
Produktionsverlagerungen deutscher Unternehmen nach China – Eine neo-institutionalistische Perspektive
Lohmar – Köln 2014 ◆ 524 S. ◆ € 74,- (D) ◆ ISBN 978-3-8441-0315-1

Band 135
Kerim Galal
Strategic Positioning in the Consulting Industry – An Emperical Analysis of Strategic Groups and Performance
Lohmar – Köln 2014 ◆ 200 S. ◆ € 49,- (D) ◆ ISBN 978-3-8441-0365-6

JOSEF EUL VERLAG

Reihe: Planung, Organisation und Unternehmungsführung · Band 135

Herausgegeben von Prof. Dr. Dr. h. c. Norbert Szyperski, Köln, Prof. Dr. Udo Winand, Kassel, Prof. (em.) Dr. Joachim Griese, Bern, Prof. Dr. Harald F. O. von Kortzfleisch, Koblenz, Prof. Dr. Ludwig Theuvsen, Göttingen, und Prof. Dr. Jan Marco Leimeister, Kassel

Dr. Kerim Galal

Strategic Positioning in the Consulting Industry

An Emperical Analysis of Strategic Groups and Performance

With a Foreword by Prof. Ansgar Richter, PhD,
EBS Universität für Wirtschaft und Recht

EUL VERLAG

Bibliografische Information der Deutschen Nationalbibliothek

Die Deutsche Nationalbibliothek verzeichnet diese Publikation in der Deutschen Nationalbibliografie; detaillierte bibliografische Daten sind im Internet über <http://dnb.d-nb.de> abrufbar.

Dissertation, EBS Universität für Wirtschaft und Recht, Wiesbaden, 2013, unter dem Titel: Strategic Positioning in the Consulting Industry: Strategic Groups and Performance

ISBN 978-3-8441-0365-6
1. Auflage November 2014

JOSEF EUL VERLAG GmbH
Brandsberg 6
53797 Lohmar
Tel.: 0 22 05 / 90 10 6-6
Fax: 0 22 05 / 90 10 6-88
E-Mail: info@eul-verlag.de
http://www.eul-verlag.de

Bei der Herstellung unserer Bücher möchten wir die Umwelt schonen. Dieses Buch ist daher auf säurefreiem, 100% chlorfrei gebleichtem, alterungsbeständigem Papier nach DIN 6738 gedruckt.

FOREWORD

Over the past 30 years, strategy scholars from different schools of thought have argued that in order to outperform others, firms need to "position" themselves carefully against their competitors. However, not all companies in the industry of a given firm are of equal importance as competitors for the firm concerned: A firm may be relatively similar with some firms on many dimensions, and thus compete more directly with these firms, than with those others with which it shares very few characteristics except for their belongingness to their respective industry. "Strategic groups" are those groups of firms that follow relatively similar positioning strategies, so that these firms compete "head on" with one another. This very similarity raises the question as to how firms – in particular new market entrants trying to take market share from their established competitors – can offer distinct product or service propositions that will induce customers to transact with them. "Strategic balance theory" – an approach spearheaded by authors such as Deephouse (1999), Porac et al. (1989) and Semadeni (2006) – proposes that a firm's optimum positioning strategy balances the advantages of differentiation and uniqueness with those of similarity with established companies at the core of a strategic group e.g., in terms of increased legitimacy and greater recognisability.

In his work, Kerim Galal applies strategic group theory to the German management consulting industry, and provides an empirical test of the performance effects of alternative positioning strategies of management consulting firms. Due to its explosive growth since the 1960s, the consulting sector constitutes an important, yet largely under-researched industry, and little is known about the strategies of the players in this industry. By addressing both descriptive and explanatory research questions, Galal's work casts new light on these issues. At its core is its empirical research, specifically the analysis of the "service expositions" through which consulting firms communicate the nature of their services to clients. In order to ascertain these service expositions, Galal conducts content analysis of the websites of 233 consulting firms active in the German market. He then uses the findings in order to cluster the firms into distinct strategic groups and tests for associations between the positioning of firms within their respective group and their performance.

Overall, Galal finds evidence of three distinct strategic groups of consulting firms that operate in the German market, which he describes as "Standardized Solution Providers", "Functional Specialists" and "Functional Generalists". For the former two groups, his analyses confirm the predictions of strategic balance theory that "secondary firms" outperform "core" firms, as they reap the advantages of both positioning near to and away from other competitors. In contrast, for Functional Generalists the opposite holds true. This "mixed" finding provides the author with a strong basis for raising important questions about the generalizability of strategic balance theory. Furthermore, he finds support for the notion that young firms that position close to "core" firms reap performance advantages from this approach, whereas older firms should differentiate themselves more in order to carve out distinctive positions. Overall, the author shows that the core insight of strategic balance theory – regarding the benefits of positioning on the "competitive cusp", especially for new market entrants – holds in some, but not in all strategic group settings. As a result, he concludes that strategic balance theory applies only under certain boundary conditions.

Kerim Galal's work provides an important analysis of strategic positioning efforts of firms in the German consulting market. It is rich in terms of both empirical evidence and theoretical discussion. As such, it offers insights that are likely to be valuable for different groups of audiences. Practitioners and industry observers are going to find this thesis uniquely helpful as it provides clarity on both the macro- and the micro-strategies of consulting firms active in Germany i.e., the overall service portfolio choices they make (which types of services to offer at all), and the specific communicative positioning of these service offerings vis-à-vis their clients. Strategy scholars will benefit from the in-depth discussion of the strengths and limitations of strategic group theory in general, and of strategic balance theory in particular. It is to be hoped that this book finds the wide readership it deserves.

Frankfurt, June 2013 — Prof. Ansgar Richter, PhD

ACKNOWLEDGMENTS

This thesis is a result of my work as a doctoral student and research assistant at the Department of Strategy, Organization and Leadership at the EBS Business School in Oestrich-Winkel, Germany, and as a visiting researcher at Università Commerciale Luigi Bocconi in Milan, Italy, between March 2007 and July 2009. During this time I had the privilege of working together with a number of exceptional people to whom I express my deepest gratitude.

First, I would like to thank my supervisor, Professor Ansgar Richter, who continuously encouraged me to follow my path and provided constructive feedback and helpful advice throughout my work. Without his support this thesis would not have been possible. I also owe thanks to my second supervisor, Professor Alexander Pohl who was so kind to supervise my thesis and provide me with valuable feedback. Furthermore, I would like to thank Professor Michael Gibbert who contributed to my project during my time in Milan.

In addition, I would like to thank my colleagues at EBS specifically at the Department of Strategy, Organization and Leadership, who made my doctoral experience meaningful. Furthermore, I thank my closest friends who constantly motivated and challenged me to engage in this project.

Without the unconditional support of my family to who I express my warmest gratitude and love, this thesis could not have been possible.

I dedicate this doctoral thesis to my beloved parents.

Stuttgart, June 2013 Kerim Galal

TABLE OF CONTENTS

List of Tables

List of Figures

LIST OF ABBREVIATIONS

cf.	Compare with
Consultant	External management consultant
e.g.	For example
etc.	Et cetera
HR	Human resources
i.e.	Id est
IO	Industrial organization
IT	Information technology
LR	Likelihood ratio
M	Arithmetic mean
N	Number of observations
NIE	New institutional economics
P	Probability
R^2	Coefficient of determination
RBV	Resource-based view
SD	Standard deviation

1 INTRODUCTION

1.1 Background and motivation

In his seminal paper on the dynamic theory of strategy Michael E. Porter (1991) stated that in *competitive markets firms need to develop competitive positioning strategies carefully relative to their competitors* in order to *achieve enduring competitive success.* In my research, I intend to determine what impact strategic positioning in the competitive management consulting market has on firm performance.

Strategic similarity is the underlying concept, which constitutes a firm's different positioning possibilities in relation to its competitors (Deephouse, 1999). Deephouse (1999, p. 148) defines strategic similarity "as a firm-level construct representing the extent to which a firm's strategic position resembles the strategic positions of other firms competing in its market at a particular point in time". Ecological research offers the concept of 'competitive intensity', which is analogous to strategic similarity. Competitive intensity stands for the nearness of a firm to other firms in terms of a set of shared strategic dimensions (Baum & Mezias, 1992). Chen (1996, p. 101) defines competitors as "firms operating in the same industry, offering similar products/services, and targeting similar clients". He adds that a firm will experience "different degrees of competitive tension, the extent to which the firm would consider a given competitor as a primary competitor, from each of its competitors" because of existing differences along strategic dimensions. In line with this, competitive asymmetry theory suggests that a given pair of firms may not pose an equal threat to each other. Within this research, I aim to respond to Semadeni's (2006, p. 183) criticism that "competitive asymmetry has been largely absent from strategy research, particularly in research on positioning".

In its two extremes, strategic management research suggests that a firm has two dichotomous options to position itself in a market: to position near to or to position far from its competitors (Deephouse, 1999; Galal & Richter, 2007; Porac, Thomas, & Baden-Fuller, 1989; Semadeni, 2006). However, both positioning efforts impose advantages and disadvantages on the respective firm. While there are advantages to positioning one's services close to those of other established market players, e.g. in terms of increased legitimacy (Suchman, 1995) in an increasingly crowded market place the relative benefits of positioning differently from competitors should increase. Porter (2008) sums up that the appropriate positioning strategy can build defenses against competition or find a position where competitive forces are low.

Developed within cognitive research, strategic management scholars introduced a third hybrid positioning strategy which proposes that strategists need to balance positioning efforts on the "competitive cusp" (Porac, et al., 1989). Research on strategic positioning proposes that firms seek 'balance' between the forces pulling them toward or pushing them away from each other to maximize the advantages (and minimize the disadvantages) of both proximity and distance (Deephouse, 1999; McNamara, Deephouse, & Luce, 2003; Semadeni, 2006). In other words, firm strategists need to balance the positioning between simultaneous pressures both to conform and to differentiate from competitors (Deephouse, 1999; McNamara, et al., 2003; Porac, et al., 1989; Semadeni, 2006). In line with this, Abrahamson and Hegeman (1994) found that strategic conformity between firms diminishes not only competitive risk, but at the same time opportunities for competitive advantage. Empirical evidence in the strategic management literature supports this notion of the theory of strategic balance (e.g. Deephouse, 1999; McNamara, et al., 2003; Semadeni, 2006). For instance, Deephouse (1999) analyzed the trade-off between legitimacy and differentiation with regard to similarity between commercial banks, finding that successful banks try to establish balance between the conflicting forces in the individual asset portfolios.

If strategic balance theorists are right than positioning on the competitive cusp is always superior and is not dependent on industry or firm specifics. However, the range of strategic balance theory is not sufficiently examined and empirically analyzed, yet. I propose that the temporal and contextual factors that set the boundaries of generalizability of the strategic balance theory are not comprehensively addressed and well defined. The theoretical objective of this research is to cast doubt on the generalizability of strategic balance theory and shed light on the boundary conditions of the theory. Herewith, I respond to Whetten's (1989) general statement that "few theorists explicitly focus on the contextual limitations of their propositions". He underlines the responsibility of theorists to discuss the limits of generalizability. Furthermore, he recognizes that the boundary conditions are most likely to be discovered while applying a theory empirically in various settings. In line with this argument, I apply strategic balance theory to the market for management consulting services in order to find evidence for boundary conditions.

Porter's outlined fundamental principle addresses three crucial issues related to the underlying research motivation of this thesis. First, the market for management consulting services – as part of professional service industries – is considered a highly competitive market (Nissen, 2007; Richter & Niewiem, 2004; Semadeni, 2006). Hence, the market for consulting services is characterized by both an external and an internal "unboundedness". The external unboundedness constitutes itself by three attributes. First, the market consists of low barriers to entry and to exit and has no institutional protection (Galal & Richter, 2007; Keeble & Schwalbach, 1995; Semadeni, 2006). Hence, market entry is comparably easy for new consulting firms as it requires only limited investments, mainly in human capital. Furthermore, due to missing institutional protection any firm can claim itself a provider of consulting services without institutional approval. Second, the term 'consulting service' is not clearly defined as there is no broadly accepted definition of what constitutes a consulting service. Third, the external unboundedness is marked by high market dynamics resulting in numerous market entries as well as exits. One third of the firms operating leave the market within five years (Keeble & Schwalbach, 1995). As a consequence, the market is steadily evolving, which fosters a dynamic and competitive market environment. The internal unboundedness of the consulting market results mainly from three aspects. First, there exist no formal requirements for what constitutes a consulting service. Second, service line classifications are largely based on firm reputation. Third, the market is characterized by low mobility barriers and a high intransparency.

In recent years the consulting industry has faced far-reaching changes. Both the demand side and the supply side expanded in the past, which led to overall market growth. As a result, the consulting industry has established high growth rates and mainly above-average profit margins. In addition, the industry has recovered from the severe dip in 2002-2004 and achieved dynamic growth rates (e.g. German consulting market: CAGR 2005-2011 7.8%, according to BDU 2012) despite the negative impact of the financial crisis in 2009 (3.1 % market growth).

The constantly growing demand for consulting services is influenced by the significant increase in complexity of industries, markets, organizations and management responsibilities. Consulting clients face multiple challenges in maintaining high performance levels of their companies. They need to stay up-to-date with recent market developments, process rising quantities of information, adapt to changing needs of their clients and employees, deal with organizational challenges and outperform competing market participants. Established literature on behavioral science and managerial roles calls this a "role overload" – managers have to carry out more roles than they are able to do at the same time (S. P. Brown, Jones, &

Leigh, 2005; Harste, 2008; Jones, Chonko, Rangarajan, & Roberts, 2007; Mintzberg, 1975). In order to fill arising knowledge blanks, to deal with the role overload and to react appropriately to new challenges, managers rely on consultants to profit from their specific knowledge and experience. As a consequence, in many organizations consultants are engaged frequently and have become part of the organizational day-to-day life.

Attractive market opportunities have piqued the interest of numerous new market entrants and of competitors who object to enlarge their market share. A major outcome was an increase in competition and competitive intensity (Armbrüster, 2006; Richter & Schmidt, 2006; Weyrather, 2004). Due to its tremendous growth on the supply as well as on the demand side over the last decades, the market has become highly intransparent to both consultants and clients. This increasing level of competition led to a broader range of choices available to potential clients. However, there exists only limited in-depth information on different positioning efforts and multidimensional segmentations of consulting providers to overcome intransparency and resulting uncertainty. The rising intransparency correlates with increasing levels of uncertainty on both sides of the market. Existing consulting typologies derived by consulting experts or cognitively perceived by managers cover merely the full multidimensional scale of consulting providers. As a result, clients encounter challenges in screening and selecting consulting providers suitable to their specific needs.

On the supply side, transparency on competitors is also limited due to constant entry and exit in the consulting market. In a market with high market participant turnover it is challenging to keep pace with the evolving competitive landscape. As particularly the weaker providers leave the market, overall level of competition is constantly increasing. Furthermore, limited mobility barriers in the market facilitate diversification of the service portfolios of established consulting providers. In order to adapt appropriately to the changing competitive environment it is mandatory for consulting providers to constantly monitor the positioning efforts of their competitors.

Over the last years the consulting market has started to turn into a mature market (Richter & Niewiem, 2004; Toppin & Czerniawska, 2005; Weyrather, 2004) with first symptoms of saturation. The market growth rates are continually decreasing as no fundamentally new service lines arise and frequent users of consulting services are connecting the engagement of consulting to concrete profitability targets. In addition, although demand for consulting services has grown, the demand curve has become more elastic, indicating greater buyer professionalization (Böcklund & Werr, 2005; Galal & Richter, 2007; Hooley, Broderick, &

Moller, 1998). There is evidence that through an increased use of consulting services clients have become more experienced and more cautious in engaging consulting providers (Haferkamp & Drescher, 2006; Werr & Pemer, 2007). In line with this, buyers of consulting services expect a precise value proposition from consultants. Existing research concludes that the balance of power in the consulting-client relationship is shifting towards the client side (Ebrahimchel, Mohe, & Sternzeld, 2006; Galal & Richter, 2007; Richter & Niewiem, 2004). As a consequence, consultants encounter a loss of distance from clients diminishing the unique selling proposition of consulting services.

In line with Porter's second fundamental principle (1991), consulting firms need to develop competitive positioning strategies carefully vis-à-vis their competitors responding to increasing market challenges. The expectation is that consulting firms would benefit from cautiously analyzing their competitors' market positions and improve their own strategic position. Anticipation of future market developments and of dynamic positioning efforts of competitors seems to be a mandatory prerequisite for enduring success. Increased competition, greater buyer professionalization and the resulting shift in the client-consultant relationship pressure consulting firms to professionalize their positioning efforts. Mintzberg (1978) considers competitive positioning to be among the core tasks of managers involved in shaping and implementing a company strategy. Consulting managers need to ensure that the consulting firm's own positioning strategy is adaptive, dynamic and suitable to market conditions. It is no longer sufficient to rely on existing personal relationships with clients or established business relations in order to acquire client assignments. To stay competitive and to attract additional clients, consulting firms need to highlight their contribution and excellence in adding value for their clients. Clear propositions of what is comprised in the service offering, how interaction with clients is intended and what should be the outcome of the service provision are mandatory. Clear-cut strategic positioning in the consulting market segments competitors and allows clients to identify the consulting firm best suited to their individual problem. In addition, the more dominant clients become, the more value they receive by enforcing decreased prices and demanding increased service at a higher quality (Porter, 2008). Furthermore, consulting firms should profit from improving their market exposition as a reaction to the increasing 'war for talent'. Consulting firms compete for the same decreasing pool of talent as their clients do. Thus, top talent as the main asset of consulting firms becomes more expensive to recruit and more difficult to retain.

The third principle addressed by Porter (1991) states that different strategic positioning efforts hold for deviating performance rates. Porter argues that the overall aim of strategic positioning is to achieve superior and sustainable competitive advantage (2008). For a consulting company choosing the right positioning strategy is just as crucial as it is for any other company (Werr & Pemer, 2007). As described, arising market challenges should increase the relative attractiveness for firms to position themselves carefully relative to their competitors. Only few researchers have focused on the positioning efforts of professional service firms and its influence on performance. So, there is still a lack in analyzing the multi-facetted positioning efforts of consulting firms in-depth (Leask & Parker, 2007; Semadeni, 2006). Consulting market experts argue that enduring success in the consulting industry depends on the ability of focusing on appropriate market position and differentiating from competitors (Sommerlatte, 2004; Weyrather, 2004).

Established consulting providers face the danger of loss of uniqueness due to the increase in competition and the fact that barriers to market entry are low. Uniqueness is a particularly important aspect of strategic positioning, especially as competition for grown-up and demanding clients increases. While uniqueness decreases and danger for substitutes increases margins come under pressure and performance rates drop. However, differentiating from competitors does not only hold for advantages as positioning is a constant tradeoff between proximity and differentiation. Proximity to competitors offers also advantages in terms of increase of legitimacy, reduction of uncertainty and potential for spill-over effects (Deephouse, 1999).

Therefore, the tradeoff between differentiation and proximity to competitors – as proposed by strategic balance theory - should be analyzed in-depth for the consulting market in terms of their influence on performance. I expect to find significant differences in how management consulting firms advertise their services to potential clients and in the resulting success.

1.2 Research Objectives

In my research, I will apply strategic group theory to the professional service industry, more specifically, to the market for consulting services in Germany. Professional service firms are of rising interest as they are presumed to be different from other companies and demand for distinct management theories arises (Greenwood, Li, Prakash, & Deephouse, 2005; Maister, 1993; von Nordenflycht, 2010). Professional service research agrees that especially empirical research beyond law and account firms is needed (von Nordenflycht,

2010). In general, research on strategy of professional service firms is still limited (Ou & Chai, 2007). As described the consulting market is highly intangible and research has not taken its full complexity into account. In my research, I aim to determine what effect the careful strategic positioning of consulting firms' offerings in the market has on performance.

The question of positioning near to or far from competitors in professional services and its implications on firm performance has not been sufficiently addressed in strategic group literature (Greenwood, Deephouse, & Li, 2007; Greenwood, et al., 2005; McNamara, et al., 2003; Semadeni, 2006). While there are advantages to position one's services close to those of other established service providers, e. g. in terms of increased legitimacy, in an increasingly crowded market place the relative benefits of positioning differently from other providers should increase. The outlined changes of an increasingly competitive market suggest that service firms should benefit from positioning their service offerings carefully in the market. Services in particular are hard for buyers to define ex ante and difficult to evaluate ex post (Clark, 1993, 1995; Ebrahimchel, et al., 2006; Ernst & Kieser, 2002; McLachlin, 2000; Nachum, 1999). Due to the specific characteristics of services, professional service firms have to rely on verbal expositions of their service offerings. Especially, firms that have not had the opportunity to build up reputation and brand, need to use service expositions in order to capture the interest and imagination of their potential clients and to communicate their positioning. However, little is known so far about how consulting firms position themselves in the market.

On the basis of strategic positioning, professional service firms – consulting firms active in the German market – will be examined with respect to the existence of strategic groups and performance differences. In order to determine existing positioning efforts and their impact on performance closely, I will apply strategic balance theory. This leads to a deeper understanding of the existence of strategic groups in the German consulting market and of how strategic positioning efforts influence the performance of professional service firms.

Furthermore, this research aims to shed light on the existence of boundary conditions that limit the generalizability of the strategic balance theory. Rather that merely reaffirming theory, the objective is to contribute to the definition of limiting constraints and the range of the theory.

To summarize, I will address the following three research questions:

1. **Given the economic characteristics of consulting services, into which strategic groups is the German consulting market segmented?**

2. **What is the effect of strategic positioning on the performance of consulting firms in Germany?**

3. **What do we learn from this for strategic positioning theory in general?**

1.3 Research Approach

1.3.1 Defining the Research Approach

The outlined research objectives have particular implications regarding the research approach. The underlying theoretical foundation, unit of analysis, data collection, measures, and methodology of my thesis are described in the following.

I will draw my research on the body of literature on strategy, strategic positioning, strategic groups and professional service firms. In more detail, the theoretical foundation of my research will be built on strategic balance theory and strategic group theory.

My twofold empirical research is described as both: exploratory and deductive. First, within my empirical strategic group analysis on German consulting firms, I will provide a new segmentation to the consulting market and expect the detection of strategic groups. Second, I will use the outcome of this empirical study to further test hypotheses and propositions derived from existing theory on the relation between strategic positioning and its impact on performance.

Management literature provides only little empirically approved approaches to asses positioning without relying on perceptional constructs. Even though efforts have been made towards the conceptualization and development of positioning typologies, results to this point are not convincing (Blankson & Kalafatis, 2004). Results are either descriptive, based on limited empirical evidence or reflect managerial views. The main challenge is to assess divergent positioning efforts of single firms and to find a plausible way to relate them to one another. Most studies analyze positioning from a demand side perspective and thereby utilize the perceptions of managers and customers of different competitive positions. As proposed earlier, the focus of this work lies on the communicated strategic positioning and is not based on perceptions of individuals.

I will concentrate my research on the supply-side of the market for consulting services. The objective is to focus on the existing differences in strategic positioning. I will intentionally leave the perceived positioning - by clients and competitors - out of my research focus (cf. Figure 1). Therefore, the strategic positioning of professional service firms - consulting firms active in the German market - as exposed on their websites will be the unit of analysis. In order to collect representative data, I will involve independent raters who are instructed to apply well-defined rating rules to compare the strategic positioning of German consulting firms in-depth.

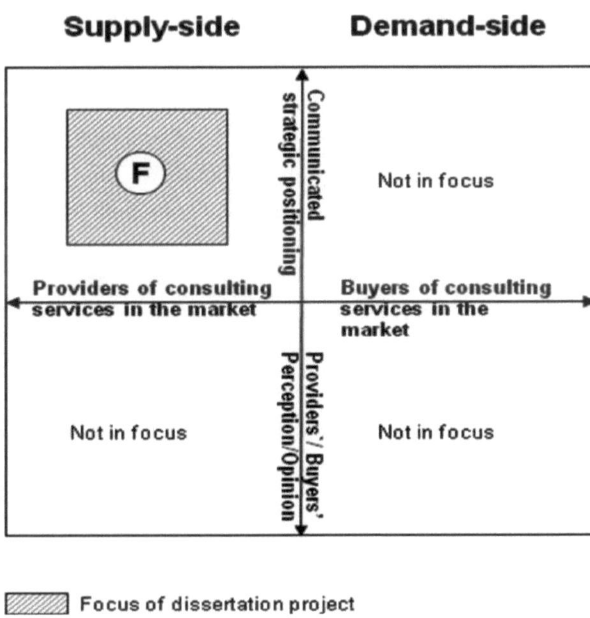

Figure 1: Focus of the Research Approach

To determine differences in strategic positioning between consulting firms I use three key dimensions: the type of service model, intended relation with the client, and degree of functional and sectoral specialization. In addition, I use a number of firm characteristics in order to shed light on firm specifics and their influence on competitive positioning.

1.3.2 Defining the Consulting Market

Dranove, Peteraf, & Shanley (1998) state that "anyone who has ever struggled over market definition knows: To define industries, is more art than science". Obviously, to define industries - like management consulting - that are highly dynamic and characterized by low barriers to entry and exit with limited institutional protection of the profession is even more challenging. However, the aim of this section is to shed light on the definition of management consulting services as part of the professional service industry and the market analyzed within this study.

Professional service firms represent an intensively studied area and over recent years a substantial body of knowledge resulted (e.g. Greenwood, et al., 2007; Richter & Schroeder, 2008; von Nordenflycht, 2010). However, existing research is providing merely undefined or indirectly defined characteristics and classifications of professional service firms. To this end, a lack of boundary conditions and a correlating ambiguity of what professional services comprise burden research on the distinctiveness of professional service firms. From an economist's perspective, professional services are subsumed under the primary services as they are carried out explicitly by service providers. They differ from secondary services in that these services are delivered by product companies as a supplement (Niewiem, 2005).

Nordenflycht (2010) reviewed 52 recent articles on professional services in reputable publications and derived three distinctive characteristics to describe and classify professional service firms: knowledge intensity, capital intensity, and a professionalized workforce. Different levels of these dimensions result into separate classes of professional service firms. Greenwood et al. (2005, p. 661) define professional service firms from an input-output perspective as "those whose primary assets are a highly educated (professional) workforce and whose outputs are intangible services encoded with complex knowledge". Some researchers assert that professional service firms create indistinguishable credence goods (Armbrüster, 2004; Fincham, 1999; Harste, 2008).

Commonly, the main characteristics of professional services are described as intangibility, inseparability, heterogeneity, and perishability (Blankson & Kalafatis, 2007; Clark, 1993; Harste, 2008). In other words, professional services are individual and mostly customized, intangible services which are regularly developed in interaction with the client. Furthermore, professional services are produced and consumed at the same time. Building on this, management consulting services are subsumed under the "narrow set of canonical industries" of professional services (von Nordenflycht, 2010, p. 155). However, Nordenflycht (2010) states that existing literature focuses mainly on accounting and law firms which deviate to some extent from other professional service firms e.g. management consulting. Management consulting services differ from professional services in terms of more diverse body of knowledge, limited professional standards, and lower entry barriers (Niewiem, 2005).

Based on the general characteristics of professional services, Greiner & Metzger (1983, p. 7) describe consultants that deliver management consulting services as "specially trained and qualified persons who assist, in an objective manner, the client organization to identify and analyze management problems, recommend solutions and help in the implementation of those solutions.

Within this research, the analyzed supply side of the German consulting market is defined as the sum of all external management consulting firms active in Germany. However, the German market for consulting services is a little delineated market and the population of consulting providers can hardly be comprehensively determined. Any precise and exhaustive lists of consulting firms active in the German market do not exist. As a consequence, I rely in my empirical research on a compilation of the available lists of consulting firms in deriving the sample for this research (cf. Chapter 3.2.1).

According to estimates of the Bundesverband Deutscher Unternehmensberater (BDU), a German industry association, around 14.250 consulting firms were offering consulting services to clients in Germany as of 2006 (BDU, 2006). The total market size in terms of revenues is estimated to account for EUR 14.7 billion (the selling unit booking the revenue is localized in Germany). The estimates are based on the in Figure 2 depicted definition of consulting services and consulting providers. However, this estimation is likely to be conservative as calculations are based on the limited number of members of the industry association.

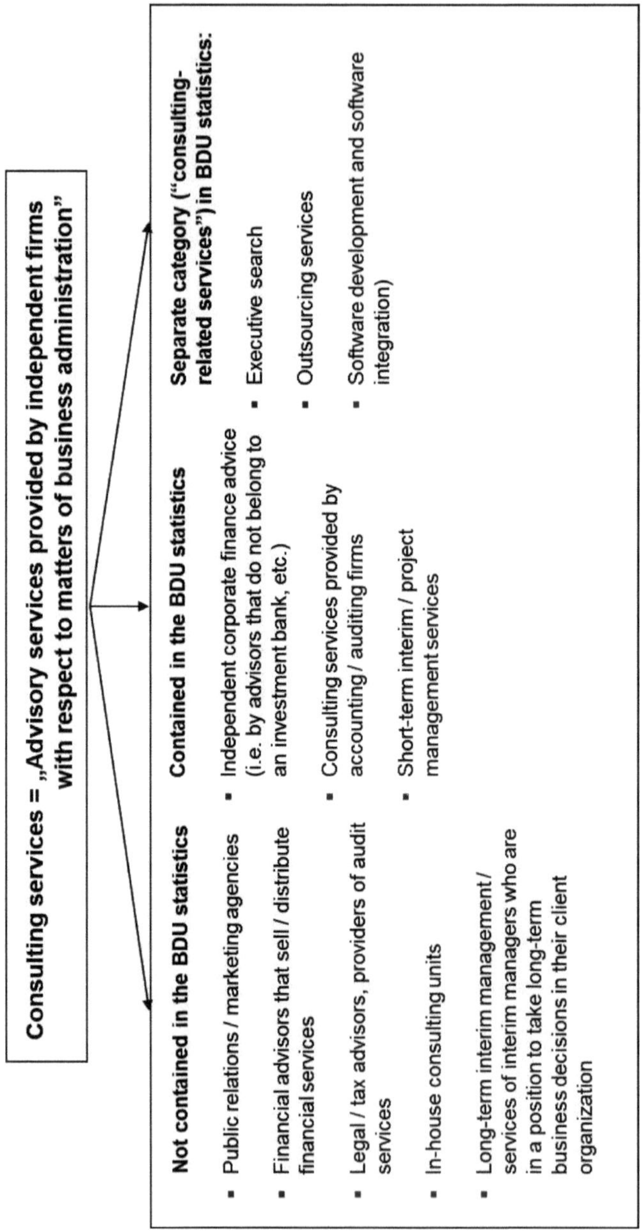

Figure 2: Definition of Consulting Firms active in the German Market

1.4 Structure of the Thesis

This thesis comprises six chapters. Chapter 1 gives an introduction to the motivation and background of my study. The research objectives, research questions and the research approach are derived.

Chapter 2 gives an overview of existing theory on strategic positioning and strategic groups. The discussion of the notion of strategic positioning and different key dimensions of positioning is followed by an examination of the three main positioning strategies. Next, strategic group theory is comprehensively introduced. A special focus is given to strategic groups as an intermediary perspective between industry and firm level. This is followed by a literature review and an evaluation of theoretical approaches and concepts in strategic group research. The next section includes empirical evidence on the existence of strategic groups and on the relationship between strategic groups and performance. Based on the discussion of theoretically derived arguments, four research hypotheses are developed pertaining to the existence of strategic groups and the relationships between strategic groups, strategic positioning and performance.

Chapter 3 introduces the empirical approach and the methodology applied. It contains the description of the data collection, operationalization of the variables and rating rules and a depiction of the analytical methods employed in the empirical study.

Chapter 4 presents the results of my analysis. First, I provide the strategic group structure derived from cluster analyses. Second, descriptive statistics of the main variables used in the cluster analysis and additional firm characteristics are described. Third, the results of additional empirical analysis as well as the results of the regressions on performance are exhibited.

Chapter 5 discusses the findings. It reviews the results in light of the research hypotheses and refers to the objectives of the study. It concludes with a discussion of practical implications for consulting firms and their clients.

Chapter 6 summarizes the outcome of the study and presents starting points for future research.

2 THEORY ON STRATEGIC POSITIONING AND STRATEGIC GROUPS

2.1 Strategic Positioning

2.1.1 Theoretical Background

In the following chapter the theoretical foundation for this research is introduced. First, strategic positioning is defined and discussed with respect to the market for consulting services. Second, the concept of key dimensions within strategic positioning is presented. Building on this concept, strategic dimensions relevant for this research are derived and explained.

2.1.1.1 The Notion of Strategic Positioning

In order to remain successful in the long run, a firm has to carefully position itself in the market vis-à-vis its customers and competitors (Blankson & Kalafatis, 2004; Blankson, Kalafatis, Cheng, & Hadjicharalambous, 2008). In his seminal work on strategy, Porter (1996) asserts support for the relationship between strategic positioning and the long term success of firms. In addition, he stresses the argument that opting to focus on strategic positioning rather than on operational efficiency leads to advantageous benefits of successful long term growth. In the strategic management literature, strategic positioning is defined as the deliberate crafted actions of a firm that impel the firm to achieve a competitive position within a given market structure (e.g. Kalafatis, Tsogas, & Blankson, 2000; Porter, 1991; Ries & Trout, 1986; Trout, 1996). By matching company abilities with market requirements, strategic positioning represents the way a firm faces competition in those markets the firm serves (Hooley, et al., 1998). Scholars conceptualize strategy in this context as a firm's realized position in its competitive market (Mintzberg, 1987; Porter, 1980) and as the management's efforts to create a unique and valuable position in the market place (Porter, 1996). Managers deem to strategically position their firms relative to their competitors in order to be successful in the long run (McKenna, 1986; Ries & Trout, 1986; Wright, 1997). In consequence, managers are obliged to concentrate not only on the firm's own strengths and the given market opportunities, but also to consider the actions of their competitors. From a market perspective, the aim of strategic positioning is to keep the customer focused on the added value of a firm's offering (Ries & Trout, 1986; Trout, 1996).

For the purpose of this research, strategic positioning is defined as:

The long term oriented deliberate crafted actions that the management of a firm undertakes in order to position the added value of the firm's offerings (products or services) relative to competitors and vis-à-vis potential customers in a given market structure.

Perspectives on strategic positioning

In order to further identify important characteristics of strategic positioning, two perspectives are referred to structure the main influencing factors of strategic positioning (Barney, 1991; Hooley, et al., 1998): the internal and the external perspective on strategic positioning. In addition to these two perspectives, I will introduce a third perspective on strategic positioning: the communicated positioning.

First, the internal perspective relates to the strategic choices a company takes in regard to resources and associated activities. In line with this, each company's strategic position is dependent on its resources and capabilities (Barney, 1991). This reflects the commonly shared notion that resources and positions are two sides of the same coin (e.g. Deephouse, 1999; Wernerfelt, 1984). From an organizational theory perspective, a firm's realized strategic position corresponds to an organization's actual domain, which is the markets an organization serves and the resources and capabilities it uses to serve them (Deephouse, 1999; Haveman, 1993; Levine & White, 1961). The internal perspective will not be considered in this study.

I suggest an extension of the internal view, the 'intended strategic positioning'. The notion of the 'intended strategic positioning' implies that managers aim at certain market positions for their firms and try to alter strategic actions of the firms accordingly. Nevertheless, the extent to which a firm realizes the intended market positioning depends on a variety of influences. Therefore, the intended positioning might deviate significantly from the actual realized positioning of a firm in the market. Furthermore, the management of a firm might intentionally keep elements of the intended positioning strategy within the firm and not communicate them externally, in order to secretly pursue a strategy. This diminishes the threat of imitation by competitors. However, other market participants might also differ significantly in their perception of the firm's market position. So, there is certainly a discrepancy between the intended positioning, the perceived positioning and the realized positioning. Nevertheless, an analysis to relate the perspectives is not included in this thesis.

Second, the external perspective considers the competitive advantage a company achieves relative to other companies within the same market. A common definition describes competitive advantage as the condition "when a firm earns a higher rate of economic profit than the average rate of economic profit of other firms competing within the same market" (Besanko, Dranove, & Shanley, 2000, p. 389). In consequence, the competitive advantage can be regarded as the outcome of strategic choices that managers take. However, competitive advantage is not anymore – especially in service industries – based on physical 'bricks-and-mortar' assets, but more on 'invisible assets' like brand, customer loyalty and reputation (Makadok, 1998). In addition, as features of competing firms' offerings are becoming less distinctive, intangible factors gain significance. However, invisible assets are merely externally perceived and not directly subjected to or influenced by managerial strategic choice. Conversely, some scholars state that invisible assets are in general easier to imitate and to circumvent by substitutions (Itami, 1987; Makadok, 1998). Therefore, recent strategic management research challenges the traditional perspective, namely the 'sustainability model' that argues that competitive advantage is sustainable. Researchers state that in today's economic environment the notion of sustainability is outdated (cf. Makadok, 1998). Today's economies are characterized by fast-paced, dynamic developments in increasingly global markets. Consistently, in these dynamic, 'hypercompetitive' markets (e.g. professional service industries) competitive advantage increasingly based on invisible assets is not sustainable in the sense it used to be in oligopolistic, static markets with high barriers to entry and exit (Gimeno & Woo, 1996).

For these reasons, managers have to position the offerings of their firms in a way that succeeds in gaining positive external perception and contributes positively to their set of 'invisible assets'. Thus, strategic positioning of the firm and its offerings in the marketplace – including the management of reputation and manipulation of consumer perceptions – gains even more importance (Blankson, et al., 2008). In line with this, strategic positioning is considered by academics as well as by practitioners to be one of the key elements of modern management (Blankson & Kalafatis, 2004).

As an extension of traditional perspectives, I introduce the concept of the 'communicated positioning', which serves as a bridging element to the external and internal perspectives on positioning. It is linked to both perspectives as it is derived from the internal view, but reflected in the external view on positioning. Hereby, I define the positioning efforts of a firm that are externally perceivable and explicitly expressed (e.g. verbally) by the management of a firm. This concept influences the actual market position of a firm as it is objectively observable by the organizational field of a firm. Especially within service industries, communication as a means of marketing to promote a firm's service offerings within relevant markets is of significant importance. As a consequence, the communicated positioning serves as a means of placing a firm's offerings in the market as services are merely promoted through rhetoric. This is relevant because the communicated positioning is generally not identical with the 'intended strategic positioning' and the perceived strategic positioning. However, all three contribute to the realized strategic positioning. Therefore, managers' interest should be to align the intended, communicated and perceived strategic positioning of their firms.

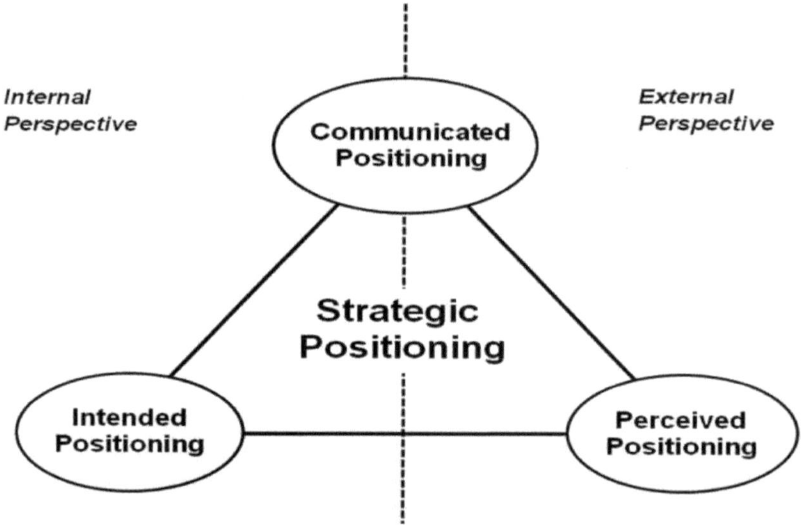

Figure 3: Perspectives on Strategic Positioning

The overall aim of strategic positioning is to achieve competitive advantages over competitors and to thereby realize superior and sustainable performance. Furthermore, a firm's ideal strategic positioning highlights these strategic dimensions that are either distinctive from or similar to those of competitors depending on the followed strategy.

Within this research, I concentrate on the external perspective of strategic positioning and on the communicated positioning within this research. In a sense, this draws attention to the strategic positioning of firms as perceivable by customers and competitors. Nevertheless, the perspective of this thesis is based on the company view. It omits that marketing research defines positioning from the perception of the customer or client (Kalafatis, et al., 2000). Consistently, positioning is conceptualized as "a complex multidimensional construct that attempts to positively adjust the tangible characteristics" of a firm's offering and "the intangible perceptions of the offering in the marketplace in relation to competition" (Blankson, et al., 2008). With this thesis, I aim at analyzing strategic positioning of professional service firms on the basis of comparing their service offerings as communicated by the firms themselves. Thus, I will not focus on perception-based concepts e.g. customer loyalty, reputation, and brand name of a firm within this research. These aspects are only measurable based on the perceptions of market participants and consistently not the focus of this research.

Although considerable research exists on strategic positioning, key areas remain still unexplored (e.g. Semadeni, 2006). Research on positioning has in large parts concentrated on industries with tangible products with well-known characteristics, e.g. automotive industry (L. Thomas & Weigelt, 2000), semiconductors industry (Stuart & Podolny, 1996), well-defined services such as radio market positioning (Greve, 1998) or hotel lodging (Baum & Haveman, 1997). The question that remains largely unanswered is whether the implications found by these previous positioning studies hold for industries such as professional services that are marked by specific characteristics and challenges to clearly define relative market positions between competitors (Semadeni, 2006). In order to address this existing research gap, this thesis focuses on the strategic positioning efforts of consulting firms.

Strategic positioning of consulting services

For consulting firms, strategic positioning is particularly important due to the nature of services concerned (Galal & Richter, 2007). While the principles of strategic positioning apply to both products and services, the explicit characteristics of services have certain implications on strategic positioning efforts. Recognition of the presence of certain distinctive characteristics remains important in order to understand positioning options of professional service firms (Easingwood & Mahajan, 1989; Levitt, 1981). The fact that services are "essentially acts or experiences" implies that services are characteristically inseparable – produced and consumed simultaneously (Devlin, Ennew, & Mirza, 1995; George & Berry, 1981). The characteristic of inseparability points to the essential role that customers have in the production of services. In line with this, the categorization of services more as an act than an object emphasizes the individuals who provide the service and their interactions with the customer (Devlin, et al., 1995; Skaggs & Youndt, 2004). Therefore, the service quality is highly dependent on personal interactions and potential for variability exists. The interaction between consultant and client in the provision of services leads to another typical service characteristic, namely heterogeneity. Consulting services are heterogeneous due to their interactive character and the fact that the delivered services are the result of dialectic between the client and the consultant. Consequently, the outcome of intangible, experience-intensive consulting services is heterogeneous and hard for buyers to define *ex ante* and to evaluate *ex post* (Clark, 1993, 1995; Ebrahimchel, et al., 2006; Ernst & Kieser, 2002; McLachlin, 2000; Nachum, 1999). Nevertheless, the extent of some of the distinctions between products and services has been questioned by management scholars (Levitt, 1981; Middleton, 1983). For instance, the characteristic of intangibility of services in contrast to tangible products has been subject of extensive discussion within management research. Scholars argue that creating a distinct dichotomy in the positioning of products and services solely based on the characteristic of intangibility neglects the fact that even products are intangible to a certain degree (Cowell, 1989; Levitt, 1981). For example, the functionality of a product remains intangible ex ante a product is bought.

However, the impact or success of a service is difficult to measure even after service delivery (Armbrüster, 2004). Consequently, significant information asymmetry between the providers and the buyers of consulting services exists (Clark, 1993; Sharma, 1997). It is difficult for clients to determine how services are actually produced and to compare the service offerings across competing firms (Skaggs & Youndt, 2004). This fact makes it difficult to find the right value and pricing for the delivered consulting services (Mitchell, 1994). In addition, consulting contrary to other professional services (e.g. medical doctors, accountants and lawyers) is not a legally protected profession. Therefore, clients have no institutional certainty about the quality of consulting firms (Armbrüster, 2004). In line with this, consulting services have only limited intellectual property protection. This complicates comparative evaluations of the quality of the offerings across firms (Makadok, 1998; Semadeni, 2006). Due to the confidentiality of the delivered services and the often close involvement of clients in the provision of the services, consulting firms are not able to provide samples of their work a priori (unless they are for very routinized services) (Galal & Richter, 2007). This means, at the time of sale the belief in the rhetoric being espoused by the consultants is of high importance to the client.

The outlined characteristics of consulting services suggest that a consulting firm should benefit from putting significant effort in shaping its service exposition in order to point out its market positioning to potential clients and competitors. Furthermore, a clear description of what the consulting firm does and how it adds value for clients enhances client satisfaction and the probability of future success (Ou & Chai, 2007). However, the specific characteristics of consulting services, especially their intangible nature and the difficulties to create and maintain a competitive advantage on the strength of service-level features, put considerable emphasis on reflection of the organization as a whole (Devlin, et al., 1995). In order to precisely analyze the positioning of a consulting firm, it is of great importance to consider its service model as well as its specific firm characteristics (e.g. age, size, internationality, origin) in accordance.

Intangible assets such as reputation and brand name serve as means to preserve a dominant and successful market position for professional service firms (Lange, Lee, & Dai, 2011; Shamsie, 2003). Dominant and established consulting firms use information asymmetries on competitors and providers of substitute services in order to maintain their superior and reputable market position vis-à-vis their clients and competitors. Therefore, even established consulting firms are declined to provide meaningful service expositions to attract new clients and maintain their existing client base. Moreover, in particular, young and small consulting firms that have not had the opportunity to build up reputation and strong brand image are obliged to draw on service expositions. They need to do so in order to capture the interest and imagination of potential clients. Furthermore, service expositions serve as indicators to whether and how a firm's services are similar to or different from those of established competitors (Galal & Richter, 2007).

In summary, due to their specific characteristics, strategic positioning of consulting services can be more complex than the positioning of products because of the challenge to communicate vague and intangible benefits to the client (Blankson & Kalafatis, 1999). Consequently, consulting firms espouse their service offerings in form of rhetoric to potential clients. Consulting firms use service expositions as a means of communicating their strategic positioning in the market.

2.1.1.2 Dimensions of Strategic Positioning

Strategic positioning is conceptualized as a complex construct, consisting of multiple interconnected dimensions that are mutually exclusive and complementary (Blankson, et al.,

2008; Hooley, et al., 1998). As a consequence, strategy researchers seek to determine the factors that lead to failure and long term success of a firm within its respective market environment (Porter, 1991). As stated above, the importance of examining strategic positioning is supported by assertions of a positive relationship between firm performance and well-formulated, clearly defined positioning strategies (Porter, 1996). Nevertheless, there is only limited clear empirical evidence on strategic positioning and its effects on firm performance (Hooley & Greenley, 2005; Suzuki, 2000). However, the aim is to understand the causes of success for firms, relative to their competitors, in order to adjust firm strategy accordingly. Isolating the determinants of success and failure leads to a fine-grained comparison of firms based on their market positions, which they obtain vis-à-vis their clients and relative to their competitors. By identifying relevant strategic dimensions and relating them to success, a firm can determine its performance based on a set of strategic dimensions in relation to competing firms. As a result, the appropriate selection of strategic dimensions outlines a firm's strategic position on its market by differentiating it from its competitors and comparing performance differences.

Within strategic management literature various dimensions have been conceptualized and applied to assess strategic positioning efforts within different industries. Scholars have designed various positioning typologies in order to structure analyses of firms' positioning efforts. However, review of existing literature reveals that most of the positioning typologies are purely conceptual (e.g. Aaker & Shansby, 1982; Blankson & Kalafatis, 2004; Collier & Meyer, 1998; Silvestro, 1999; Wind, 1982). In addition, many typologies are based on limited empirical evidence (e.g. Arnott, 1992; Easingwood & Mahajan, 1989; Kalafatis, et al., 2000) or reflect in particular perceptional managerial views (Blankson & Kalafatis, 2004). Therefore, numerous scholars call for further research on strategic dimensions that focus consistently on the specific industry and type of firms examined (e.g. Blankson, et al., 2008; Hooley & Greenley, 2005; Hooley, Greenley, Fahy, & Cadogan, 2001; Kalra & Goodstein, 1998; Miles & Mangold, 2005).

In line with this, Semadeni (2006) criticizes positioning research that considers only single dimensions as "an incomplete and potentially inaccurate perspective on positioning dynamics". The management scholar argues that by probing multiple dimensions, a more precise understanding of positioning will evolve. Consequently, he suggests to consider multiple strategic dimensions to precisely evaluate what affects the strategic positioning decision of a single firm and to analyze it in relation to the firm's competitors (cf. Devlin, et al., 1995). Literature on professional services, specifically consulting services, agrees with this notion and argues for a multidimensional assessment of consulting service models and positioning efforts that result from them (e.g. Armbrüster, 2006; Galal & Richter, 2007). In the following, subsequent to a brief definition of what constitutes a service model and an explanation of service expositions, a set of strategic dimensions relevant for the consulting market is introduced and discussed.

Service model

The decision of what strategic positioning to pursue is influenced by the notion of a firm's service model (Galal & Richter, 2007; Galal, Richter, & Wendlandt, 2012; Richter & Schmidt, 2006):

A service model is a system of mechanisms and procedures through which providers use heterogeneous resources to generate and deliver services that they can sell to clients.

This model draws strongly on input-output models used in economics, which are often illustrated with examples from manufacturing industries (e.g. Adam Smith's famous example of the production of pins). Consulting firms use individual and organizational capabilities as well as financing and physical resources in combination with client access and brands as input factors in order to generate and deliver services. The interaction with the client is of major importance within the process of service provision and delivery (Skaggs & Youndt, 2004). The degree and quality of client interaction relies heavily on the human capital of a service provider. Skaggs and Youndt (2004) found that the right fit between human capital of the service firm and interaction with the client results in superior performance.

However, the notion of the service model is less complex in comparison to the concept of a firm's business model. The business model of an organization is defined as "a concise representation of how an interrelated set of decision variables in the areas of venture strategy, architecture, and economics are addressed to create sustainable competitive advantage in defined markets" (Morris, Schindehutte, & Allen, 2005, p. 727). The service model is more closely related to the functional and economic nature of the service (i.e., the economic good) concerned. It tends to be less susceptible to variations in firms' choices as to how to compete with other firms than is the case with the business model, as defined above. The service model should be more easily discernible in situations where competition among a multiplicity of service providers forces companies to adopt particular practices for efficiency reasons and thus to avoid strategic experimentation. The underlying service model shapes the consulting firm's possible strategic positioning options and consequently determines positioning efforts. In other words, depending on the approach of how a consulting firm tries to provide its services, strategic positioning options diminish.

Service exposition

Due to the nature of consulting services described above, consulting firms rely on verbal expositions of their services in order to strategically position themselves in the market vis-à-vis their clients and competitors. Consulting firms are merely selling rhetoric in describing their service models that must be reified to the buyer. Nevertheless, these expositions are imperfect in at least three respects (Galal & Richter, 2007). First, they offer only a rough substitute for the service experience a firm offers to its clients. Second, firms address a broad audience with their service expositions at the cost of missing a certain specificity which is a general key characteristic of the actual service. Third, the author of the service exposition can only impart little meaning to it; it is rather the recipient by reading and interpreting who adds meaning to the service exposition. As a consequence, it must be the consulting firm's objective to phrase its service expositions as carefully as it possibly can in order to ensure that ambiguities about what the service entails are minimized and customer expectations that cannot be met are not raised in the first place.

However, the service exposition goes beyond a mere description of the consulting process steps within the provision of services. However, a detailed description of the process steps that consultants go through may expose consulting firms to the danger of imitability (Galal & Richter, 2007). Due to the specific characteristics of services, service expositions are of immense importance to consulting providers in order to position themselves in the market and raise the awareness of potential clients. Service expositions include detailed insights into the service model and therefore into the specific positioning dimensions of consulting firms.

In the following, relevant positioning dimensions for consulting firms are defined and illustrated in further detail. I have identified three categories of key positioning dimensions for the consulting market. The first category comprises those dimensions that define the type of service model. The second category contains dimensions that define the intended relationship and interaction with the client. The third category focuses on dimensions that define the degree of functional and sectoral specialization of a consulting firm.

Type of service model

The type of service model provided by a consulting firm is described by a set of dimensions. This set of the dimensions comprises, for instance, the degree of standardization of the services offered and the level of individuality of the services. A central element for the description relates to the extent to which a service is 'standardized' (Galal, et al., 2012) or 'procedural' (Maister, 1993) in nature. Within extant professional service literature, few scholars refer to the question of what constitutes a standardized service. Drawing on the literature on task 'programmability', incentives and control (e.g. Eisenhardt, 1989; Eisenhardt & Bourgeois, 1988) and on recent literature on standardization (Brunsson, Rasche, & Seidl, 2012), I distinguish between three central characteristics that define a standardized or procedural service:

- *Ex-ante specifications:* Extent to which a service requires a particular succession of steps that can largely be specified well in advance of the steps being taken. In the case of unforeseen contingencies, the steps to be taken until the next junction can be determined with relative ease.

- *Repetitiveness during service provision*: Extent to which the steps to be taken during the process are repetitive or similar to another, enabling the provider to deploy the same capabilities on a repeat basis.

- *Ex-post monitoring*: Extent to which the provision of the service can be assessed in terms of both quality and efficiency, the outcomes of the service can be adequately described and assessed in terms of their functionality, and can be used as benchmarks for further service provisions.

This definition suggests that consulting services, which are straightforward to specify ex ante a service provision, are to a certain extent standardized. Providers of standardized services offer a set of well-defined service "modules" or "packages" to their clients. Clients can choose particular service modules from the offered set that suit their specific consulting demand best. If a specific consulting demand can be met with the provision of standardized consulting service modules, the demand will be comparable across clients. As a result, similar demands allow the repetitive provision of these services to different clients. Although standardized services are provided within different client settings, these kinds of consulting demands request only little customization of consulting service. For efficiency reasons some consulting firms rely heavily on the repetitive provision of standardized services, which is grounded in their service model.

For example, the provision of IT consulting services is more of procedural nature than that of strategy consulting services(Nissen, 2007). IT consulting services related to the implementation or modification of a software system, for instance, are highly standardized with a predefined succession of milestones and comparably limited customization to specific client settings. The outcome of procedural services can be adequately defined ex ante and measured ex post both in terms of efficiency and quality. In contrast, for most strategy consulting projects it is challenging to define concrete milestones or measurable components of the outcome ex ante. Furthermore, the outcome of a strategy consulting project is difficult to assess shortly after project completion as long term effects of a new strategy are not yet observable or measurable. Strategy development within a specific client's setting has, due to its creative character and tailor-made conception, a limited degree of standardization. Moreover, standardized services incline the possibility to be used as benchmarks for further service provisions. The repetitively occurring process steps enable comparisons of different service deliveries across clients. Furthermore, this facilitates consulting firms' efforts to reach higher efficiency levels in providing their service.

As an extension to the already discussed attributes of what defines a service model that emphasizes standardization, I introduce different levels of standardization within the provision of consulting services. I propose a three-layer model of standardization within a specific consulting firm drawing on recent research on standardization (Brunsson, et al., 2012). Each layer relates to a certain degree of standardization of the specific services of a firm.

At lower level of standardization, consulting firms use if anything standardized methods and analytical tools to structure the processes of consultation. Consultants apply a certain set of methods and procedures in order to structure the consultation work. These methods and tools are independent from the particular content of the consulting project and specific client situation. This set of methods is of strong procedural nature and can be described as a 'consultant's toolbox'. This toolbox is applied for the most part at the beginning of a consulting project in order to comprehensively asses the client's situation and to generate data and information within the client's organization and on markets of interest. The gathered information often builds the basis for a variety of tasks that clients are not able to perform on their own (Armbrüster, 2004). It may comprise specific statistical analyses, project management methods, and further means of analysis.

At the medium level of standardization, consulting firms apply predefined solutions to specific client settings in combination with standard methods. The application of standardized solutions indicates a higher degree of standardization than the mere use of standardized methodology. Standardization of solutions implies a certain extent of repetitive use of conceptual content, which goes further than just a repetition of procedural methodology. These predefined solutions are to a certain extent storable and repeatedly usable. Different parts of these solutions are set together in a modular system and applied to the consulting requests of a particular client. Nevertheless, standardized solutions are only partial elements of the overall solution, which results from the consultation process. These solutions need to be customized to a certain client setting and conceptually adjusted to the specific needs of relevance of certain clients. The implementation of standardized solutions enables and often fosters further provision of benchmark services. In particular, as the repetitive use of standardized solutions allows for comparisons of clients within and across different industries.

The highest level of standardization is characterized by the use of 'standard products' as the essential part of the provided service and/or the provision of standardized 'consulting products'. For instance, if clients are looking for highly specified information, consultants can deliver their expertise as if it were a product. However, a piece of market research may still require limited interaction with the client and adaptation the client's needs. Nevertheless, these consulting products are typically documented by means of a written or electronic file, so that the service (i.e. the generation of the required information) has a physical correlate (Galal & Richter, 2007). Moreover, the definition of standardized consulting products may be advantageous to consulting firms as it facilitates the provision of relatively unambiguous descriptions of a consulting firm's services, and thus provides greater transparency with respect to the price, time and other resource requirements (Galal & Richter, 2007). Standardized products (e.g. software packages, IT equipment) that are applied within the consulting process share even more characteristics with highly standardized industry products. Both are created for mass production, are storable and permit only limited customization to clients' specific needs. Consequently, if a firm sells 'off the shelf' products to its clients that need any or only little adjustments to the client's specific problem, the highest level of standardization is established. Adding to this, consulting services that accompany the provision of a particular product tend to be relatively standardized themselves, as the nature of the service is partially determined by the technical specification of the product (Scarbrough, 1996). Richter & Schröder (2008) conclude from this that consulting firms, whose services relate to the provision of technical products, also tend to provide relatively standardized consulting services. Nevertheless, it is of importance that the selling of standard products has to be one of the essential elements of the consulting process, in order to establish the highest category of standardization.

The complementary dimension to the level of standardization is the degree of individuality of a consulting service. Service firms differentiate themselves from competitors by the extent to which they customize the service offering for individual clients (Normann, 1984; Skaggs & Youndt, 2004). The lower the level of standardization, the higher is the level of individuality in the service provision. A consulting solution that is created almost from scratch is highly tailor-made as consultants are engaged in particular to solve a client's individual, specific and new problem. However, it seems that most consulting firms tend to describe their services as highly individual and as always adjusted to each of their clients' situations. Consulting firms seem to believe that clients are more attracted by the promotion of individual service offerings than by high levels of standardization. Nevertheless, empirical evidence from different service industries indicates that service customization has a negative effect on firm performance (Skaggs & Youndt, 2004). The negative performance effect seems to suggest that high levels of individuality in the service provision may be costly and/or not adequately valued by clients. To be more precise, service customization may have high costs of production and delivery without corresponding pricing power and therefore it erodes profit margins (Skaggs & Youndt, 2004). Nevertheless, a certain degree of standardization also reflects consulting experience, high levels of consulting efficiency and offers the possibility to conduct significant benchmarks across different clients and industries. Besides that, a certain degree of standardization offers possibilities for economies of scale and scope for consulting firms, which results in reduced price offerings.

In addition to the previous dimensions, Maister (1993) derived a three-partite typology of consulting services based essentially on two characteristics of consulting services. He discusses the degree of service standardization and the type of knowledge required. The first type of service concentrates on the intellectual expertise of the consulting service provider ("brain projects"), which is of particular importance for clients with complex and unusual problems. The second type is characterized by a high level of experience of the consultants ("grey-hair projects"). Consultants are engaged not for their sheer brain power, but for their experience from past projects. The main focus of the third type of consulting services lies on efficiency ("procedure projects"). Clients expect consultants to ramp up quickly, and execute the given task and project at low cost with a high level of efficiency. Although this classification concentrates on two characteristics of services, the spectrum of consulting services is still uni-dimensional and suggests that consulting services are rather homogenous (Galal & Richter, 2007).

Intended relationship with the client

As stated above, consulting services are by definition of a highly interactive nature. Hence, service expositions include a description of the intended relationship and interaction with the client. Galal & Richter (2007) suggest that the intended relationship with the client comprises three interrelated aspects. In addition, Schein's (1978, 1988, 1998) three types of consulting-client relationships will be further explicated and analyzed within this research.

First, the intended relationship specifies the extent to which the client is involved in the execution of the consulting process or to which he interacts with the consultant, observed from the perspective of the consulting service provider. Therefore, client involvement in this context describes the degree to which clients are involved in the process of consulting on a day-to-day basis. The definition also includes how the client interacts in a trusted and permanent exchange with the consultants. High degree of client involvement implies that consultants and clients cooperate on a permanent basis and build an interacting project team that solves the challenges jointly. Low client involvement implies that consultants and clients interact only in predefined intervals and service provision is carried out merely by the consultants. As clients of consulting firms interact within the service provision process, the variance in their demands creates uncertainty for the firm (Mills & Moberg, 1982). When a high degree of variability is introduced to the service provision process, consulting firms depend on the skill, knowledge and expertise level of their consultants in order to be able to address this variability and successfully satisfy client needs (Skaggs & Youndt, 2004). Skaggs & Youndt (2004) contend that employees with high skill levels are able to better deal with uncertainty in the task environment. This argument aligns with existing research and supports human capital theory.

The second aspect is the relation between individuality of the service and the degree of client interaction. The more client-specific the consulting service, the greater the degree of interaction between consultants and clients. Here, the consultants spend more time with the client in order to ascertain client requirements and develop a joint set of expectations. So, if a consulting firm requires a lot of information from each client before providing the service, it can be considered a highly individual as well as interactive service provision. On the contrary, more standardized consulting services tend to require only a limited degree of interaction between clients and consultants. The potential disadvantages of limited interaction with clients, due to high levels of standardization, include a loss of perceived individuality and the danger of imitability. Furthermore, to build up intimate, trust-based relationships with clients is more challenging to consulting firms that offer standardized services.

The third aspect related to the intended relationship between consultant and client is the extent to which the consulting firm seeks to become actively involved in the client's organization on an ongoing basis, i.e. beyond the scope of a time-delimited project. Many consulting firms have realized the clients' demand for an enduring support throughout all stages of a project and beyond. Consequently, consulting firms try to respond to upcoming criticism that consultants provide merely conceptual advice to executives and then leave further project tasks to the clients (O'Shea & Madigan, 1997). As a result, consulting firms have begun to developed service models that involve an ongoing support of their clients also during the implementation phase of a project, following the provision of conceptual advice. With this offering, firms tend to prove that their developed concepts are applicable and practical, and that they are confident enough to share in the responsibility for the implementation. In addition, as clients have begun to become more professional in their use of consulting services, they insist on consulting firms to take over responsibility of their developed concepts on an ongoing basis and even relate remuneration to measures of project success. In sum, I expect consulting firms to emphasize their client involvement throughout the implementation phase and position themselves not only as conceptual advisers, but also as providers of applicable solutions.

The dimension of client involvement plays an important and central role in relation to a consulting firm's service model. In other words, the degree of client involvement in the process of consulting depends on the service model that the consulting provider pursues. Some service models require intense interaction with the client in order to jointly find a solution to a firm-specific problem, while other service models do not necessitate constant personal interaction with the client, e.g. service providers focused on the implementation of standardized IT solutions. As some types of consulting services evolve strongly around unique asset that the consultant may be able to provide, a lower degree of client involvement can be favorable. However, most consulting services require a high level of labor input. In addition, as it is not possible to mechanize the delivery process, the adequate level of client interaction should be a key component to the success of the consulting project. However, Skaggs and Youndt (2004) provided empirical evidence that the intensity of client interaction has no significant influence on firm performance when a high level of human capital is involved. In contrast, for firms drawing on low human capital, high client interaction is preferable over low interaction in order to reach high performance rates. In other words, high client interaction moderates for different levels of human capital in influencing firm performance.

As a matter of fact, the degree of client involvement determines a range of decisions concerning the consulting project setting. The level of client involvement has implications for the composition of the consulting team, the skill and experience level of the consultants, the leverage ratio (amount of junior consultants working under the supervision of senior consultants of the team) and the fees that can be charged for the consultants. Furthermore, consulting clients take the expected interaction level into account in the decision whether to engage a consulting firm due to implications for their own resource planning. This requires consulting firms to clearly specify in their service exposition the degree of involvement clients would have during the consulting process.

In line with this, the intended relationship with the client is strongly influenced by the role the consulting firm assigns to its consultants during the consulting process. Schein (1978, 1998) introduced a relationship model in which he identifies three types of consultant-client relationships that occur within the setting of consulting projects. The three relationships were distinguished by Schein on the basis of two opposing dimensions that consultants may provide 'content expertise' versus 'process expertise'. Schein relates 'content expertise' to the nature of the problem that a client may require the help of a consultant to solve it on his/her behalf. However, 'process expertise' focuses rather on how to solve problems and tasks (Rockwood, 1993). Two potential relationship outcomes are described by Schein's mode: Neutrality/independence of the consultant in contrast to closeness of the relationship between consultant and client. Depending on the defined relationship model different levels of neutrality of the consultant and closeness of the relationship are established.

The so-called 'purchase of expertise' consultation model relies for the most parts on content expertise. Consultants serve in this context as external experts and offer clients their expertise or some specific kind of information that conforms to a client's well-specified request. In a sense, consultants in this view offer expertise consulting products to their clients. In fact, the expertise content provided is typically documented by means of a written or electronic file, so that the service has a physical correlate, almost like a product. The client has a specific issue which needs to be resolved by consultants who are positioned as experts within the respective field. Although the consulting experts provide the client with the required expertise or information, the client needs to draw conclusions by himself. As Teece (2003) has shown, profitable consulting operations can be developed on the basis of the purchase of an expertise model. In this consulting model, consultants are sharply delineated from their clients. Therefore, the provision of expertise is primarily independent of the client and conducted with a low degree of closeness to the client.

Within the 'doctor-patient' consulting model, consultants are hired by the client in order to diagnose the causes of a prevalent problem and prescribe a treatment/solution to it. This model relies moderately on content expertise. The consultant conducts several in-depth analyses on the client's situation or area of interest and tries to find a solution to the matter. Although the client is helping with the analyses, the consultant is the dominant partner in the relationship and determines the treatment/solution to the problem. In order to conduct sound analyses, the consultant interacts with the client and tries to establish a trustful relationship with the client. Even though the consultant finally advises the client how to solve the challenging issue, the client is required to take remedial action himself.

In Schein's third relationship model, the 'guide-mountaineer' model, the client hires a consultant in order to better understand and reflect his own situation. This model stresses the enabling role of consultants and their process expertise. The consultant guides the client throughout the process of diagnosing and finding a solution to a specific problem. In a moderating position the consultant supports the client's internal decision processes. Both, the consultant and the client heavily interact within this close relationship and jointly shape a solution. Thereby, they take the necessary steps together and establish a trustful relationship with each other. Nevertheless, it is the client's organization as a collective that undergoes this process of solving a problem via communication and interaction among its members (Massarik & Pei-Carpenter, 2002; Schein, 1978).

The neutrality of the consultant decreases with intensity of interaction with the client. The more the consultant gets involved in clients' processes and merely focuses on the delivery of content expertise, the less neutral his involvement in the client's organization is. At the same time, involvement in the clients' organization rises, the relationship gains in closeness.

Degree of functional and sectoral specialization

An important strategic dimension in order to comprehensively analyze positioning efforts of a consulting firm is the degree of specialization of the offered services. In terms of functional positioning there exist different levels of functional and sectoral specialization. In the extremes, I expect consulting firms to position either as generalist or specialist firms.

A high level of functional specialization implies a focus on few functional areas. Functional specialization corresponds in a sense to the pursuing of a differentiation strategy within the competitive market space. Specialist consulting firms try to differentiate themselves from competitors by positioning as experts on a certain functional area. The aim is to build up reputation as a provider of functional expertise and to cultivate visibility throughout the relevant market. As a successfully established provider of specialist consulting services, a firm may be able to realize above-average returns and reach high performance rates. Another form of specialization is the focus on certain client sectors. Consulting providers intentionally concentrate in their service provision on specific client sectors and promote their specific expertise to potential clients.

A provider of a low level of functional specialization is not concentrating on few functional areas (e.g. strategy, process, IT) in the provision of consulting services, but aims at broadly meeting client demands at all functional levels. Successful positioning as a generalist provider reflects to the client that the consulting provider is capable of dealing with complex business challenges in different functional areas. Positioning as a functional generalist might be advantageous in cases of top-level strategy development projects where interdependent areas of the client's organization are concerned and at the same time implications throughout the whole organization occur. Due to their expertise in all functional areas, in particular generalists are able to react to organization-wide interdependencies of complex project structures, even throughout a strategy implementation phase. Furthermore, generalists are predominantly large, often well established firms that signal both high levels of experience and large capacities to potential clients. In addition, large, successful generalists have the opportunity to build up reputation due to their great visibility to both competitors and clients in the market for consulting services.

To summarize, I argue that the strategic positioning of a consulting service firm is a complex, multidimensional construct. By defining and providing descriptions of the type of consulting service provided, the level of standardization of the service model, the intended relationship with the client, the functional and sectoral specificity of the offerings described in their service expositions, consulting firms seek to position themselves near to other competitors, e.g. as members of a particular school, or far from them, i.e. as service differentiators that intentionally seek to address one or several dimensions differently as exposed by other firms.

The following chapter focuses on three basic positioning strategies and discusses them with respect to their applicability to the consulting market. Thereby, how positioning in relation to competition affects firm performance will be discussed.

2.1.2 Positioning Strategies

As introduced strategic similarity is the underlying concept that constitutes a firm's different positioning possibilities in relation to its competitors (Deephouse, 1999). Considerable research exists on the strategic act of positioning from an external perspective, which is broadly defined as determining where a company locates itself relative to its rivals (Semadeni, 2006). However, strategic management researchers have mostly paid attention to one side of the similarity issue: either what is the value of positioning far from competitors, or what is the value of positioning near to competitors (DiMaggio & Powell, 1983; Hannan & Freeman, 1977; Rumelt, Schendel, & Teece, 1991). In addition, studies have examined different dimensions of geographic positioning (Baum & Haveman, 1997), product market positioning (L. Thomas & Weigelt, 2000), radio market positioning (Greve, 1998), and technological positioning (Stuart, 1998; Stuart & Podolny, 1996).

As described, strategic balance theory proposes both to position near to and far from competitors at the same time. Each of the three positioning strategies are outlined in the subsequent sections and discussed with respect to their implications for the consulting market.

2.1.2.1 Positioning near to Competitors

Based on the concept of strategic similarity, Deephouse (1999) elaborated on the view that firms should be the same as others – positioning near to competitors – in order to achieve superior performance and calls it "conformity proposition". He derived it primarily from resource dependence view and new institutional theories. Streams within strategic group research also suggest that the pursuit of similar positioning strategies increases firm performance. The proposition stemming from strategic group research is that as two firms recognize their interdependence and their similar positioning in the market, they collude in order to both increase their firm performance (Caves & Porter, 1977; McNamara, et al., 2003). Another explanation for positioning strategies near to competitors can be derived from the theory of spatial competition, which states that firms over time assimilate their positioning efforts (Hotelling, 1929; Tang & Thomas, 1992) (cf. Chapter 2.2.2). In summary, the common proposition is that positioning near to competitors is beneficial in three ways: it increases legitimacy (Suchman, 1995), decreases uncertainty (DiMaggio & Powell, 1983), and raises potential for spillover effects (Baum & Haveman, 1997; Makadok, 1998). Yet, at the same time the persistent lack of differentiation raises the likelihood of an increased competition for resources and clients (Barney, 1991).

Legitimacy

Over the years, the notion of legitimacy has raised considerable attention in particular within social science literature (cf. Suchman, 1995). In order to apply this theoretical construct to management literature, Suchman (1995, p. 574) defined legitimacy as "a generalized perception or assumption that the actions of an entity are desirable, proper, or appropriate within some socially constructed system of norms, values, beliefs, and definitions". Firms seek to gain legitimacy for their actions within their natural market space for different reasons. The level of legitimacy affects not only the way a firm is perceived within its market environment, but influences also how different parties interact with it. A highly legitimate firm is perceived as more worthy, more meaningful, more predictable, and as a consequence even more trustworthy (Suchman, 1995). Thus, a gain in legitimacy enhances the credibility of a firm. On the contrary, firms that lack legitimacy face the challenge of being perceived as unnecessary or confronted with diminishing credibility among other market participants. As firms in an established market compete with each other for both clients and also for suppliers (Chen, 1996), the level of legitimacy is of high importance to firms in order to successfully perform business operations.

Therefore, in line with density dependence theory (Hannan & Carroll, 1992), positioning near to established competitors increases the perceived legitimacy of the firm and its service offering (Suchman, 1995). However, density dependency theory further argues that legitimacy grows at a decreasing rate within industries with a high density of competitors, whereas competition grows at an increasing rate. On the contrary, at low levels of density, industry growth serves primarily to legitimate existing competitors (Haveman, 1993). Firms gain legitimacy and benefit from it by focusing on a well-established, respected service model (DeSarbo & Grewal, 2008; DiMaggio & Powell, 1983; Grewal & Dharwadkar, 2002) and pursue a commonly accepted strategy. More generally speaking, the proposition is that organizations receive legitimacy if they conform their strategic actions to contemporary norms – as determined by professional and scientific authorities (Scott, 2002; Semadeni, 2006).

Research proposes that managers and strategy researchers develop a cognitive consensus about the strategies that lead to success in a certain industry and thus are acceptable within a firm's organizational field (Deephouse, 1999; Reger & Huff, 1993). A firm's organizational field consists of competitors, suppliers, clients, market regulators (DiMaggio & Powell, 1983). As the outcome of an iterative isomorphic legitimization process (Scott, 1995) a range of acceptable strategies – also called 'industry recipes' (Spender, 1989) – evolves. Following this, a firm's strategic positioning is legitimate, if it is aligned with cognitive consensus and accepted as an industry recipe by its organizational field (Porac, et al., 1989). Within this stream of dependency theory research, March (1981) introduced the notion of 'obligatory action'. The notion suggests that members of an organizational field do things a certain way and that this course of action becomes taken for granted or institutionalized. Subsequently, new entrants to the organizational field undertake that course of action without thinking and try to imitate it (Haveman, 1993). The outlined concepts help to further explain why and how firms position near to competitors.

An implication of these propositions is that firms have to become similar to one another and strategically positioning alike, in order to increase the probability of organizational survival and performance (Roberts & Greenwood, 1997). As legitimacy is considered to be an intangible asset that determines the ability of organizations to acquire capital and personnel, it thereby influences organizational survival (Hannan & Freeman, 1989; Rao, 1994). However, as competing firms strive for similar resources, positioning near to competitors increases the perceived legitimacy in the resource acquisition process and thus enables a firm to procure resources required for its operations. Deephouse (1999, pp. 152-153) developed three reasons for his argument that a "legitimate firm obtains resources of higher quality and at more favorable terms than a firm whose legitimacy is challenged". First, a potential exchange partner that does not comprehend a firm's strategy or accept it as rational will not provide any resources to the firm and thereby restrict its resource supply. Second, an exchange partner may require greater inducements to contract with a firm whose legitimacy is challenged. Third, since less legitimate firms are perceived as more likely to fail (DiMaggio & Powell, 1983; Singh, Tucker, & House, 1986), exchange partners will demand higher risk premiums in contracts. In sum, firms that are dissimilar from legitimate competitors face a legitimacy challenge, which encumbers resource acquisition, and results in reduced firm performance and lower probability of organizational survival.

In addition, reputation is considered in large measure as an outcome of the legitimization process (Lange, et al., 2011; Rao, 1994). Increasing legitimacy fosters the reputation of a firm over time. As firms with a high legitimization are well-accepted and trusted within their market environment, their reputation develops over time and spreads within the market. Therefore, firms try to gain legitimization in their market environment to build up and protect their established reputation (Semadeni, 2006). The specific importance of reputation especially within professional service industries has been emphasized by Greenwood et al. (2005).

Empirical evidence has been presented that supports the proposition that legitimacy increases the probability of organizational survival of young firms as well as firms undergoing organizational transformation (Semadeni, 2006; Singh, et al., 1986). Still, the question arises how strategic positioning near to competitors that have a high level of legitimacy, influences the performance of small and young firms. In more detail, the question is whether young firms will be able to establish similar performance rates like large reputable firms resulting from similar market positioning.

Uncertainty

A high degree of uncertainty coincides with the strategic positioning process of a firm. Managers have to decide, which strategic path to follow without reliable assurance of the consequences and future success of their strategic ambitions. Deciding on a strategic positioning is inherently uncertain as it requires commitment to certain actions that influence future business operations of the firm (Cyert & March, 1963). As a consequence, uncertainty is "a powerful force that encourages imitation" (DiMaggio & Powell, 1983, p. 151) and time decreases differentiation forces in the same way. Therefore, scholars propose that under conditions of uncertainty, firms mimic actions of their competitors (DiMaggio & Powell, 1983). In order to reduce uncertainty, firms imitate strategies that provide a high probability of future success, strategies that have been pursued successfully by other industry participants in the past (Haveman, 1993; Reger & Huff, 1993). As stated above, cognitive industry consensus results in an array of strategies that have the potential for future success (Spender, 1989). According to Haveman's empirical evidence, firms imitate rather large and profitable firms than similarly sized firms in order to reduce uncertainty (Semadeni, 2006). As a consequence, firms choose to position near to their direct competitors in order to gain legitimacy and reduce uncertainty.

Spill-over effects

Another argument that emphasizes the advantages of positioning near to competitors is the increasing potential for beneficial spillover effects. Spillover effects occur when firms produce positive externalities to their organizational field and similarly positioned firms benefit from it. Consequently, companies profit from close, successful competitors, e.g. in terms of pricing or in terms of knowledge already developed by the incumbent firms. For instance, pricing efforts of small firms can be positively influenced by successfully established pricing efforts of similarly positioned larger competitors (Baum & Haveman, 1997). The potential for spillover effects is even higher in new markets with low entry barriers – such as the consulting market - and is supposed to offer the same benefits to both early movers and first movers (Makadok, 1998). In sum, the anticipation of spillover effects decreases differentiation efforts and moreover increases incentives to position near to competitors.

However, the process of imitation of another firm's strategic positioning is characterized by a high level of complexity. Given the fact that competitive positions can be achieved in various ways, firms face different challenges in pursuing the strategy of positioning near to competitors. First of all, the essential problem for the imitating firm is to understand the complex interplay of strategic dimensions that have created a firm's specific market position, in the first place (Hooley, et al., 2001). Secondly, a firm's ability to realize a certain setting of strategic dimensions is influenced by many dynamic factors (e.g. institutions, competitors, clients, resource supply, and additional economic factors) and dependent on the specific market environment. In particular, imitation is impeded by the fact that these environmental factors can hardly be intentionally influenced, but at the same time play a significant role in achieving a certain market position. In addition, resource requirements that enable the realization of a certain market position are generally difficult to fulfill in highly competitive markets. Especially in markets characterized by low entry barriers and high competition, it is highly demanding to imitate a competitor's strategic positioning.

Positioning near to competitors in the consulting market

As described above, the specific characteristics of consulting services demand a careful positioning of service offerings vis-à-vis potential clients and relative to competitors. Due to the nature of consulting as a credence or an experience good that relies on the trust between provider and buyer (Armbrüster, 2004), positioning the service offering near to the more well-established competitors may be particularly attractive (Galal & Richter, 2007). Legitimate providers of consulting services draw largely on their established public reputation for quality and reliability. This is in line with recent empirical findings on the determinants of client loyalty in the consulting industry (Harste, 2008). Non-economic factors such as trust, legitimacy and reputation outweigh economic factors such as transaction-specific assets and dependence. This finding emphasizes the dominant role of trust and reputation for client loyalty and herewith its relevance for strategic positioning in the consulting market. In order to increase legitimacy, many small consulting firms openly advertise the fact that their consultants have spent some time at one of the leading brand names in the industry, and that they apply the skills learned in these firms in their present work (Galal & Richter, 2007). In sum, positioning near competitors seems beneficial especially to young, small consulting firms. Young, small consulting firms should try to establish legitimacy and reduce uncertainty and aim to benefit from spillover effects. Still, established, older consulting providers should gain from pursuing differentiating positioning strategies. This is in line with Semadeni's (2006) empirical findings, as his results indicate that young firms position near to other firms, while old, established firms locate their service offerings farther from competing firms. The reason is that old established firms do not longer need the legitimacy resulting from positioning near to other firms.

On the other hand, positioning effects of a young and small consulting firm near its established competitors makes it hard for potential clients to distinguish the firm's service offering from those of its competitors. Especially, if small firms provide services that are seen as largely identical to those offered by large firms, they have hardly any means to compensate for the lack of reputation – the most important buying criterion for clients (Armbrüster, 2006) – apart from lower prices. Nevertheless, Dawes, Dowling, & Patterson (1992) and Page

(1998) found that price or cost criteria tend to play a subordinate role in clients' decisions on which consulting firms to engage.

However, a high number of similarly positioned firms, results in increased competition for resources as the consulting market is characterized by a limited carrying capacity and a finite level of resources (Deephouse, 1999; Hannan & Freeman, 1989). The developing fight for resources increases selection pressures and raises incentives for firms to differentiate themselves from their competitors to pursue dissimilar positioning strategies and to establish new market niches (Galal & Richter, 2007; Simon, 1983).

2.1.2.2 Positioning far from Competitors

The disadvantages of positioning near to competitors - e.g. an increased competition for resources and customers leading to selection pressures - raise incentives for firms to differentiate themselves from their competitors. Strategic management research proposes that by being different and positioning far from competitors firms benefit from less competition, ceteribus paribus (e.g. Barney, 1991; Deephouse, 1999; Porter, 1991). As the market for resources is assumed to have a finite level, they are divided among competitors if their realized strategic positions focus on the same resource niches (Porac, et al., 1989). A firm that positions next to numerous similar competitors, limits its own supply of resources and thereby the market potential of its specific competencies. Baum and Sigh (1994) defined a high number of firms competing for the same resources as high "niche overlap density". Overlap density in this context is the aggregate overlap of an organization's resource requirements with those of all other organizations in the market (Baum & Haveman, 1997). In order to limit the level of overlap density, firms follow a differentiation strategy and thereby benefit in their resource procurement processes from less competition (Deephouse, 1999). A high level of niche overlap density and high competition for resources significantly limits a new entrant firm's growth potential. Furthermore, conformation of firm strategy to strategies of others bears the risk of an increased failure rate and performance limitations (Baum & Singh, 1994; Henderson, 1996).

As a consequence of these limitations, firms pursue rational differentiation strategies in order to reduce competition, to increase performance and facilitate higher earnings (Baum & Singh, 1994; Porter, 1979, 1991). Deephouse (1999, p. 151) argues that "a firm selects a distinct position in what it *ex ante* perceives to be an unexploited or underexploited niche". He consents with Porter (1991) who states that a firm needs to stake out a distinct position from its rivals, in order to preserve a competitive advantage and potential for above-average performance. In order to follow a differentiated strategic positioning, firms seek to offer services or products with exceptional attributes that are highly valuable to target customers. Potential for above average profits arises, when customers are willing to pay a price premium that exceeds the additional costs of offering a differentiated service (Porter, 1980). Potential for differentiation in service industries includes e.g. brand image, service specialization, expert knowledge offerings, human capital, quality of services, or other variations in the service models that distinguish a firm from existing service offerings. Furthermore, positioning far from competition shields firms from the bargaining power of clients and protects against substitutes. Besides that, this positioning results in lower price sensitivity and thereby limits rivalry. For that reason, within an environment of low competition, firms are enabled to gain advantages from individual pricing of their products or services (Carmeli & Tishler, 2004). Nevertheless, deficient legitimacy can arise and possibly outweigh the advantages of lower competition with respect to resources and client project acquisitions.

However, the persistence of a distinct market position and superior performance is to a large account dependent on competitors' success in their imitation efforts and success. Especially in markets and industries that are characterized by business models, which are easy to imitate, firms face a limited persistence of a distinct market position. In industries with low mobility barriers (e.g. brand loyalty, scale economies, switching costs, and preemption of strategic assets (Deephouse, 1999)), firms that occupy market niches are not able to protect and maintain superior market positions e.g. with the erection of barriers to entry and exit from competing firms in the long run (cf. chapter 2.2.1). Therefore, in case of low mobility barriers and a permanent threat by competitors, firms are obliged to identify profitable new strategic opportunities for their core competencies in order to reestablish distinct market positions (Prahalad & Hamel, 1990; Zook, 2007).

Positioning far from competitors in the consulting market

Professional service industries, e.g. consulting services, have lower barriers to imitation compared to regulated and asset specific industries e.g. banking or pharmaceuticals. The characteristics of consulting services facilitate imitation efforts, especially as consultants are merely selling rhetoric, which is espoused to potential clients ex ante the actual service provision. Furthermore, due to missing institutional protection of consulting as a profession, market entry is comparably easy. The first mover advantage is comparably limited in these types of industries and imitation attempts are more likely to succeed in the long run. However, continuity in consulting service provision and resulting experience raise clients' awareness for a legitimate, trustworthy consulting firm. In line with this, young consulting firms face high competition for resources as well as for clients when they position next to established firms. The advantages of positioning near to established firms – increased legitimacy, reduced uncertainty, potential for spillover effects – may be outweighed by the disadvantages of not being able to establish a distinct market position. Especially, young, small consulting firms may need to propose their services in a distinct way from established players in order to raise the attention of potential clients and to achieve above-average returns.

In line with this, Carroll (1985) and Baum & Haveman (1997) suggested the notion that high competition among generalist firms to establish within the center of a market, opens opportunities for peripheral resources that are likely to be exploited by rather small specialist firms. The argument is that in concentrated markets with a few large generalist firms, small firms that position differently can exploit more of the available resources without being in direct competition with the established generalist firms (Baum & Haveman, 1997). Following this argumentation leads to the proposition that increased concentration among generalists firms will increase failure among large generalists and reduce failure among small specialists. Empirical evidence supports this theoretical proposition (cf. Baum & Haveman, 1997).

However, concerning the market for consulting services, Caroll's notion may not be supported. I agree with the suggestion that specialist firms that follow a differentiating positioning strategy are likely to profit from intense competition among generalist firms as niches naturally develop. Nevertheless, I am not convinced that within consulting markets a large concentration of generalists will lead to failure among generalist firms and in parallel decrease failure among specialists firms. As the success of a consulting firm is heavily dependent on firm reputation, legitimacy and brand name, I expect a concentration of generalists to establish a self-reifying community. On the contrary to Carroll's proposition, generalist firms should profit from positioning similar to each other as they prove themselves as trustworthy by promoting the same service offerings as their competitors and thereby establishing an accepted industry recipe. The relationship between the positioning of small consulting firms and large generalists will be the subject of the following empirical analyses.

To summarize, competition for resources and clients can be reduced by differentiating from other companies in a market, increasing the probability to generate higher returns (Barney, 1991; Peteraf, 1993). On the other hand, to be different from other market participants bears the disadvantages of decreasing legitimacy, increasing uncertainty, and limiting potential benefits from spillovers.

2.1.2.3 Positioning on the 'Competitive Cusp'

In the strategic management literature, as described above, two basic – at first sight – dichotomous perspectives on positioning exist. The first argues that firms will benefit from positioning near to competitors by establishing legitimacy, mitigating uncertainty, and capturing benefits from spillover effects. While on the contrary, the other perspective argues that firms will benefit from positioning distant from other firms by avoiding competition through differentiation. Conversely, it is not essentially a unconditional bipolar dichotomy between being positioned near to or far from competition. In markets with strong competition and institutional forces, both the conformity and differentiation proposition can be important at the same time. Semadeni (2006) states that the positioning decision is largely focused on being close enough to competition to establish the advantages of proximity, but not so close as to engage in direct competition. Hence, the suggestion is that firms are motivated to position both near to and far from their competitors at the same time.

Drawing on this concept, strategic balance theory states that firms benefit from positioning on the 'competitive cusp' between similarity and differentiation (Deephouse, 1999; Porac, et al., 1989). As outlined above, at least a marginal level of similarity and herewith legitimacy to other firms is obligatory in order to tap into the same resource niches as established competitors. The suggestion is that a firm with a moderate level of strategic similarity to its competitors faces reduced competition for resources and at the same time establishes organizational uniqueness. Consistently, its performance should be higher than that of firms of the highly similar or dissimilar type. But, in order to be successful and to be even superior in obtaining resources, a firm needs to create and sustain organizational uniqueness (e.g. Porter, 1980). However, the threat of direct competition pushes firms far away from similar competitors while the opportunities of complementary differences pull firms close to dissimilar competitors. At the same time, spillover effects from adjacent competitors (agglomeration economies) and institutional forces pull firms close to similar competitors. With their notion of the 'competitive cusp', Porac et al. (1989) describe the level or the balance point, where the dual of isomorphic and differentiating pressures meet that a firm needs to find to ensure its uniqueness among essentially similar firms. However, a firm is obliged to remain within the range of strategic similarity, so that the organizational field will not challenge its legitimacy. Following these propositions, a firm is expected to "achieve maximum performance at the level of strategic similarity, where the gains from reduced competition are equal" to the costs of legitimacy, uncertainty and spillover challenges (Deephouse, 1999, p. 154). Thus, the range of strategic similarity marks the positioning span, where firms successfully balance differentiation and conformity pressures.

Strategic balance theory integrates strategic management concepts as well as organizational theories. While strategic management research contributes to the proposal that competition decreases the benefits of institutional isomorphism, resource dependency theory contributes to the notion that legitimacy facilitates a firm's efforts in gaining resources (Deephouse, 1999). In short, this hybrid theory states that firms need to balance between the forces pulling them towards or pushing them away from competitors in order to maximize the advantages and minimize the disadvantages of both extremes conformity and differentiation (Semadeni, 2006). The implication being that the process of strategic positioning is of a multidimensional nature (Baum & Haveman, 1997) along a set of strategic dimensions in dependence of the industry examined. Hence, strategists need to optimize their firm's strategic positioning along multiple dimensions and decide along which particular dimension to conform to competitors and along which dimensions to differentiate in order to establish a successful market position.

However, due to different interpretations of selecting and implementing positioning strategies, variation in firm's realized market positions arises. For that reason, Reger and Huff (1993) introduced the notion of 'core' firms, which follow strategic recipes closely and 'secondary' firms that follow industry recipes less closely. By following industry recipes less closely, secondary firms differentiate themselves to a certain extent from core firms who imitate each other's strategies closely. This positioning strategy builds on strategic balance theory as it tries to combine the advantages of both positioning far from and near to competitors. Solitary firms are defined as firms that do not share a strategic recipe with other competitors. They are defined to exist when single clusters of firms emerge (DeSarbo, Grewal, & Scott, 2008).

In this context, Deephouse (1999) introduced the "range of acceptability" of strategic similarity, in which a firm maintains legitimacy. This refers to the notion that firms can be different to some extent from their competitors, but still maintain legitimacy to a certain extent in the perception of their organizational field. Although strategic positioning efforts of secondary firms are different to some extent, members of the organizational field are indifferent to certain efforts of differentiation and do not perceive these firms as less legitimate. Consistently, firms perceived within the range of acceptability maintain their established level of legitimacy. On the contrary, firms who select strategies, which fall out of the range of acceptability, face questions and actions challenging their reliability, legitimacy, and rationality by their organizational field (Deephouse, 1999; DiMaggio & Powell, 1983; Hambrick & D'Aveni, 1992; Suchman, 1995). As a consequence, legitimacy challenges weaken a firm's ability to acquire resources from potential exchange partners. However, the pursuit of a different positioning strategy offers firms the potential to exploit above-average returns resulting from lower competition in a specific niche (Carroll, 1985).

Positioning on the competitive cusp in the consulting market

Due to the characteristics of internal and external unboundedness, the market for consulting services is marked by a high level of competition. Consequently, as consulting firms are selling merely a rhetoric, they have to position their service offerings carefully vis-à-vis potential clients and relative to competitors. Nevertheless, the decision to position near to or far from competitors may differ over time and with growing firm age of the consultancy. It was proposed that young consulting firms should benefit from positioning near to competitors to raise legitimacy and reduce uncertainty. But, as innovation and flexibility are opposing to a close positioning, it can also be assumed that young firms prefer distant positioning. In addition, established market players should favor a distant market positioning with reduced competition as they face less reputation and legitimacy challenges. Similar propositions can be made with regard to the size of consulting firms. Smaller firms might try to replicate processes and behaviors of larger consulting firms to increase legitimacy, but may also position in distance to take advantage of new market niches and benefit from being strategically different. Larger consultancies should favor less similar positions to establish potential for growth or develop new markets.

The propositions of strategic balance theory have not sufficiently been applied to the consulting market. However, the specific market characteristics deem for an in-depth examination including an evaluation of performance implications for consulting firms that try to position on the competitive cusp. Especially for consulting firms, it seems important to balance the advantages and disadvantages of the two positioning extremes. As noted, clients heavily rely on legitimacy and reputation when it comes to buying a consulting service. At the same time, clients often engage consulting providers that they have already relied on in the past. Therefore, in order to acquire new clients and to convince them to switch their preferred supplier of consulting services, competitors have to offer to a certain extent similar services, but at the same time differentiate their service offerings from that of competing firms.

Empirical evidence on the strategic balance theory

Deephouse (1999) empirically tested the theoretical propositions on positioning on the competitive cusp in a longitudinal study among commercial banks. In his seminal paper on strategic balance theory, Deephouse used the construct of strategic similarity as his independent variable by assessing the strategic deviation of firms within his sample of banks (cf. Abrahamson & Hegeman, 1994; Finkelstein & Hambrick, 1990). The management scholar measured strategic deviation by comparing individual banks' strategic positions to industry means. Empirical evidence proved the hypothesis positive that a curvilinear, concave relationship exists between strategic similarity and performance. Hence, the results indicated that intermediate levels of differentiation and similarity provide the best performance rates. In summary, by examining the legitimacy–differentiation trade-off between commercial banks, Deephouse found evidence for his theoretical proposition that successful firms seek balance between these opposing forces and strategically position on the competitive cusp.

McNamara et al. (2003) found, in their analysis of strategic positioning efforts of commercial banks, that firms that manage to position on the competitive cusp outperform their competitors. The authors used a perception based approach in their study. They assessed managerial cognitive perceptions of the strategic distance between different banks within a delineated regional area. Following this, from a strategic group perspective, the researchers identified core and secondary firms within strategic groups on the basis of strategic similarity to their direct competitors. Secondary firms are defined as members of a specific strategic group that follow a specific group strategy less closely and therefore differentiate themselves to a certain extent from core members of a strategic group. Further empirical analyses showed that secondary firms achieved significantly higher financial performance levels than core and solitary firms that occupy market niches. The findings are consistent with strategic balance theory as secondary firms manage to benefit from both legitimacy that results from being a member of a certain strategic group and at the same time from a somewhat unique market position that secondary firms manage to generate. In summary, the empirical evidence of McNamara et al. (2003) also indicates that successful commercial banks are balanced on the competitive cusp so as to be different as legitimately possible.

Overall, few scholars conducted empirical studies on strategic positioning within professional service industries and analyzed its implications on performance. One possible reason for the limited amount of studies on professional service firms is that many service firms are held privately and therefore have less rationale to expose their financial performance. This results in difficulties to convince professional service firms to respond to surveys that request precise performance data (Boxall & Steeneveld, 1999). Nevertheless, there have been few efforts to find empirical evidence concerning the strategic balance theory within professional service firms.

In a recent study, Semadeni (2006) was one of the first researchers to empirically examine strategic positioning efforts of the 50 largest consulting firms (in terms of revenues) within the U.S. market. With a sample of service mark fillings, the strategic management scholar conducted research on the effects of age, similarity, size and of prospective services on strategic positioning of consulting firms. The primary finding of the study is that firms strike a balance between the advantages of positioning near to or far from other firms along certain dimensions. In more detail, the results provide evidence for the assumption that especially young firms locate near to older firms to gain legitimacy, reduce uncertainty and benefit from spillovers. At the same time, Semadeni also observed a tendency of firms to position distant from larger firms to avoid direct competition with established consulting providers. However, with growing firm age and increasing legitimacy, young firms tend to reposition their services farther away from those of other firms. At the same time, firms that grow larger locate their services near to other firms. Semadeni argues that positioning near to competitors should be seen as an indicator for growth and the capability to withstand the effects of competition. In summary, Semadeni's study supports the empirical findings of Deephouse (1999) and McNamara et al. (2003) and provides further evidence for the applicability of the strategic balance theory in professional service industries.

Limitations of previous studies and research opportunities

As stated above, if the propositions of the strategic balance theory are right than positioning on the competitive cusp should be always beneficial and is not dependent on industry or firm specifics. However, the range of strategic balance theory is not sufficiently examined and empirically analyzed, yet. From my examination of existing research I find that the temporal and contextual factors that set the boundaries of generalizability of the strategic balance theory are not comprehensively addressed and well defined. The theoretical objective is to shed light on the generalizability of strategic balance theory and the boundary conditions of the theory. Herewith, I respond to Whetten's (1989) general statement that "few theorists explicitly focus on the contextual limitations of their propositions". Furthermore, he admits that the boundary conditions are most likely to be discovered while applying a theory empirically in various settings. Drawing on this statement, I will apply strategic balance theory to the market for management consulting services in order to define evidence for boundary conditions.

One of Deephouse's (1999) identified opportunities for future research was to apply strategic balance theory in the context of strategic group research. Hereby, the question, whether strategic balance theory applies at the strategic group level, implies the identification of firms in strategic groups that distinguish themselves from the center of the group in order to reduce competition. Following strategic balance theory positioning on the competitive cusp within different strategic groups will always be beneficial. If existing strategic balance research is correct than there will be performance differences among firms based on their ability to position on the competitive cusp. If this relation is depending on firm specifics or on strategic group structures than strategic balance theory is depending on boundary conditions. McNamara et al. (2003) have applied strategic balance theory within their seminal paper on the commercial banks industry in the metropolitan area of Minneapolis-St Paul. However, as stated earlier they applied strategic balance theory to a highly regulated market with little competitive forces and high barriers to entry and to exit. Consequently, the question still remains of how strategic balance theory alters the understanding of firms' behaviors in dynamic, large and unregulated markets with low barriers to entry and exit. This research has the objective to further strengthen this promising stream of research by testing it in a context which, relative to the highly regulated banking industry in McNamara (2003), is characterized by lower mobility barriers, less regulation and more intense competition.

Furthermore, Deephouse assumed in his theory that firms did not collude. Within industrial organization economics, research indicates that similar firms collude in order to increase their performance. Following this argumentation, if the balance point within an industry is closer to similarity than to differentiation, it is likely that tacit collusion will be present (cf. Chapter 2.2.1). In line with this, the question arises of how much similarity is needed to avoid legitimacy challenges. Concerning performance implications, research opportunities exist when it comes to the question of how rapidly performance is declining when firms move beyond the strategic balance point (Deephouse, 1999). Moreover,

Deephouse stated that the particular relationships between strategic differentiation, competition, and resulting firm performance have not been convincingly demonstrated. Besides, scholars call for future research on the strategic balance theory within markets that face strong competitive pressures and consist of limited barriers to entry and to exit (e.g. Deephouse, 1999; McNamara, et al., 2003).

Although Semadeni investigated the market for consulting services, he merely focused on the 50 largest consulting firms. His argument to limit his sample to large consulting firms was that the highest "growth in consulting revenues has been among the very largest firms in the industry". Nevertheless, with the exclusion of small- and mid-sized consulting firms, an important part of the analyses of positioning efforts in the consulting industry is missing. In addition, a concentration on the largest players in the market is not appropriate in order to examine legitimacy issues as large firm size already implies a certain degree of establishment in the served markets. Thus, established firms are less challenged by legitimacy issues as they have mastered a certain firm growth and have already resisted competition within their organizational field. In consequence, the empirical outcome focused on a specific market segment is neglecting the full industry picture.

As outlined above there is little empirical evidence probing into positioning and its effect on firm performance. Nevertheless, the use and preservation of positioning strategies and their effect on performance has long been established (Fisher, 1991). McAlexander, Becker, & Kaldenberg (1993) stress the argument that the selection of the right positioning strategy is significantly correlated with financial performance of a firm. Although this research gap has gained attention, assertions were raised that positioning and its impact on performance is in danger of being underresearched (Blankson & Kalafatis, 2004). Thus, my research answers the call from management scholars for further research on positioning strategies and contributes to an 'evolving discussion related to the impact of positioning strategies on firm performance' (e.g. Blankson, et al., 2008; Hooley, et al., 1998; Kalra & Goodstein, 1998; Langerak, 2003; Suzuki, 2000).

In order to fully address and test the theoretical propositions of strategic balance theory, it is mandatory to use a representative sample of firms of an industry. Accordingly, analyses should not be limited to one specific firm type prevalent in an industry, but try to derive a sample that mirrors the existing diversity of an industry closely. Consequently, I will include not only large but also mid- and small-sized firms active in the German consulting market in the sample. Hereby, my research comprehensively covers the existing diverse market environment for consulting services. Furthermore, this research helps to advance strategic positioning research methodologically by using a multi-dimensional, non-perception based, and supply oriented measure of strategic positions based on content analysis of the service offerings communicated on the consulting firms' websites. Within this research, I will address the outlined limitations and research challenges introduced by strategic management scholars. I will apply strategic balance theory to the highly competitive consulting market that is marked by limited institutional protection and low barriers to entry and exit. I expect that my research has significant implications for strategic balance theory and that the theory has to be modified, i.e. that moderating factors such as the structural characteristics of the "local" competitive environment have to be included.

2.2 Strategic Groups

In the following chapter, the theoretical concept of strategic groups is introduced in four steps. First, a definition of the basic theory of strategic groups is derived. Second, the concept of strategic groups is explicated as an intermediary level between industry- and firm-level. Third, theoretical approaches and different streams of literature within strategic group research are presented. Forth, empirical evidence on the existence of strategic groups as well as on the relationship between strategic group membership and performance is discussed.

2.2.1 Theoretical Background

2.2.1.1 Defining Strategic Groups

Since Hunt's (1972) seminal work on competition, in which he coined the term 'strategic group' a substantial body of literature has addressed research questions on strategic groups. A basic and widely accepted definition states that a strategic group is "a group of firms in an industry following the same or similar strategies along strategic dimensions" (Fiegenbaum, Sudharshan, & Thomas, 1987; Hunt, 1972; McGee & Thomas, 1986; Porter, 1979, 1980). The membership of firms within a strategic group is based on similar characteristics of firm strategies and delineating differences of firms to other strategic groups. According to Cool and Schendel (1988), firms of an industry naturally build strategic groups when their actions are more homogenous than those of industry incumbents in general. In an extreme case, there might be only one strategic group within an industry that comprises all market participants or every company within an industry could form an individual group. Conversely, a limited number of strategic groups exist in most industries that reflect the essential dimensional differences. In consequence, companies within a strategic group are similar to each other and at the same time differ along strategic dimensions to other groups (Hinterhuber & Kirchebner, 1986; Porter, 1980).

Hunt's seminal research

Hunt (1972) developed the concept of strategic groups within his unpublished dissertation. He designed an empirical study to examine the U.S. home appliance industry that was characterized as a highly concentrated and competitive market in the 1960s. Although market concentration was high, industry profitability was dismal (Cool & Dierickx, 1993; Hunt, 1972). Hunt attributed this unexpected finding to the existence of - so far undefined - structural factors. During his course of investigation Hunt detected different sources of asymmetries between firms within the industry and found certain groups of firms behaving in similar ways. He followed from his analyses that different groups of firms in the same industry pursue similar strategies along the detected asymmetries. Consistently, Hunt proposed to group and to analyze firms further within an industry along certain strategic dimensions and he labeled the results 'strategic groups'. Industry in this context is defined as a compilation of organizations that produce comparable or even homogeneous products or services for a specific target group (Fiegenbaum & Primeaux, 1987; Hunt, 1972).

Hunt applied strategic dimensions that were in line with the detected asymmetries: differences in product differentiation, degree of product diversification and extent of vertical integration (Hunt, 1972; McGee & Thomas, 1986). Along these strategic dimensions, Hunt identified four strategic groups in order to ensure minimized economic asymmetry within each group. Consequently, he stated that companies within a strategic group pursue similar strategies and are to a certain extend homogeneous (Fiegenbaum & Primeaux, 1987; Hunt, 1972). He further argued that entrants to an industry face different entry barriers depending on the strategic group they intend to position in (Hunt, 1972; McGee & Thomas, 1986). According to Hunt, strategic groups are surrounded by barriers influencing the likelihood for outside firms to enter and for inside firms to exit the group. As a consequence, he identified entry barriers in dependence of his four strategic groups. Furthermore, he argued that dividing industries in aggregated units is of practical relevance to top management in order to achieve competitive advantages. In summary, Hunt focused in his analysis on competitors active in the same principle markets and allocated firms to strategic groups on the basis of homogeneity of operations within the same basic businesses (McGee & Thomas, 1986).

Strategic dimensions

The question of what strategic dimensions comprise has been subject of debate among strategy researchers. The notion to differentiate along strategic dimensions itself is only of limited specificity and allows instrumenting various firm differentiating aspects in competitor analyses. Mascarenhas & Aaker (1989) define strategic dimensions as the chosen firm strategy or key factors that are crucial for a specific group or a total industry, e.g. assets or special skills. Strategy – in this context – is understood as a firm's combination of strategic valuables and of what a firm does, its activities (Hunt, 1972; Mascarenhas & Aaker, 1989). Consistent with this, Chang et al. (2006) comprehend strategic dimensions as a way to describe characteristics and the resource allocations of different business providers. It includes e.g. positioning strategies, manufacturing strategies, functional-level strategies, pricing strategies, targeting (of sub-markets) strategies, and distribution strategies (Mascarenhas & Aaker, 1989). Hence, if a pattern of similar or common strategies becomes obvious, firms build a strategic group. Consistently, some scholars point out that to some extent strategic group structure is the result of strategic choices (Dess & Davis, 1984; Porter, 1980; Tang & Thomas, 1992). Firms strategically position by choosing to be similar or to be different to their competitors and acting accordingly. Therefore, understanding the formation of strategic groups helps business providers to act upon the most suitable strategy and to better allocate their limited resources (Asker, 1995; Chang, et al., 2006; Cool & Schendel, 1987). As Ketchen et al. (2004, p. 29) put it "knowing what your competitors are doing, and how to respond, is clearly important to a firm's success". Nevertheless, Tang and Thomas (1992) insist that strategic choice is not enough to explain the existence of groups of firms. Over time, strategic groups naturally evolve and structure the positioning of single firms within an industry.

Furthermore, key factors exist depending on the examined industry that influences the building of strategic groups. In the relevant literature, strategic dimensions such as vertical integration (Hunt, 1972; Newman, 1978), product lines (Cool & Schendel, 1987), product differentiation and specialization (Feka, Xouris, & Tsiotras, 1997; Oster, 1982), technology (Cool & Schendel, 1987; Ghazanfar, McGee, & Thomas, 1987), brand identification (Feka, et al., 1997), and size (Porter, 1979; Primeaux, 1985) have been used to classify firms into strategic groups.

Mobility barriers

From a complementary perspective Mascarenhas and Aaker (1989, p. 475) define strategic groups as "a grouping of businesses within an industry that is separated from other groupings of businesses by mobility barriers, barriers to entry and exit". In their argumentation, the main driver of strategic group definition is the analysis of mobility barriers and not the one of pursued strategies. Porter (1979, p. 215) states that strategic groups are "persistent structural features that are bounded by mobility barriers". Mascarenhas and Aaker (1989) agree with Porter and consider mobility barriers to be at the core of the concept of strategic groups. They consent with Caves and Porter (1977) who state that firms' investments in mobility barriers play a decisive role in defining and differentiating strategic groups. Mobility barriers are defined as structural factors – barriers to entry and exit, which are specific for every strategic group and protect its members from invasion of adjacent competitors by retarding imitation efforts (Caves & Porter, 1977; Dranove, et al., 1998; McGee & Thomas, 1986; Sudharshan, Thomas, & Fiegenbaum, 1991). Caves and Porter (1977) argue that mobility barriers prevent industries from consolidating into one group of firms. Conceptually, mobility barriers are the intra-industry equivalent of barriers on an industry-level (Porter, 1980; Tywoniak, Galvin, & Davies, 2007).

Mobility barriers can be seen as a collective investment for members of strategic groups, sometimes in intangible assets whose benefits are shared between the members. For example, groups of firms invest in advertisement and the establishment of brands to differentiate themselves from other groups of firms. Thereby, firms erect mobility barriers to protect themselves from strategic group entrants (Tang & Thomas, 1992). However, other scholars consider mobility barriers as structural forces impeding firms from freely changing strategic positioning and as substantially independent of firms' actions (Cool & Schendel, 1988). Tang and Thomas (1992) doubt that a behavioral explanation of mobility barriers is sufficient. They argue that mobility barriers are also dependent on structural basic conditions of the industry, e.g. relocation costs. Porter (1980, 2008) identifies product differentiation, cost advantages, economies of scale, capital requirements, access to distribution channels, and government policy as the main drivers of entry barriers. However, it is necessary to differentiate between the conceptual definition of mobility barriers and the building up of mobility barriers in reality. Especially, the intention to protect strategic groups from the invasion of competitors seems to be far from perfect.

Depending on the industry different barriers to entry and exit apply. With respect to service industries, tangible assets (e.g. firm size), special skills (e.g. knowledge, experience, educational level of the workforce) as well as intangible assets (e.g. reputation, brand name, customer loyalty) are plausible entry barriers (Ferguson, Deephouse, & Ferguson, 2000; Ketchen, Thomas, & Snow, 1993; Mascarenhas & Aaker, 1989; Peteraf & Shanley, 1997). Furthermore, Semadeni (2006) suggests that service marks can be utilized by firms to prevent competitors from entry to certain industry groups. Complementary to entry barriers, exit barriers restrain firms within strategic groups from leaving and switching to other groups. Examples of this type of barriers are sunk costs, switching costs or government policies (Caves & Porter, 1977). Furthermore, specialized assets (e.g. labor, customer or distributor commitments; long-term contracts with suppliers; managerial pride) are also considered as structural forces impeding companies from unreservedly changing their competitive market positioning (Cool & Schendel, 1988; Olusoga, Mokwa, & Noble, 1995). Considered over time strategists face the challenge of increasing entry barriers whilst decreasing exit barriers (Mascarenhas & Aaker, 1989).

In general, mobility barriers are not static, but develop over time. Hereby, they provide possibilities for companies to change into different groups, or even build new strategic groups (Chang, et al., 2006; Porter, 1979, 2008). As a consequence, the structures of strategic groups evolve reflecting further expansion and growth in the affected industry. Therefore, different strategic groups show different financial performance over time regarding the competitive strategies they adopt (Asker, 1995; Fiegenbaum & Thomas, 1990; Hunt, 1972; Newman, 1978). In contrast, McGee and Thomas (1986) consider mobility barriers as being highly stable because barriers reflect decisions and behaviors that are long-term, costly and difficult to change. They argue that it is difficult for firms to reposition and move from one strategic group into another. Mobility barriers impede firms from entering strategic groups, which offer higher performance potentials (Ketchen, et al., 1993). Certainly, the type of industry investigated plays an important role in this discussion. Industries that require heavy initiating investments for product development and that provide high switching costs are likely to have high and stable mobility barriers. For example, the pharmaceutical industry provides high mobility barriers due to heavy financial investments in research and development, highly specific asset requirements and a high degree of governmental regulation (Cool & Schendel, 1987).

However, professional service industries - for instance the consulting industry - are marked by comparably low mobility barriers. Initiating investments to enter the consulting market are limited as consulting services are mainly dependent on human capital and the skill set of its employees (Richter & Schmidt, 2006). In other words, the suggestion is that the consulting industry is marked by comparably low capital intensity (von Nordenflycht, 2010). Furthermore, institutional protection of consulting as a profession is missing and business models are comparably easy to imitate. In addition, I consider existing intangible market barriers like reputation, brand name and customer loyalty as intra-market barriers other than barriers hindering market entry. Market entry in consulting is comparably easy to achieve. However, intra-market barriers hinder new entrants from establishing in market segments with above-average performance rates and thereby serve as barriers to successful growth and performance. Concluding, I consider the consulting industry as a market with low barriers to entry and exit. In line with the previous argumentation, I propose to take a closer look at intra-industry mobility barriers in industries with low barriers to entry and exit the market.

Summary and definition underlying this thesis

In summary, Mascarenhas and Aaker (1989) foster a less action-dependent focus like common strategy conceptualization of strategic groups and emphasize on a stronger resource dependence approach. Dranove et al. (1998) admit that mobility barriers serve a critical role in limiting access to strategic group entry and enhancing group interactions. Nevertheless, they state that mobility barriers can only sustain group-level differentials, but have no direct influence on defining strategic groups and on enhancing group-level effects (Dranove, et al., 1998). Leask (2007, p. 192) tries to combine these complementary views and defines strategic groups as "stable intra-industry structures separated by mobility barriers in pursuit of different strategies that may be expected to yield significant performance differences in terms of outcome".

The definition underlying this thesis with respect to my focus on the professional service industry is as follows:

Strategic groups are defined – in the light of service industries - as groups of firms within a service industry that follow the same strategic positioning and are similar along specific strategic dimensions that are of key importance to the respective industry. Firms within a strategic group differ from firms in other groups on the grounds of key strategic dimensions (e.g. business/service model, intended client relationship, positioning, service offering). Strategic groups build structural intra-industry mobility barriers impeding members of other strategic groups from freely changing their competitive market position.

In the following chapter, I will explain why the strategic groups-level analysis serves as an important intermediate that complements industry- and firm-level analyses.

2.2.1.2 Strategic Groups between Industry- and Firm-Level

Researchers in the fields of economics and strategic management have argued that merely focusing on aggregate industry- or on individual firm-level leaves out an important and useful sub industry aggregation, the strategic group-level (e.g. Caves & Porter, 1977; Hatten & Schendel, 1977; Hunt, 1972; McNamara, et al., 2003; Nair & Kotha, 2001; H. Thomas & Venkatraman, 1988). While economists in industrial organization (IO) research concentrate on industry-level and strategic management researchers originally focus on firm-level, strategic group research serves as an intermediary level combining ideas and concepts of both perspectives. Thus, strategic group theory created a new important and complementary unit of analysis and enriches existing research within both economics and strategic management (Sudharshan, et al., 1991). Both groups of scholars find strategic group research intelligible and credible as it represents a theoretical compromise between traditional IO theory and traditional strategy theory (Barney & Hoskisson, 1990). While it deepens intra-industry knowledge, it adds to the body of knowledge on firms. In addition, it does not totally reject the assumption of heterogeneity between firms like IO theory, but at the same time it analyses groups of firms that resemble each other closely (Barney & Hoskisson, 1990). In a nutshell, with strategic group analyses economists come to understand differences within industries while strategists come to understand commonalities across firms (Michael, 2003).

Within IO research, industries are the unit of analysis and firms within an industry are assumed to be homogeneous (Bain, 1959). The general assumption is that firms are alike in all important dimensions except for their size (Porter, 1979). In that sense, economists expect true variation to be prevented by competition and competitive imitation (Michael, 2003). In addition, all firms are defined to obtain the same profits. The particular aim is to detect industry dynamics, patterns of conduct – a central industry strategy – and to compare industries with respect to performance differences by conducting inter-industry analyzes (Scherer & Ross, 1990).

Strategic group theory was intentionally developed as an extension of IO theory (Caves & Porter, 1977; Hunt, 1972; Howard Thomas & Pollock, 1999). This theory extends IO theory as it shows that there is not only one optimal strategy, which all firms in an industry should pursue. As a consequence, strategic group theory introduces heterogeneity to industry examinations as the concept allows firms to differ along multiple dimensions, including strategy and profits (Michael, 2003). Moreover, IO's structure-conduct-performance (S-C-P) paradigm postulates that structure (environmental factors) determines conduct (strategic managerial actions), which in turn determines industry performance (Bain, 1959). Strategic group theory turns this around by arguing that the conduct (the strategy) of the firm directly influences both the structure (group structure) and the performance of the industry (Cool & Schendel, 1987; Tang & Thomas, 1992). Furthermore, strategic group theory helps to explain performance differences beyond IO theory's proposition that performance differences between firms exist solely due to relative application of scale (Bain, 1959). Since Hunt's (1972) and Porter's (1979) seminal theory building efforts strategic group research intends to explain performance differentials between firms within the same industry, mainly across strategic groups. Contrary to IO's orientation toward analyses of industry performance merely on cross-sectional industry samples strategic group research is mainly concerned with the analysis of firm performance typically confined to a single industry (Cool & Schendel, 1987; Dess & Davis, 1984).

However, strategic group researchers argue that firms within the same industry coalesce around a limited array of competitive approaches (Leask & Parker, 2007; Short, Ketchen, Palmer, & Hult, 2007), and that some approaches offer higher performance potential than others (Fiegenbaum & Thomas, 1990). Moreover, some streams within strategic group literature modify IO's concept of entry barriers and argue that firms within a strategic group are likely to collude to build up mobility barriers (Barney & Hoskisson, 1990; McNamara, et al., 2003). As described earlier, mobility barriers facilitate the preservation of exclusive conditions and high profitability within certain strategic groups (Michael, 2003). Thus, strategic group research made the concept of collusion more plausible as the smaller the number of firms that colludes within an industry, the more likely collusion leads to higher profitability. Following this line of argument leads to performance differences across groups and similar performance potentials within groups. Nevertheless, it is up to the single firm within a strategic group to successfully position itself within a given group structure to optimize its individual performance.

Strategic management research initially focuses on firm-level and concentrates on single firms as the unit of analysis. Consistently, strategic management research has its origins in the study of the decisions of a single firm that is adapting its resources and skills to the unique business environment it faces (Rumelt, et al., 1991). Thus, firm performance differences are – in line with the resource-based view (RBV) – resulting from different levels of resources and the result of superior skills firms obtain (Barney, 1991; Demsetz, 1973). From this perspective, performance is considered as a function of a company's ability to obtain and deploy the resources bundle needed to achieve sustained competitive advantage for its organization (Barney, 1991; Wernerfelt, 1984). In this manner, the economics' concept of collusion is de-emphasized while similar performance is attributed to common patterns of resources and skills (Michael, 2003). Consistent with this, the RBV suggests that companies should strive to position themselves in such a way so that no other company can imitate their unique set of resources and skills (Short, Palmer, & Ketchen, 2002). In contrast, strategic group research argues that mutual interdependence among organizations exists and impacts company success within its strategic group. Hence, strategic group theory originally implied that some determinants of performance are unique across different groups, but similar within groups (Short, et al., 2002). Nevertheless, strategic group research has acknowledged that differences in strategic key dimensions and performance exist not only between but also within strategic groups (McNamara, et al., 2003; Reger & Huff, 1993).

Despite the differences, more emphasis has recently been put on the RBV of the firm within strategic group research (Michael, 2003). Essentially, the suggestion from the RBV is if firms within an industry invest in similar 'valuable' and 'rare' resources, they form hereby a strategic group (Barney & Hoskisson, 1990). In line with this, if it is difficult to imitate or substitute the resources, the strategic group can achieve above normal profits (McNamara, et al., 2003) and try to build mobility barriers. This is complementary to strategic group theory, as the history of a firm influences strategic investments which is also observed by strategic group analysis (Leask, 2007).

In summary, strategic group theory provides the perspective of an intermediary level between industry- and firm-level. It efficiently fills the existing research gap by borrowing ideas and concepts from IO research as well as from strategic management research. As an intermediary level, the strategic group level facilitates in-depth analyses of market competitor interactions and thorough analyses of performance variances of industry participants across and within group structures (Dranove, et al., 1998). Consequently, strategy researchers have taken this third intermediate unit of analysis into account when comparing performance effects within industries across different firms (e.g. Kotha & Nair, 1995; Michael, 2003; Short, et al., 2007; Tywoniak, et al., 2007). In addition to this, Porac et al. (1989) distinguish an additional market sublevel and call it competitive groups. Competitive groups are defined as groups of firms that compete from a demand side perspective. In contrast to this limited perception-based perspective, strategic groups offer a more fine-grained approach to analyze how firms compete (Leask, 2007; Leask & Parker, 2007; Sherer) along multi-dimensions.

In general, strategic group theory has been well established in strategic management research. It is considered as one of the concepts that have a high impact on strategic management literature (DeSarbo & Grewal, 2008; Fiegenbaum & Thomas, 1995; McGee, Thomas, & Pruett, 1995; Porter, 1979). Scholars have shed light on the concept of strategic groups from various perspectives and applied numerous related theories to deepen the development of a grounded strategic group theory. The following section provides an overview and discussion of theoretical approaches applied within the framework of strategic group research.

2.2.2 Theoretical Approaches in Strategic Group Research

Basically two streams of strategic group research have developed over the years. The first body of literature concentrates on performance implications of strategic group membership (e.g. Caves & Porter, 1977; Cool & Schendel, 1988; Fiegenbaum & Thomas, 1990; McNamara, et al., 2003; Pandian, Thomas, Furrer, & Bogner, 2006; Short, et al., 2007). The second stream focuses more on behavioral implications of strategic groups (e.g. Dranove, et al., 1998; Ketchen, Snow, & Hoover, 2004; Peteraf & Shanley, 1997; Tywoniak, et al., 2007). Complementing the two streams, two methodological approaches applied in strategic group research are presented and discussed.

Streams of strategic group research

A substantial body of literature has built up on the basic research question of what constitutes performance differences between strategic groups. While strategic group research is well-established in strategic management literature, scholars criticize inconsistent empirical evidence on group effects that help to explain performance differences between firms in an industry. However, this *first stream of literature* reported mixed results on the strategic group-performance relationship throughout a large scale of industries. Some scholars present empirical evidence for significant linkages between strategic group membership and performance (e.g. Ketchen, et al., 1997; Nair & Kotha, 2001) while others observe contradictory evidence and opposite effects (e.g. Barney & Hoskisson, 1990; Cool & Dierickx, 1993; Marlin, Ketchen, & Lamont, 2007; McGee & Thomas, 1986). As a consequence, critiques question the existence of strategic groups in general (Barney & Hoskisson, 1990; Hatten & Hatten, 1987; H. Thomas & Venkatraman, 1988) and formulate the concern "whether the study of intra-industry groups provides any information that cannot be gleaned from the study of industries and individual firms" (Dranove, et al., 1998, p. 1029). Hatten and Hatten (1987) and Dranove et al. (1998, p. 1030) even suggest „that the concept of strategic groups may be nothing more than an analytical convenience - a way to summarize and examine firm-level data efficiently". Ketchen et al. conclude in their meta-analysis of studies in strategic groups literature that "ambiguity still surrounds the strategic groups-performance relationship" (2004, p. 796). Subsequently, scholars call for future research on the contingencies that shape the nature and strength of between-group performance differences (Ketchen, Snow, & Hoover, 2004; Marlin, et al., 2007).

The critique led to a parallel evolving *second stream* of strategic group literature that did not solely concentrate on group effects on firm performance as the key contribution of strategic group research (Tywoniak, et al., 2007). In a nutshell, scholars proposed that strategic group theory is valid and meaningful to deepen our understanding of firms' strategic behaviors and/or industry rivalry patterns (Chen, 1996; Cool & Dierickx, 1993; Cool & Schendel, 1988; Mas-Ruiz, Nicolau, & Ruiz-Moreno, 2005; Peteraf & Shanley, 1997; Reger & Huff, 1993; Smith, Grimm, Wally, & Young, 1997) merely focus on the detection of performance effects. Furthermore, scholars call for recognition of the value of the multidisciplinary perspective of strategic management in theorizing about strategic groups (McNamara, et al., 2003; H. Thomas & Venkatraman, 1988). Researchers argue that besides traditional IO economics and strategic management theories other perspectives like cognitive psychology, social psychology, organization theory, and behavioral science should be included.

Within the second stream of strategic group literature, scholars are for instance concerned with the question, whether strategic group members influence each other's strategic behavior. Researchers affirm this question by considering strategic groups as reference points to firms (e.g. industry entrants) within their strategy finding processes (Fiegenbaum & Thomas, 1995; Tang & Thomas, 1992). Fiegenbaum and Thomas (1995) argue that especially successful firms at the core of a strategic group serve in some industries as reference points. These reference firms are considered as benchmarks to competitors as they are close to ideal with respect to the industry's key dimensions, pursued strategy and firm performance. The suggestion being that their success leads to mimicry attempts from minor successful companies who try to establish similar profit potentials.

In the following, three concepts rivalry, spatial competition and strategic group identity are presented in further detail.

Rivalry

The impact of rivalry on firms' behavior in strategic group structures has been of interest to scholars within the second stream of strategic group research (Chen, 1996; Cool & Dierickx, 1993; Mas-Ruiz, et al., 2005; Peteraf, 1993; Smith, et al., 1997). Given the contradictory evidence of the effects of strategic group membership on performance, Cool and Dierickx (1993) question the existence of a direct link between group membership and performance. They propose the idea that the concept of rivalry might play an intermediate role in the strategic group membership-performance-relationship. Rivalry in this context refers to the competitive movements of individual firms – the actions firms take and the responses to them by competitors (Mas-Ruiz, et al., 2005). Within strategic group literature, discussion arose on the question whether intra-group rivalry or between group rivalry has greater influence on individual firms and their performance (Dranove, et al., 1998).

Scholars base their line of arguments to some extent on IO economics and argue that rivalry between strategic groups is greater than intra-group rivalry (Mas-Ruiz, et al., 2005; Porac, Thomas, Wilson, Paton, & Kanfer, 1995; Smith, et al., 1997). The assumption is that firms take collusive actions within strategic groups, which reduce intra-group rivalry. It suggests that in order to reduce the threat of competitors from outside the own strategic group, firms collude and build up mobility barriers (Caves & Porter, 1977; Fiegenbaum & Thomas, 1990). Collusion arises when managers from different firms recognize mutual dependence and take into account e.g. pricing, advertising, capacity expansion or other investment activities of other firms as they make decisions on those issues for their own firms (Michael, 2003). Collusion is not explicitly based on meetings and formal agreements, informal or tacit collusion is also likely to occur within certain industries (Shapiro, 1989). Dranove et al. (1998) add to this with their findings on rivalry. They argue that the greater the number of groups within an industry and the more equal their market shares, the greater the rivalry among them. Furthermore, they prove that the greater the "strategic distance" (i.e. how different the groups are along key dimensions), the greater the rivalry. According to the authors, another driver of rivalry is - high market interdependence (i.e. the degree to which groups target the same customers). As a consequence these factors affect firm performance indirectly in that the effects come through the mediating factor of rivalry. Furthermore, firms across strategic groups face - per definition - increased strategic distance, which from an IO perspective intensifies competition and rivalry between firms across strategic groups (Cool & Dierickx, 1993).

Scholars who focus more on behavioral aspects than merely on performance implications of strategic group research contradict this view and argue that intra-group rivalry is higher than between groups (Chen, 1996; Mas-Ruiz, et al., 2005; McNamara, et al., 2003; Porac, et al., 1995; Smith, et al., 1997). Herewith, they challenge the general assumption that firms in strategic groups collude. Empirical studies of collusion found that the ability to effectively collude can be limited among firms, "due to coordination difficulties and differences in the costs and benefits of collusion among industry members" (McNamara, et al., 2003, p. 166). In addition, Fiegenbaum and Thomas (1995) specifically tested for collusion in strategic groups and found no supporting evidence. On the contrary, they found evidence that firms are likely to focus on their own competitive position within their group. They do so in order to "be more aware of and reactive to the actions of their own group members" than to members of other groups. Adding to this is the finding that managers perceive their strategic group as a reference point to benchmark against competitors and experience higher rivalry with firms within their own strategic group than with firms in other groups (Fiegenbaum & Thomas, 1995; McNamara, et al., 2003; Porac, et al., 1995). In this regard, researchers argue with contestable markets theory, which states that firms that are highly similar to each other face higher competition and rivalry (Cool & Dierickx, 1993; Hatten & Hatten, 1987). McNamara et al. (2003) conclude from their evaluation of existing research that rivalry is more likely than collusion and intra-group rivalry is higher than between-group rivalry.

Spatial competition

Tang and Thomas (1992) link the theories of spatial competition and cognitive taxonomy to strategic groups. Thereby, they respond to the criticism that the concept of strategic groups is not an analytical convenience, but a theoretical construct. Based on the idea of strategic choice, they argue that in order to understand the formation of strategic groups it is necessary to explain why firms choose to position near to or far from competitors. Their proposition is to apply spatial competition to fill this research gap. Hotelling (1929) pioneered the idea of spatial competition that describes the assimilation of product offerings of competitors. The fundamental theory of spatial competition is built up on the following set of assumptions (Hotelling, 1929; Tang & Thomas, 1992; Howard Thomas & Pollock, 1999):

(1) Two firms are competing in a market characterized by a linear product space,

(2) Relocation cost is zero,

(3) Customer density function is uniform along the product space,

(4) Price elasticity of demand is zero.

If a firm positions itself in a market arbitrarily rather than in the center of a linear market, the market is divided into a long and a short segment. A new entrant firm will try to position close to the existing firm, but so that it faces the longer segment of the market. Consequently, the first firm will imitate the positioning strategy of the second firm and reposition so that it faces the longer segment and gains higher profits. In a 'leapfrogging' process both competitors will reposition and try to gain higher profits. Over time this process leads to a market situation where both competitors meet in the center of the linear market and face equally sized market segments. This result indicates a tendency to minimum differentiation of products or services between firms (Boulding, 1966; Tang & Thomas, 1992). Further research has shown that the principle of limited differentiation also applies for industries with large numbers of firms and in multi-dimensional product or service space (Eaton & Lipsey, 1975). Eaton and Lipsey (1975) call this the "principle of local clustering", which is interrelated to the concept of strategic groups. Therefore, this principle and spatial competition provide theoretical foundations to strategic group research, as they suggest that over time competitors assimilate their strategic positioning efforts to these of their closest competitors, which results in the building of strategic groups (Tang & Thomas, 1992; Howard Thomas & Pollock, 1999). However, I will not include spatial competition within my empirical research as it requires data from different time periods to analyze the positioning development.

Strategic group identity

Scholars of the second stream of strategic group research imported concepts from other sciences (e.g. behavioral sciences, psychology, and sociology) to widen the scope of how strategic groups are conceived. One of these perspectives perceives strategic groups as cognitive communities that help managers to cope with complex market situations. By allocating competitors to cognitive strategic groups, managers are capable of dealing with market complexity, reducing uncertainty, and conserving on bounded rationality (Levinthal & March, 1993; Peteraf & Shanley, 1997; Tang & Thomas, 1992). The cognitive structuring of market participants into strategic groups goes beyond a mere categorization of competitors as it influences firms' behaviors and attributes. It helps managers to effectively position their own firms within their competitive environment. Peteraf and Shanley (1997) further elaborate on the theory of cognitive strategic groups and introduce the concept of a strategic group identity:

> *A strategic group identity is a set of mutual understandings, among members of a cognitive intra-industry group, regarding the central, enduring, and distinctive characteristics of the group.*

This concept is comparable to the notion of organizational identity (Albert & Whetten, 1985). Firms develop a group identity within their cognitive strategic group. Arguing with social learning theory, firms observe and learn from competitors who face similar threats and opportunities. Furthermore, managers utilize the gained information to inform current firm strategy and to alter their behaviors and attributes, accordingly. As managers also gain experience in inter-organizational actions they reflect upon the outcome of past decisions. This supports management decisions whether to position near to or far from competitors. This dynamic process leads to the emergence of strategic groups that share strategic identities (DeSarbo & Grewal, 2008; Ferguson, et al., 2000; Peteraf & Shanley, 1997). Strategic identity in this sense facilitates that group members align their activities to a great degree with those of other strategic group members.

Deephouse (1999) introduced the theory of strategic balance to strategic group research. He builds on the concept of strategic identity with a certain strategic group. It states that firms have three options to position in a strategic group structure: positioning near to, positioning far from competitors or on the 'competitive cusp' which balances differentiation and received legitimacy (cf. Chapter 2.1.2).

Heterogeneity in strategic groups

However, DeSarbo and Grewal (2008, p. 295) state that "strategic group researchers have begun to recognize that heterogeneity may exist in the extent to which firms pursue strategic group recipes". Building on cognitive psychology and on the concept of strategic identity, Reger and Huff's (1993) differentiation of core, secondary, and solitary firms is applied within strategic groups analysis. The distinction is based on the degree to which firms associate with the strategy recipe of a strategic group or the shared strategic group identity (Peteraf & Shanley, 1997). Core firms associate tightly with group strategy and key dimensions, whereas secondary firms follow the group's strategic recipe less closely (DeSarbo & Grewal, 2008; Ketchen, et al., 1993; McNamara, et al., 2003; Peteraf & Shanley, 1997). Solitary firms do not identify with a specific strategic group and consequently pursue niche strategies. This notion establishes "a supplementary level of complexity, according to which core firms compete more intensely with one another, but less intensely with secondary firms, and vice versa" (DeSarbo & Grewal, 2008, p. 302).

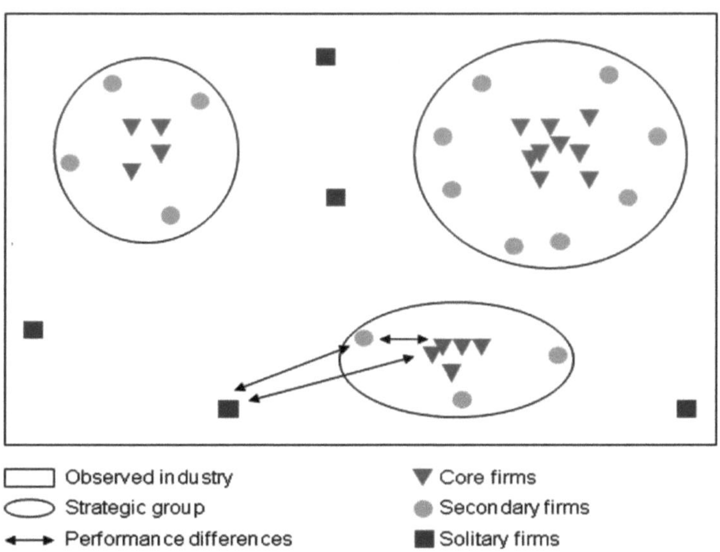

Figure 4: Distinction of Core, Secondary and Solitary Firms

DeSarbo and Grewal (2008) further develop strategic group heterogeneity with their introduction of hybrid strategic groups. This concept helps to identify firms that combine strategic recipes from different strategic groups to develop their own unique strategic position. Herewith, they differ from secondary firms that follow the group's strategic recipe less closely than core firms and solitary firms that pursue own strategies. Hybrid firms are loosely aligned with multiple strategic groups and borrow strategic recipes from different strategic groups. These firms are expected to occur in industries with low barriers to entry and exit. The suggestion is that strategic groups that are surrounded by low mobility barriers enable hybrid firms to blend strategic recipes across multiple strategic groups.

In recent years scholars tried to integrate the achievements of the first two waves of strategic group literature. Doubts, whether strategic groups exist and whether this intermediary level provides additional information, were rejected (Dranove, et al., 1998; Esper, Mas, & Murillo, 2008; Leask, 2007; Short, et al., 2007).

Strategic group research framework

In order to structure the inconclusiveness of theoretical approaches and empirical results in the two previous streams of research, Tywoniak et al. (2007) suggested a framework to comprehensively study strategic group structures. They transpose concepts of the New Institutional Economics (NIE) to expand the understanding of existing strategic group research and to provide conceptual and methodological structure for further research. Research in the field of NIE examines how economies work at the country level and how economic, political, legal, social, and cultural institutions influence the economies' performance (Platteau, 1994a, 1994b). The relationship with strategic group research seems unexpected. This is due to the fact that NIE is concerned with higher aggregate levels than strategic group research and due to differences in aims, scope, and underlying assumptions. Nevertheless, Tywoniak et al. argue (2007) the transposition of selected NIE concepts through analogical reasoning contributes to strategic group research in two ways. First, NIE offers an over-arching analytical framework that helps to forge links between behavioral and performance analyses. Second, the framework helps to incorporate the influence of all relevant institutions on intra-industry structure, which has been missing in strategic group research so far. In summary, the authors suggest that analyzing structures within industries is analog to analyzing structures within national economies. The framework, adapted from Williamson (1998, 2000), consists of 4 interrelated levels of analyses each of which corresponds to a different layer within industries and strategic groups (Tywoniak, et al., 2007).

Level 1 is that of social embeddedness, which comprises analyses on informal institutions such as norms, tacit knowledge, customs, and behavioral rules. Williamson refers to it in a sports metaphor as 'spirit of the game'. Research on the influence of institutional isomorphism (social pressures to conform to informal norms of conduct) on strategic behavior in strategic groups (Deephouse, 1996; McNamara, et al., 2003), falls in this category. Scholars argue that the existence of communities of practice (J. S. Brown & Duguid, 1991) contributes to the emergence of strategic identities within strategic groups (Peteraf & Shanley, 1997; Reger & Huff, 1993). At this level, the basis for patterns of rivalry or collusion between firms is defined.

Level 2 defines the institutional environment: formal industry regulations, government policies, industry standards, and codes of conduct. In the sports metaphor, this level sets the 'rules of the game' by imposing constraints to strategic choice in a given industry setting. These factors have to some extent been subject of analysis in strategic group research. In particular, analyses of barriers to entry and exit imposed by industry regulations fall in this level. Strategic group researchers acknowledged the importance of these institutional factors and the influence on strategic groups (Lee, 2003; McNamara, et al., 2003; Peteraf, 1993). Nevertheless, Tywoniak et al. (2007) criticize that these institutional factors have rarely been directly incorporated in the analyses as common opinion is that all industry participants are equally affected by the institutional environment.

The strategic direction and configuration of individual firms is subject of analysis at level 3. Firms are allocated to strategic groups in dependence of how they deploy resources and competencies. Metaphorically speaking, firms are grouped by the way they 'play the game' (Williamson, 2000). Many of the studies concerned with the detection of strategic groups as industry substructures are concerned with this level. Level 4 comprises the 'execution of the play'. Analyses include short-term firm-level effects, the ability of firms to dynamically deploy and subsequently realize the potential of their resources (Mehra, 1996; Tywoniak, et al., 2007). This involves reactions to changing market conditions: adjustments of price or of employment. In addition, mobility barriers imposed by group members following firms' commitment of firm resources and skills are analyzed at this level.

Tywoniak et al. (2007) state that the strategic group perspective offers a more complex view of firms than that from a NIE perspective. In strategic group research economic (asset endowment, resources and competencies), behavioral (cognitive structures, strategic identity) and social (network embeddedness) dimensions are integrated. This implies that firm-level effects are the outcome of complex, multi-dimensional influences. In sum, the framework helps to structure the relations of various strategic group studies and allocate them to different levels of analysis. The first two streams of strategic group literature were in particular concerned with level 3 and 4 analyses.

Inductive vs. deductive configuration of strategic groups

From a methodological perspective, Ketchen et al. (1993) evaluated in an influential analysis theoretical approaches of organizational configuration and its performance implications. They compared the application of inductive and deductive approaches to configure strategic groups. Basically, within a deductive approach, researchers have a priori expectations about the specific nature of groups. When an inductive approach is applied there are no such expectations (Short, et al., 2007). Furthermore, Ketchen et al. (1993, p. 1280) tested, whether the applied configuration approach led to difference variances in terms of performance-strategic group relationship and they state:

> *Two major approaches for defining and comparing organizational configurations have arisen in the strategic management literature. The historically dominant approach focuses on empirical classification of organizations in order to define inductively a set of configurations appropriate to a given context. Essentially, the inductive approach concentrates on maximizing internal validity while sacrificing generalizability. The second approach focuses on producing configurations generated deductively from prior theory. Deductively derived configurations apply broadly and are not dependent on particular industry contexts.*

Ketchen et al.'s (1997) meta-analysis on empirical studies of strategic groups finds that eight percent of the variance in firm performance is related to group membership, and that this result holds for deductively as well as inductively defined groups. This result implies that there is no approach that should be preferably applied to generate reliable results.

2.2.3 Empirical Evidence on Strategic Groups

As described in the previous chapter, different theoretical approaches have been applied to identify strategic groups in a large array of industries. In the following chapter, a summary of empirical evidence on the existence of strategic groups and the performance-strategic group relationship is presented.

2.2.3.1 Evidence on the Existence of Strategic Groups

Following Hunts seminal empirical work on strategic groups in the U.S. white goods industry, many researchers presented empirical evidence for the existence of strategic groups as industries substructures (e.g. Cool & Dierickx, 1993; Cool & Schendel, 1988; DeSarbo & Grewal, 2008; Fiegenbaum, McGee, & Thomas, 1988; Hatten, Schendel, & Cooper, 1978; Leask & Parker, 2007; McGee & Thomas, 1986; Newman, 1978; Oster, 1982; Porter, 1979). Due to the fact that every industry has its own recipes for success and of how to do business (DeSarbo & Grewal, 2008; Spender, 1989) it is difficult to generalize empirical evidence on strategic groups throughout various industries (Nair & Kotha, 2001). Therefore, it is necessary to analyze strategic group structures and their effects in different industries, separately. Leask (2007) suggests to analyze strategic groups on the basis of national specific markets, due to the assumption that strategy is both market and segment specific and should therefore be measured in these terms. Consistently, strategic dimensions have to be chosen with careful consideration of specific industry characteristics as well as national market specifics in order to ensure compelling results (Houthoofd & Heene, 2002).

In particular, in the first 20 years of strategic group research, empirical research has concentrated on consumer goods industries (e.g. Cool & Schendel, 1987; Cool & Schendel, 1988; Fiegenbaum & Primeaux, 1987; Hatten & Schendel, 1977; Hunt, 1972; McGee & Segal-Horn, 1990; Porter, 1979). Hereafter, the pharmaceutical industry has often been subject of empirical studies and still is today (e.g. Cool & Schendel, 1987; Fiegenbaum, Sudharshan, & Thomas, 1990; Leask & Parker, 2007; Lee, 2003; McGee, et al., 1995; Pandian, et al., 2006). Leask & Parker (2007) explain this observation with three reasons. First, the pharmaceutical industry has the mix of market heterogeneity and difficult-to-replicate resources that indicate the presence of strategic groups (Mehra & Floyd, 1998). Second, strategic groups are likely to exist within this industry, because many pharmaceutical companies share common historical origins and have developed in parallel (Bogner, Thomas, & McGee, 1999). Third, pharmaceuticals are constantly one of the highest performing industries in the world. Nevertheless, companies assume enormous risk in terms of research expenditure and the time-frames across which they operate. Under these circumstances, better strategies should produce superior performance (Leask, 2007).

In addition, a mere practical reason to investigate this industry is its manageability and the availability of firm data throughout the market due to a high rate of publicly owned firms. Evidence for the existence of strategic groups in pharmaceutical markets is compelling and convincing throughout different studies (e.g. Cool & Schendel, 1988; Leask & Parker, 2007; Lee, 2003). Even cross-checks conducted by authors employing different methods to the same market scope and time period, resulted in similar strategic groups (Cool & Schendel, 1987; Osborne, 1996). In all cases a number of moderately constant strategic groups was observed, even though significant changes to group composition were detected over time (Leask & Parker, 2007). In their study Leask and Parker (2007) examined the U.K. pharmaceutical market over a period of five years, implementing many methodological recommendations of former studies. They found statistically significant evidence "for a strong intra-industry structure within the U.K. pharmaceutical industry that consists of between six to eight strategic groups".

From the 1990s on, strategic group research has shifted the empirical focus to service industries (e.g. Fiegenbaum & Thomas, 1990, 1993, 1995; McNamara, et al., 2003; Nath & Gruca, 1997; Pegels & Song, 1997). Nevertheless, most scholars focusing on services have investigated the financial service industries – banks and insurances (e.g. Fiegenbaum & Thomas, 1990; Fiegenbaum & Thomas, 1993, 1995; Fiegenbaum, Thomas, & Ming-Je, 2001; Mas-Ruiz, et al., 2005; Mehra, 1996; Reger & Huff, 1993) Only few studies were concerned with other service industries, i.e. airline industries (e.g. Kling & Smith, 1995; Ryans & Wittink, 1985) and health care industries (Nath & Gruca, 1997; Pegels & Sekar, 1989; Short, et al., 2002). Due to the constantly rising importance of service industries and their heavy impact on economies (e.g. service organizations constitute almost 75 percent of employment in the United States and in Germany) many strategic group scholars continually concentrate on the analysis of service industries today (Esper, et al., 2008; Ferguson, et al., 2000; Leask & Parker, 2007; Short, et al., 2007). Nonetheless, professional service industries have hardly been subject of investigation so far. These industries are expected to further gain in importance and are marked by heavy competition, but still lack empirical manageability. Therefore, it is relevant to investigate positioning efforts, strategic group structures within these industries and resulting performance effects.

In their study, Nath and Gruca (1997) based their analysis of the existence of strategic groups on three interrelated perspectives: economic factors (strategic groups), perceptual factors (cognitive strategic communities), and organizational factors (networks of interacting firms). The aim of their study was to compare the results of three different methods of strategic group formation with each other. They used archival measure, perceptual measure and direct measure to conduct their threefold analysis integrating three different viewpoints.

First, they employed the most common method of identifying strategic groups within the strategic management literature and analyzed archival data using clustering methodology. Second, the authors applied multi-dimensional scaling on perceptual measures from managers. In a third step, they asked managers in the industry to directly identify competing firms. Finally, after they compared the resulting strategic groups, they found empirical evidence for the convergence of all three alternative methods of strategic group formation (Nath & Gruca, 1997).

In the following chapter, empirical evidence of the strategic group membership-performance relationship will be further elaborated.

2.2.3.2 Evidence on the Strategic Groups-Performance Relationship

The degree of the influence of strategic group membership on firm performance has attracted considerable attention within strategic management literature (e.g. Caves & Porter, 1977; Cool & Schendel, 1988; Fiegenbaum & Thomas, 1990; McNamara, et al., 2003; Pandian, et al., 2006; Short, et al., 2007). Almost all studies on strategic groups across different industries directly or indirectly try to assess performance implications of strategic group membership (Dranove, et al., 1998; Ketchen, et al., 1997). As pointed out by numerous scholars, theoretically, performance differences exist *across* and *within* strategic groups (e.g. Caves & Porter, 1977; Ketchen, et al., 1997; Ketchen, Snow, & Hoover, 2004; Leask & Parker, 2007; McGee & Thomas, 1986; McNamara, et al., 2003; Tang & Thomas, 1992).

Marlin et al. (2007) challenge the assumption that strategic groups offer different performance potentials. They argue with equifinality, which basically states that strategic groups can be equally effective under a given set of conditions. A certain final state can be reached from different initial conditions and from a variety of different paths. They revise the notion that firms should try to enter the most profitable strategic group and imitate the most profitable firms. Firms should rather identify a strategic path that leads to high performance within their own range of possible strategies. This colludes with the concept of strategic positioning within strategic groups as core, secondary and hybrid firms.

However, three questions surrounding the strategic group-membership-performance relationship arise:

1. Is there significant empirical evidence for a direct/indirect influence of strategic group membership on firm and group performance?

2. Are any performance differences across groups or within groups of greater extent?

3. What determines the influence of strategic group membership on performance? (This question is relevant if questions 1 & 2 can be answered in the affirmative)

Empirical research has been able to answer these questions to some extent. Yet, empirical answers given to these questions are not unconstrained consistent. However, research assessing performance differences within strategic groups has been limited (McNamara, et al., 2003). Porter (1979) was one of the first to examine potential effects of strategic group membership on group and firm performance. As proposed by scholars from an IO perspective, a group's mobility barriers protect its likely colluding members against entry of potential competitors and confer persistent advantages to some groups over others within an industry (e.g. Mascarenhas & Aaker, 1989; Tang & Thomas, 1992; Tywoniak, et al., 2007). These barriers enable to preserve exclusive conditions within strategic groups. This leads to performance differences across groups and similar performance potential within groups. At the same time, however, Porter cautioned that these barriers only determine potential performance at the group level. Yet, realized firm performance is also a function of several firm-specific factors. Nevertheless, one central insight following this rationale is that without strategic interaction among group members, there will be no direct effect of group membership on performance (Dranove, et al., 1998; Leask & Parker, 2007).

Cool and Schendel (1987, 1988) were among the first scholars to examine the relationship between strategic group membership and performance not only across but also within strategic groups. Within their studies, they analyzed the U.S. pharmaceuticals industry over a period of 20 years. They found significant empirical evidence for performance differences *within* strategic groups in terms of market share (Cool & Schendel, 1988). Whereas, they discovered only partial support for performance differences across strategic groups as results were mixed over the years (Cool & Schendel, 1987). Nevertheless, they did not compare the results of within/across performance differences and draw theoretical and practical implications. Several studies on strategic groups in pharmaceutical industries and on strategic group membership influences on performance followed their work. However, a broad assessment of empirical strategic group research within the pharmaceutical industry indicates conflicting results. Some studies report significant performance differences across/within groups (Cool & Dierickx, 1993; Cool & Schendel, 1987, 1988; Leask & Parker, 2007; Voyer, 1993), while others find no significant performance differences between different strategic groups (Bogner, 1991; Guedri, 1998; Martens, 1988). Nevertheless, there exists congruent and consistent acceptance within the research community of the fact that strategic groups exist in the pharmaceutical industry.

In their article McNamara et al. (2003) provide a study of strategic groups and performance implications in a service industry. The focus of the study is to compare competitive positioning strategies within and across a strategic group structure in a locally delineated banking industry. Consistently, the authors also reflect on strategic heterogeneity within strategic groups and test its performance implications. Hence, performance variance differences are examined not solely across strategic groups, but also within strategic groups. In order to conduct this additional distinctive analysis of performance differences, McNamara et al. (2003) differentiate between core, secondary and solitary firms in dependence of the degree of their strategic identification with their strategic groups (in accordance with Peteraf & Shanley, 1997; Reger & Huff, 1993). However, the authors use a fairly limited systematic approach of allocating firms to the three classes. They state that "while they created a dichotomous categorization for core and secondary firms, following Reger and Huff (1993) and Ketchen et al. (1993), another way to examine this issue would be to use a more profound and continuous indicator of group identification" (McNamara, et al., 2003, p. 175). Their results suggest that performance differences within groups are significantly larger than those across groups and that some firms within strategic groups develop better competitive positions than others (McNamara, et al., 2003; Reger & Huff, 1993). A more systematic and objective allocation methodology could contribute to an improvement of empirical analyses. This improves findings as the chosen methodology of defining strategic groups sets the groundwork for all subsequent following analyses.

McNamara et al. (2003) tested to which degree firm performance variance is attributable to differences across strategic groups in contrast to interfirm differences within strategic groups. It turned out that 82.6 percent of the total performance variance is within groups but only 17.4 percent of the performance variance is across strategic groups. The results indicate that firm performance differences within strategic groups are significant, but those across strategic groups are not. Furthermore, they find that secondary firms within strategic groups financially outperform both core firms as well as solitary firms. They conclude that secondary firms are able to effectively balance the benefits of strategic distinctiveness with institutional pressures for similarity. In other words, they find that successful firms position on the competitive cusp in line with strategic balance theory.

In their meta-analysis, Ketchen et al. (1997) examined 33 studies consisting of 40 independent samples with respect to performance differences across group structures. They found that group membership does partially explain performance differences. Significant performance differences across groups were prevailing. Although group membership appeared to explain a rather modest amount, eight percent of performance differences resulting within strategic group structures (Ketchen, et al., 1997; McNamara, et al., 2003). Moreover the study revealed that involving broader group configurations, concentrating on single-industry samples and longitudinal designs are more likely to find significant relationships.

Overall, there exist mixed empirical results on the relationship strategic group membership and performance. While many studies report significant performance differences across strategic groups (e.g. Dess & Davis, 1984; Fiegenbaum & Thomas, 1990; Mascarenhas & Aaker, 1989), some studies found no significant evidence (e.g. Cool & Schendel, 1987; Lewis & Thomas, 1990; McNamara, et al., 2003). In line with this, Ketchen et al. (1997) demand future researchers to use improved methodologies of detecting strategic groups in order to achieve results with sound significance.

Potential for further research

When examining empirical studies on the existence of strategic groups, it appears that researchers concentrate on straightforward definable industries, e.g. industries that are geographically delineated. Furthermore, researchers seem to choose industries with relatively stable groups for investigation, where mobility barriers limit entry and exit. In general, in order to prove existing theory it is of great value to analyze these kinds of industries. Nevertheless, for the sake of testing whether this theory holds for more complex industry structures, industries with limited barriers to entry and exit and less delineated markets should be subject of future investigation.

Due to conflicting studies, the relationship between strategic group membership and performance remains ambiguous (Barney & Hoskisson, 1990; Ketchen, Snow, & Street, 2004; Leask & Parker, 2007; McGee & Thomas, 1986; H. Thomas & Venkatraman, 1988). Although empirical studies have confirmed that many different industries consist of strategic groups over the years, an unambiguous relation between strategic group membership and performance has yet been confirmed (McGee & Thomas, 1986; H. Thomas & Venkatraman, 1988). As a consequence, the relationship between strategic group membership and firm performance is empirically not conclusively proven, yet. Despite these assertions, however, there is strong evidence that natural groupings do occur between firms (Leask & Parker, 2007).

The mixed results and empirical inconclusiveness warrant more research to deepen the understanding of the interdependence of performance and strategic positioning besides a widening of the scope of examined industries. Recent strategic management research has stressed this need (DeSarbo, et al., 2008; Short, et al., 2007; Tywoniak, et al., 2007). Leask & Parker (2007) state that the link between performance and strategic group membership has not been conclusively empirically proven. In line with this, McNamara et al. (2003) call for further research on the influence of performance across and especially within strategic groups in other industries and professions. In particular, strategic positioning efforts within strategic groups in industries with low entry and exit barriers need to be examined more closely. So far, industries observed in previous studies (e.g. banking, insurance, health care, pharmaceutical industries) were highly regulated, fragmented, and comprised geographically delineated markets (McNamara, Luce, & Tompson, 2002). Nevertheless, constraints to use highly delineated industries facilitated a certain degree of homogeneity among the firms evaluated. Doubts still remain, however, whether previous findings on influences of strategic group membership on firm performance can be generalized to industries characterized by low regulation, low delineation, and low mobility barriers. Therefore, it seems promising to examine the influence of low barriers of entry and exit on firm performance in a strategic group structure. In addition, research calls for more profound and in-depth empirical methods for the detection of strategic group structures (e.g. Ferguson, et al., 2000; Nair & Kotha, 2001). Researchers state that improving existing methodology provides more convincing evidence on strategic group structures and performance differences (Pandian, et al., 2006).

2.3 Hypotheses

This research is to a certain extent explorative in nature as it determines the existence of strategic groups within the consulting service industry. In a second part of the empirical analyses hypotheses on performance differences between consulting firms will be examined. With this procedure, I follow Semadeni (2006) and other strategy researchers (e.g. Ketchen & Shook, 1996; Meyer, Tsui, & Hinings, 1993) who argue that such an approach is appropriate in strategic management research, especially in analyzing comparably unexplored research areas such as management consulting services. It is noted that there is still little established literature on management consulting firms. However, I develop hypotheses to test the theoretical constructs in strategic management literature as derived in the previous chapters.

First, I test for the existence of strategic groups in the consulting industry on the base of the above derived strategic positioning dimensions. In a second step, I examine the relative strategic positioning of consulting firms within the derived strategic group structure. Third, these findings are used to analyze the effect of strategic positing within a strategic group structure on firm performance.

Tang & Thomas (1992) suggest that when the underlying competitive forces of an industry are driven by easy-to-change strategic dimensions, the number of strategic groups may be small. This notion may apply for the market for consulting services, as the market is characterized by low barriers to entry and exit. Strategic dimensions relevant for the consulting market – as described above – are comparably easy to change as hardly any large investments e.g. in plants, technical knowhow, research and development are required. In addition, even the necessary buildup of reputation and brand awareness is comparably straightforward in the consulting market. Especially in comparison to industries like automotive or pharmaceutical, where a strong brand can only be built over many years as quality differences between firms are easy to assess. I expect that the German consulting market is highly diverse and marked by low barriers to entry and exit. However, I propose that firms follow similar strategic recipes and service models along defined dimensions and build different strategic groups. With this, I expect firms in certain strategic groups to establish intra-industry mobility barriers in order to sustain exclusive market conditions. Nevertheless, I propose that the underlying competitive forces of the consulting industry are driven by easy-to-change strategic dimensions. In line with this, I expect the existence of a small number of strategic groups within the German consulting market.

H_1: The consulting industry is characterized by the existence of a small number of strategic groups.

The theory of strategic positioning within strategic group structures described above develops the argument that firms positioning within strategic groups differ. I expect that depending on the actual position within a strategic group structure and specific characteristics of a firm e.g. the service model followed, different positioning strategies occur with different performance opportunities to firms.

The proposition is that the consulting market holds for various competitive positioning efforts. Furthermore, different positioning options such as near to or far from competitors are comparably straightforward to achieve within this industry. In addition, sustainable barriers to imitation are decreasing due to the high transparency and enduring professionalization within the consulting market in combination with the very characteristics of a service industry itself. The professionalization of clients' buying behaviors and the broadening of service offerings by consulting providers will lead to a twofold reaction. On the one hand, this leads to differentiation measures in order to attract clients with different service models. This implies that less similarity increases overall firm performance. On the other hand, imitation efforts are established to reduce uncertainty among clients and foster legitimacy in relation to other consulting providers. In the competitive consulting environment, legitimacy serves as a prerequisite to successful competition as it drives positive client perception. As a consequence, strategic groups consisting of established firms with a high degree of reputation should attract imitating firms that successfully position alike to gain legitimacy. This assumes that consultancies challenging legitimacy and acting outside the defined setting risk a lower public perception and hence performance differences.

As a consequence, I expect that positioning efforts within strategic group structures have a significant impact on performance. In line with strategic group theory, I expect that different strategic groups offer differing market conditions to consulting firms. Therefore, depending on which strategic group a firm positions in, different performance potentials arise.

H_2: *There are performance differences between the strategic groups in the consulting industry.*

In its extremes both strategies to position near to or far from competitors impose challenges. The above outlined theory suggests that firms that position on the 'competitive cusp' and balance differentiation and legitimacy are likely to achieve superior performance rates. The suggestion is that firms align in strategic groups to achieve legitimacy but, at the same time, differentiation within these groups is tolerated and favorable to a certain degree. This implies that firms that position far from competition, but within an acknowledged strategic group gain above-average performance rates. Herewith, consulting firms may improve individual firm performance by reducing competition while preserving the consensus of a legitimate group. However, legitimacy is not challenged but similarity decreased. A consulting company positioned on the competitive cusp as a secondary firm seeks the balance between the two positioning extremes and balances legitimacy reduction and differentiation.

Existing strategy research suggests that some firms are rather centered within a strategic group and are following a core reference strategy of the respective group. These core firms are surrounded by an outer ring of firms that are less committed to the reference strategy, so-called secondary firms.

H_3: Within a particular strategic group in the consulting industry secondary firms show superior performance as compared to core firms.

The described specific market characteristics of the consulting industry like low barriers to entry and exit, high dynamics and competitiveness impose the threat of new market entrants. Young firms follow established service models, intend the same level of client interaction and offer the full spectrum of services. Hereby, they show potential clients that they are capable of delivering the same services at the same quality level alike the well-established players in the market. If young consulting providers are convincing in their positioning efforts they should be able to establish legitimacy. Existing research (Semadeni, 2006; Singh, et al., 1986) argues that legitimacy is important for young consulting firms, especially as it increases the probability of organizational survival of young firms. In addition, as the provision of consulting services is generally perceived as replaceable, potential for spill-over effects from established to young competitors should be higher in immature markets with low entry barriers. Young firms that manage to position alike established firms should profit from existing reputation for quality and reliability. They should achieve this by e.g. openly advertising the fact that their consultants are using the same methodology and processes as established market players. This alignment of positioning efforts makes it challenging for potential buyers to differentiate the service offering from those of its established competitors. In line with the outlined theory my hypothesis is:

H_4: Young firms that manage to position near to old, established firms achieve above-average performance in the consulting industry.

The derived hypotheses are empirically tested within this study and according to the results discussed in further detail.

3 Empirical approach and Methodology

The following chapter comprises the empirical approach as well as the applied methodology of this study. The chapter is divided into three parts. First, the research design of the study is introduced. Second, details on the data collection process and the variables used within this study are provided. The operationalization of the variables and the set of rating rules will be explicated in detail. Third, the statistical methodology comprising cluster analysis, multidimensional logistic regression and analysis of performance differences will be introduced and discussed. In this study consulting firms active in the German market are the unit of analysis. In other words, not solely the country of origin is of interest, but whether the respective firm is providing consulting services to clients in Germany.

3.1 Research Design

As stated earlier, this research takes consulting firms' strategic positioning as the primary unit of analysis. In order to empirically address the introduced research questions and derived hypotheses, the research objective of this study is twofold. The first objective is to identify strategic groups in the German consulting market on the basis of strategic dimensions that describe positioning efforts. Consistently, the introduction of the key dimensions that define different strategic groups is part of the objective. The second objective is to relate single firm's strategic positioning within and across strategic groups to firm performance. The effect of strategic positioning on firm performance will be thoroughly analyzed. This has important implications for the research design of the study.

In general, strategy research is often exploratory, with a focus on theory building rather than testing (Ketchen & Shook, 1996). In line with this argument, strategic group research is per definition explorative when it comes to identifying strategic groups in given industries. Consistently, the research design is partially described as exploratory. In particular, exploratory research will be based on content analyses of consulting firms' service expositions on their websites and on additional firm characteristics extracted from commercial data bases. This is an established approach within existing literature (Campbell, 2003; Frey, Botan, & Kreps, 2000; Gray, Kouhy, & Lavers, 1995; Heldal, Sjøvold, & Heldal, 2004; Holder-Webb, Cohen, Nath, & Wood, 2009).

As service firms have to rely mainly on verbal expositions of their service offerings, the websites of a consulting firm contain firm statements and information that reflect the communicated strategic positioning closely. Therefore, a consulting firm's website can be seen as a mirror of the firm's positioning efforts and is understood as a means to raise the attention of potential clients. Existing research points out that the consulting business is based on strong relationship networks to attract clients (Harste, 2008). However, the possibilities of promoting consulting services and communicating market presence to new clients out of the relationship network are limited. This argument in combination with the spread of the Internet, firm websites have significantly gained importance (Holder-Webb, et al., 2009). Besides, strategic decision making is a team process in the majority of professional service firms (McNamara, et al., 2002). Team decisions are essential for professional service firms that build on human capital. As a consequence, firm statements on consulting firms' websites are expected to be thoroughly defined and approved by the management team of a consulting firm. Consistently, I propose that the communicated positioning stated on the website of a consulting firm builds to the strategic positioning approved by the management in team efforts.

With respect to this line of argument, consulting firms will be clustered into strategic groups on the basis of strategic dimensions gathered from website content analyses. As Barney & Hoskisson (1990) state the development of clusters, per se, cannot be used as a test of the existence of strategic groups. In line with this, the identified strategic groups will be further examined with respect to their key differentiating characteristics to verify the existence of strategic groups and differences within groups. In a second step the influence of strategic positioning in strategic group structures on firm performance will be thoroughly analyzed.

The empirical analyses on strategic positioning of consulting firms are performed on the basis of publicly available data. In order to conduct reliable empirical research within the field of strategic management, it is crucial to use data that fits the research objectives well. In order to address these requirements, I use service expositions as published on the websites of consulting firms as my primary data source to conduct content analyses.

3.2 Data and Variables

The following chapter is structured in two sections. First, it describes the data composition of this study. Hence, the process of data collection, the information sources as well as the sample composition is explained in further detail. Second, the variables applied as well as their operationalization are explicated. In line with this procedure, content analyses and the process of defining the rating rules are introduced. Furthermore, the application of the rating rules to firm websites is outlined.

3.2.1 Data Collection and Sample Composition

The sample of my empirical investigation is in large parts random. However, generating an unconditionally random sample would have been particularly difficult, especially due to the fact that the total population of management consulting firms in Germany can hardly be determined. In order to represents the consulting market closely, I use a stratified random sample (Holder-Webb, et al., 2009; Neuman, 2005). With this technique, I control the relative quantity of each stratum, to include a sizeable proportion of different firm sizes in the final sample.

As the consulting industry is not sharply delineated, firm lists that encompass the entire population of consulting firms active in Germany are unavailable. According to estimates of the Bundesverband Deutscher Unternehmensberater (BDU), a German industry association, around 14.250 consulting firms were offering consulting services to clients in Germany as of 2006 (BDU, 2006). The total market size in terms of revenues is estimated to account for EUR 14.7 billion (selling unit booking the revenue is localized in Germany). This estimation is likely to be conservative (Galal & Richter, 2007). As the BDU may not fully take small consulting service providers into account, the number of consulting firms in Germany is expected to be significantly larger.

Data collection process

However, as consulting firms are very restrictive with the publication of their financial data, I use a commercial data base to extract firm specific data as the starting point of my data collection. In order to develop a random sample of consulting firms, active in the German market, I follow a three-step process (cf. Figure 4).

First, as my initial data source, I generate a list of firms providing consulting and consulting-related services (e.g. executive search, outsourcing services, and software development), active in the German market extracted from the data base of a commercial firm data provider (Hoppenstedt). The list contains in total 3.127 firms. The firm description includes firm name, headquarters address, number of employees (as of 2006), revenues from consulting services in Germany (as of 2006), year of foundation of the firm, and the address of firm websites. Due to the commercial provider's vague definition of what composes a consulting service, many of the listed firms have to be excluded owing to their non-conformity with the targeted sort of firm to be included within this research. Within the data cleansing process, I also have to exclude a large number of firms due to missing data (Chapman, 2005). Many firms refuse to publish confidential firm data. In particular, number of employees and revenues is often missing. Furthermore, I exclude all firms that focused their offerings on consulting-related services, as well as industry associations and firms offering temporary work. The data cleaning procedures result in a final list of 443 firms offering management consulting services in Germany. The firms are grouped into five revenue classes. In accordance to the frequency of firms within each revenue class, I randomly select 185 small- and mid-sized firms (<45mn revenues per year) from the list to include in my sample. With this approach, I follow Semadeni's call to tap the competitive dynamics manifested among mid-sized and small consulting firms (Semadeni, 2001).

Second, I use an additional commercial provider (Lünendonk lists), specialized on the largest 50 consulting firms by revenues generated in the German market (Streicher & Lünendonk, 2007). The firm list derived from Hoppenstedt data base includes only a small number of large consulting firms. However, large consulting firms are of particular interest to research on professional service firms and deem for specific consideration (Semadeni, 2006). Therefore, I gathered relevant data on the 50 largest firms as of 2006 and include them in my sample. In sum, the consolidated sample adds up to 235 consulting firms active in the German market as of 2006.

Third, I conduct content analyses on the German websites of the 235 consulting firms in the sample. This marks the most critical step of the data collection process. Content of text refers to written statements containing information on the firms' service characteristics and positioning efforts (Neuman, 2005). Whereas these written statements can be empirically observed, the service itself cannot be directly observed by people other than the firms' clients. Therefore, drawing on Van de Ven & Poole (1990), I apply an investigator inference approach to data gathering (for other examples of the application of content analysis in strategic management research see Fiol (1994) and Lal, Pitt & Strachan (2004)). Due to unavailability of the websites, two firms have to be excluded from further investigation.

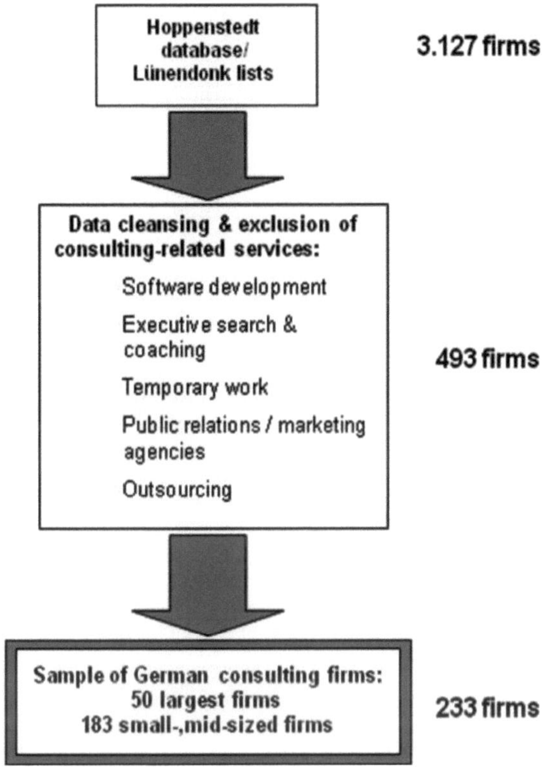

Figure 5: Data Collection Process

Sample Composition

The sample comprises a total of 233 consulting firms active in the German market. These 233 firms generated collectively about EUR 8.5 billion revenues with the provision of consulting services in Germany and employ over 48,400 employees as of 2006. Given that the German consulting market had estimated revenues of about EUR 14.6 billion in total as of 2006, the sample represents a sizeable proportion (almost 60%) of the consulting market in this geography. The number of employees comprises consultants as well as support staff.

The average number of employees within the sample is 213, ranging from 1 employee to 3996 employees. The average revenue of a firm within the sample is EUR 37.2 million, ranging from EUR 25.000 to EUR 695.9 million. The revenue and employee composition of the sample reflect the German consulting market closely (cp. Figure 4). On average the firms have 3 offices in Germany, the maximum being 33. The year of foundation of the firms ranges from 1886 to 2004. However, the great majority (2/3 of firms in the sample) were founded in the 1980s and 1990s.

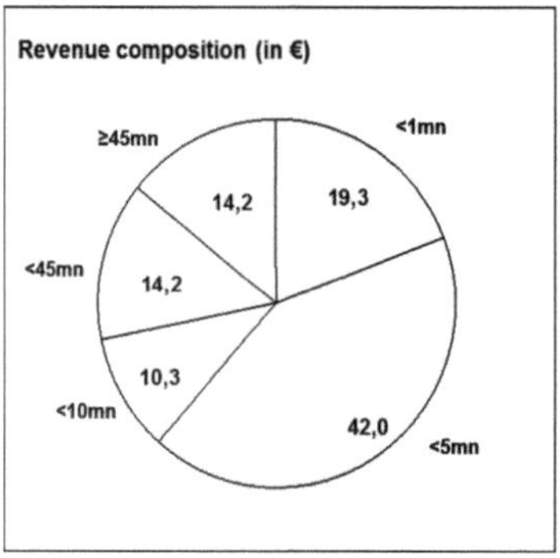

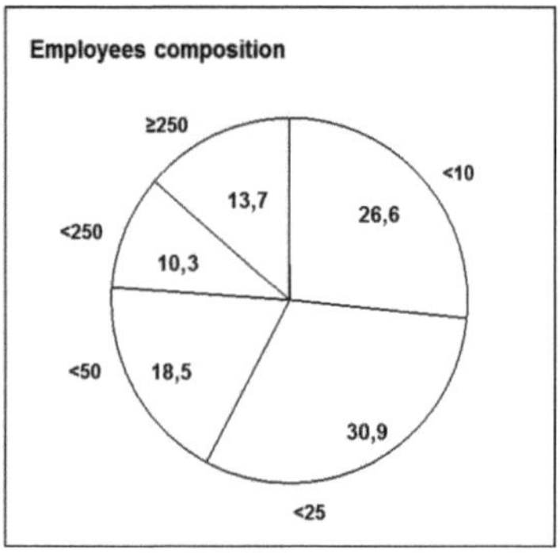

Figure 6: Revenue and Employee Composition of the Sample

Within the sample 9% of the firms are of international origin (mostly U.S. based), while 91% are of German origin. However, the majority of firms with international origin are among the largest firms of the sample. Nevertheless, approximately half of the German consulting firms (51%) offer their consulting services outside of Germany to German firms operating internationally as well as to international clients. However, half of the German consulting firms that are offering consulting services abroad operate international offices. This highlights the high degree of internationality of the research sample.

3.2.2 Variables and Operationalization

In line with the previously identified key dimensions of the consulting industry, I will examine several constructs within the research, in order to determine the positioning efforts of German consulting firms.

3.2.2.1 Content Analyses and Coding of Data

As stated above, consulting firms use verbal expositions of their services offerings to position themselves vis-à-vis potential clients and relative to their competitors. In order to minimize ambiguities about what the service entails, it must be the consulting firm's objective to phrase its service exposition carefully. To systematically capture the communicated positioning of consulting firms as exposed in the service offerings on their websites, I defined a set of rating rules to conduct the content analysis (Lacity & Janson, 1994) (cf. Appendix A) . The set contains 55 rules that explicitly determine the rating of variables that are of interest for this study. The rules were defined with the purpose to capture the constructs and underlying variables of interest to the study. The set of rules clearly determines for each examined variable along additional rating dimensions which value has to be set by the raters. In dependence of the variable examined, different dimensions apply. Strong emphasis has been put on a careful wording of the rules.

The content analysis of the websites was conducted in a three step process from December 2007 to January 2009. In the first step, a test phase was run by two independent raters. Within the test phase each rater applied the set of rating rules to the websites of a test sample of 25 consulting firms. According to the experiences the raters reported within the testing phase, I adjusted and rephrased the rating rules. With this approach, I ensured a definition of the rating rules and reduced rating ambiguity. Herewith, the wording reflected the intended constructs and variables of the study. However, within strategy research a certain level of ambiguity that leaves room for interpretation is needed.

In the second step, the two raters applied the defined set of rating rules to the websites of the entire sample of 233 consulting firms. Both raters applied the rules independently of each other to each firm of the sample. By applying the rating rules, both raters had to thoroughly examine each firm's websites and to individually decide on the ratings of each variable. The raters were not allowed to interact with each other which further ensures the reproducibility of the data set (Fleiss, Levin, & Paik, 2003). They had only limited participation in the process of defining the rating rules, in order to clearly separate the process steps of definition and application of the rating rules. This procedure ensures that the data set can be reproduced and is independent and unbiased. In summary, I worked with two independent raters, who were not in exchange with each other, in order to control for inter-rater reliability requirements.

In the third step of the websites evaluation process, a third independent rater took the position of a rating judge (Holder-Webb, et al., 2009). The rating judge did not participate in the rating process so far. This step was introduced as the inter-rater reliability - using kappa-statistic measure of agreement (Fleiss, et al., 2003) - between the first two raters was moderately (75% agreement on all variables) within the reliable range of inter-rater reliability (> 70%) (Frey, et al., 2000; Holder-Webb, et al., 2009; Neuendorf, 2002). Therefore, in cases where the first two raters differed in their ratings of single mostly binary variables, the judge was asked to apply the rating rules to the particular firm websites to take a final rating decision on a certain variable.

3.2.2.2 Variables and Rating Rules

The selection of variables is one of the most critical steps in an empirical study, in particular within strategic management research (Dawes, et al., 1992; Leask & Parker, 2007). The definition of key dimensions to distinguish strategic groups is of critical importance. However, the specification of strategic variables is always a function of the industry under study (Cool & Schendel, 1987). Nevertheless, different choices of sets of variables generate different results. Therefore, differences in the variable sets of previous studies provide a legitimate explanation for contradicting results of empirical studies within strategic group research. The number of variables chosen to identify strategic groups has varied significantly within the research community. In general, the prevailing assumption within exploratory research is that the higher the number of variables included the more profound the findings will be (Leask & Parker, 2007).

Basically, there are three approaches to identify appropriate strategic variables: inductive, deductive, and cognitive (Ketchen, et al., 1993). The *inductive* approach concentrates on an exploratory classification of observations. In other words, neither the variables nor the number and nature of the resulting strategic groups are intertwined to deductive theory (Ketchen & Shook, 1996). All factors are defined along dimensions the responsible researcher himself considers as important. McKelvey's (1975) recommendation is to use as many variables as possible in order to maximize the outcome of an analysis of differences between firms and groups. The use of a large number of strategic variables is expected to maximize the likelihood of discovering meaningful differences between strategic groups. Within a *deductive* approach, the combining facets of the research approach are closely determined by theory. The type of strategic variables, the number of variables as well as the expected outcome are strongly dependent on theory-based hypothesis building. Whereas the *cognitive* approach can be considered as a sort of 'conceptual cousin' of the inductive approach due to the fact that both avoid to make theory-based predictions (Ketchen & Shook, 1996). Contrary to the inductive approach the cognitive approach relies primarily on the perceptions of experts such as industry executives (e.g. Mascarenhas & Aaker, 1989; Reger & Huff, 1993) to define strategic variables.

With this research, I follow mainly an inductive approach in order to define the right set of strategic variables. Nevertheless, to some extent the approach used within this study has cognitive and deductive elements. To understand the relevant dimensions of strategic positioning in the consulting market, I conducted 22 expert interviews with consulting industry experts. The interviews were conducted with academics, with executive providers of consulting services, as well as with consulting clients – in order to cover different perspectives on the consulting market. The interviews were semi-structured in nature in order to achieve comparable results, but at the same time to provide enough space for open discussions. The results of the interviews in combination with reflections on theory were used as ground information within the process of defining the right set of variables and consequently deriving rating rules.

In order to characterize positioning efforts and services provided by the firms in my sample, I used a set of rank-ordered and binary measures. Despite the disadvantages of binary measures, their use is beneficial as it reduces the ambiguity in the rating process conducted on the firms' websites (Schnell, Hill, & Esser, 1999). I defined the following measures to capture the nature of services and the positioning efforts offered by the firms in the sample, as portrayed in their service expositions. The variables used are derived from three key dimensions of the consulting industry that were related to existent literature on strategic positioning in the previous chapters (cf. Chapter 2.1.1.2). For each variable a specific rating rule was defined as described above. The categories included in the cluster analysis are type of service model, intended relationship with the client, degree of functional & sectoral specialization. As control variables, I used additional firm characteristics and measures of the usability of the examined websites. As the depended variable in the analyses of performance differences, I use performance.

Performance

In previous management research performance has been measured in various ways. Researchers have discussed the measurement of performance from different perspectives (e.g. Ketchen, et al., 1997; Pandian, et al., 2006). Existing studies often use accounting-based, value-based measures of performance, such as return on assets (ROA) and return on equity (ROE) to address long-term performance differences between firms within the same industry (Pandian, et al., 2006). In line with this argument, many studies on strategic groups also rely on accounting measures of performance. Nevertheless, accounting measures of performance have several limitations in practice, including the range of managerial prudence in adjusting accounting numbers, a short-term measurement bias and their restrictions in the evaluation of tangible capabilities and resources (Barney, 2002).

In order to overcome these disadvantages researchers introduced financial market measures of performance to strategic group studies, e.g. economic profit (EP) and total market value (TMV). The suggestion is that market-based measures of performance are more relevant to strategy research as they capture expectations of future returns from firm performance (Keats & Hitt, 1988), rather than past outcomes that are reflected in accounting-based measures. Pandian et al. (2006) call for further research on the relationship between strategic group membership and financial performance on the grounds of more elaborate constructs in particular for financial performance. They argue that recent empirical results using improved financial performance measures provide a rationale for “reexamining the performance consequences of strategic group membership”.

Furthermore, total revenues have been commonly included in strategic management research (Leask, 2007). Revenues have often served as an indicator for the size of the examined sample firms. Especially within research on management consulting firms revenues provide an important measure of firm size (e.g. Galal & Richter, 2007; Harste, 2008; Semadeni, 2006). The described performance measures are not ideal for the subject of this study as consulting firms are different in many regards from financially and assets driven companies. In particular, as consulting firms mainly draw on human capital and only compose limited additional assets.

As stated above I examine within this research performance differences between firms within and across different strategic groups. In order to establish a profound measure of the performance of consulting firms I define *performance* as the relation between total *revenues* and total number of *employees* of a consulting firm. Similar approaches have been applied in research (Deephouse, 1999). The resulting revenue per employee ratio establishes a straightforward measure for the performance of a consulting firm. My interviews with industry experts confirmed that especially consulting companies use this indicator for the performance or productivity of their company as well as an indicator for the performance of individual consultants.

This performance measure responds to the legitimate criticism by Leask (2007) of studies within strategic group research that included revenues as being tautological. He argues that revenues are an outcome and not a strategic choice variable. However, the researcher especially criticizes the approach of using revenues within the process of defining strategic groups as being tautological. As I am explicitly only using variables that reflect the strategic positioning of a firm and not variables on firm characteristics as size, age or origin within the group differentiation, this criticism does not apply for this research.

Type of service model

I use nine variables to analyze the service model of a consulting firm (cf. Chapter 2.1.1.2). As described above, it refers to the system of mechanisms, which the firm uses to deliver services that it can sell to clients (Richter & Schmidt, 2006). Four of the defined variables are rank-ordered measures and six are binary measures. The corresponding rating rules are described in Appendix A.

- The variable *detail description* contains whether a consulting firm is describing its consulting process properly to its clients before the actual service provision. A detailed description serves as an indicator whether the service provision is to a certain extent a routine procedure and therefore comparable across different clients. The raters were advised to search for details on process phases or milestones within a consulting project description. Furthermore, the listing of routine tasks that will be carried out during the provision of consulting services serves as an indicator to a positive rating of the variable. If firms are describing their consulting process in detail the value is 1, otherwise it is 0.

- The variable *implement* analyzes whether a consulting firm supports the implementation of measures that were defined during the conception phase of the consulting process. This variable provides further insights on the service model of the respective consulting firm. Some consulting firms' service model is to solely focus on the conception of a strategy and derive measures that need to be implemented as a consequence of the new strategy. Consulting firms following this type of service model concentrate on analyzing the consequences of different strategic decisions within the conceptual phase of a company project rather than on the implementation. The variable is of rank-ordered nature. To reduce ambiguity in the rating decision, a set of rating dimensions concerning the wording was defined. Besides the factual dimension, i.e. synonyms for 'implementation', the raters had to take combinations of expressions for time frame, frequency and role sovereignty within the project execution into consideration. The variable takes the value 0, if a firm is not at all engaged in the implementation of identified measures and only provides its consulting services throughout the conceptual phase of a project. It takes the value 1, if a consulting firm supports and accompanies its clients to a certain extent in the implementation process but is not enduringly involved in it. The value is set to 2, if a consulting firm indicates to strongly engage during the entire implementation process.

- The variables *standardmethods, standardsolutions* and *products* serve as measures to assess the degree of standardization of the service model of a consulting firm. The variables are derived on the basis of the characteristics of standardized services and the levels of standardization introduced above (cf. Chapter 2.1.1.2). If consulting firms describe the use of a set of methods and analytical tools, it serves as an indicator of a standardized service model and consulting approach. The applied methods can be described as a consultant's procedural toolbox and are separated from the particular content of the consulting project and specific client situation. This toolbox is often applied at the beginning of a consulting project in order to comprehensively asses the client's situation and to generate data and information within the client's organization and on markets of interest. This aspect was described earlier as the lower level of standardization of a consulting service model. The dimensions that define the exact rating for *standardmethods* are the stated frequency of the use of standard methods, verbal emphasis put on the use of certain methods and the intensity of the description of specific methods and tools. If consulting firms indicate the application of specific methods the variable *standardmethods* is set to 1, otherwise 0. If the service expositions of a firm indicate a standardized consulting approach with a fixed chronology of methods and toolbox the variable is set to 2.

  As described above, at the middle level of standardization, consulting firms apply predefined solutions to specific client settings. The application of standardized solutions indicates a higher degree of standardization than the mere use of standardized methodology. However, these solutions need to be customized to a certain client setting and conceptually adjusted to the specific needs of relevance of certain clients. Standardization of solutions implies a certain extent of repetitive use of conceptual content, which goes further than just a repetition of procedural methodology. These kinds of predefined solutions are only limited storable and repetitive usable. The dimensions that set the rating framework for standardsolutions are stated frequency of application, factual descriptions and whether the concrete result of the consulting service can be defined prior to the service provision. If consulting firms describe the use of standardized solutions the variable is set to 1, otherwise 0. If a consulting firm advertises the implementation of solutions that need only modest customization the variable is set to 2.

Nevertheless, standardized solutions are still merely partial elements of the overall solution which results from the consultation process. Building on this, the variable *products* evaluates whether a firm offers predefined products such as standard software that need any or only minor adjustments to the client's specific problem. In case a firm promotes the selling of "off the shelf" products the value is set to 1, otherwise 0. The use of products during the consulting process marks the highest level of standardization of a service model.

- The variable *tailormade* describes whether a consulting firm explicitly advertises the individuality of its services. It assesses the degree to how individual or tailor-made a consulting service is. To reduce the rating ambiguity two dimensions are defined: the factual dimension, i.e. synonyms for the individuality of a service and the importance of the individuality as advertised by the consulting firm. If a firm describes its services as merely customized and tailored to a client's specific problem, the value is set to 1, otherwise 0. In case a firm describes its service model as to develop comprehensively new services the value is set to 2.

- The variable *benchmark* comprises whether a consulting firm conducts benchmarks within the consultation process. The provision of benchmarks implies a certain degree of comparability across the clients of a consulting firm. Some clients request specific industry know-how from consultants and seek comparisons with competitors in order to improve their market position. In case a consulting firm promotes benchmarks the value is set to 1, otherwise 0.

- The variables *advertclient* and *partner* indicate whether a consulting firm names its client and partner relations in order to attract new clients. The variable advertclient measures whether a firm openly promotes names of clients or whether the respective firm treats this information as confidential. In case a firm displays client names the value is set to 1, otherwise 0. The variable partner reflects whether a consulting firm openly addresses partner firms that could be of support within a consulting project. Partners could be members of a network of consulting firms with expert knowledge or firms providing services compulsory for the success of a consulting project, e.g. IT solutions. In case a firm list partner firms the value is set to 1, otherwise 0.

Intended relationship with the client

The relationship that a consulting firm intends to have with the client while performing the consulting service is used as a second dimension to assess the strategic positioning (cf. Chapter 2.1.1.2). This is done by using three categories: consulting services as simple purchases, limited involvement of the client, and high and consistent involvement of the client during the consulting (Galal & Richter, 2007). The intended relationship with the client is determined by the role the consultants carry out vis-à-vis the clients during the consulting process. In order to thoroughly asses the role of the consultant vis-à-vis their clients and the interaction during the consulting process I define items for the three types of consultant-client relationships that occur within consulting projects according to Schein's relationship model (1978). For each of the three roles, I define a variable and derive a set of rating rules. As stated earlier Schein distinguished the three roles on the dimensions content and process expertise that consultants may provide.

In order to analyze a consulting firms' intended relationship with their clients, I define four variables. One variable is of rank-ordered nature and three are binary measures.

- The variable *cooperation* measures the intensity of cooperation between client and consultant. This variable describes whether a client is involved in the execution of the consulting project and thereby mirrors the level of client involvement. In order to reduce ambiguity during the rating process three dimensions are defined to support the process. Besides a verbal description of the intended interaction (e.g. "working in teams", "close cooperation with our clients") and the order of used expressions depending on the level of intensity - frequency of naming the interaction and descriptions of the duration of interaction are taken into account. In case the level of interaction between consultants and clients throughout the whole process is described as being high and constant during the entire consulting project, the variable takes the value 2. In case the client is involved during the consulting project to a limited extent or just supports the project the variable is set to 1. On the other extreme if the client simply buys the consulting service almost like a product without contributing to the project, the value is 0.

- The variable *expertrole* represents the so-called 'purchase of expertise' consultation model that relies for the most parts on the selling of content expertise (e.g. market studies, benchmarks). The variable takes the value of 1 if a firm expresses that it sells specific content expertise to its clients and conducts its services with a limited closeness to the client, e.g. an independent market analysis with only limited need for interaction with the client. Otherwise the value is 0.

- The variable *docpatient* stands for the 'doctor-patient' consulting model. In this relationship model consultants are hired by clients in order to diagnose the causes of a prevalent problem and aim to prescribe a treatment or solution to it. In order to conduct sound analyses, the consultant interacts with the client and tries to establish a trustful relationship with the client. In case a consulting firm describes the intended relationship and its consulting provision in that way, the variable takes the value of 1; otherwise the value is 0.

- The variable *processmod* examines whether the consultant acts as a process moderator to the client and acts accordingly to Schein's third role the 'guide-mountaineer'. The consultant guides the client throughout the process of diagnosing and finding a solution to a specific problem. The consultant and the client strongly interact and establish a close relationship in order to jointly find a solution. In case the consultant guides the client in generating a solution and supports the client to enable him to address the challenges on his own, the variable takes the value of 1, otherwise 0.

Degree of functional and sectoral specialization

In order to analyze the functional and sectoral specialization of a consulting firm, a set of variables is defined (cf. Chapter 2.1.1.2). To assess the level of specialization, I follow a two-step process. In a first step, eight variables are defined that mirror the functional consulting offering of a firm. In a second step, I use a set of four variables to classify the level of functional and sectoral specialization of the sample firms.

- First, to assess the functional consulting offering of a consulting firm I define variables for each of the different functional consulting services. These variables indicate functional specializations of the respective consulting firm in the sample. I follow the BDU's definition of consulting functions (BDU, 2006). According to this definition consulting services are structured into eight functional consulting services: *strategy, organization, process, IT, HR, marketing, logistics and finance.* Each variable takes the value of 1, if a firm is offering this functional consulting service, otherwise 0.

- Second, in order to differentiate between consulting firms that follow a generalist or a specialist approach, I introduce the variable *generalist.* Consulting firms that follow a generalist approach offer a large number of different consulting services to their clients, whereas functional specialists concentrate on the performance of a limited number of consulting services. In order to differentiate generalists from specialists I count the number of functional consulting services a firm offers. If the number of services defined above equals or is larger than 5, the variable generalist takes the value of 1, otherwise 0.

- The variable *sector specialist* describes whether a firm serves as a specialist within certain client sectors. A consulting firm that states its specialization within a limited number of sectors is considered a sector specialist. The variable takes the value 1 if a firm positions as a specialist within certain, limited sectors, and otherwise 0.

- To measure whether a consulting firm openly addresses specific functional or sectoral knowledge, I define the variables *functional expert* and *sector expert.* Functional or sector experts differ from functional or sector specialist in the respect that a firm openly promotes its offerings of specific expertise and knowledge. A concentration on specific functions or sectors does not always result into a high level of expertise. However, even a generalist can also offer functional or sector expertise. Long years of experience and the accumulation of expert know-how are prerequisites to be considered as a functional or sector expert. The variable functional expert takes the value of 1, if a firm strongly positions as an expert in certain functions and promotes its functional knowhow, otherwise the value is 0. The variable sector expert takes the value 1, when a firm positions as a well-experienced sector expert and promotes its long term expert know-how within that specific sector openly, otherwise the value is 0.

Control variables

For further interpretation of the findings I take additional variables on firm characteristics into account. The intention is to relate the results on firms' service characteristics analyses to organizational characteristics like size, age, level of internationality and origin. As measures of firm size, I use *revenues in Germany* (in Euro), *number of employees* and *number of offices* (in Germany) as well as *international offices* (outside of Germany) as of 2005. The age of a particular firm is measured with the *year of foundation*. As described above the firm characteristics concerning size, age, origin were extracted from a secondary database. In addition, I gathered control data from the firms' websites. These variables are not included in the cluster analysis.

- To identify the client sectors in which a firm is active, I follow the BDU definition and take nine client sectors where consulting firms perform their services into consideration, namely *healthcare & social services, trade & distribution, tourism, energy, TIME (Telecommunications, Information technology, Media, Electronics), public sector, manufacturing, financial services, and others* (BDU, 2006). Each variable takes the value of 1, if a firm promotes to offer its services to clients in this sector, otherwise 0.

- With the variable *publications* I determine whether a firm is openly sharing its knowledge with potential clients. The question that needs to be analyzed here is: are consulting firms engaging in the generation of expert knowledge and transfer this knowledge? If a firm publishes studies, reports, or transfers knowledge in any other sort of publication on its websites the variable is set to 1, otherwise 0.

Furthermore, I use a set of four variables as proxies for the level of internationality of the firms in the sample.

- The variable *homepage language* measures whether a consulting firm is promoting its service offering in German as well as in English language. This serves as an indicator to the level of internationality as it points towards whether a firm deems to address international clients. In case a firm offers its websites in both or more languages the value is 1, otherwise it is 0.

- The variable *services international* measures whether a firm verbally advertises the provision of its services internationally. In case a firm openly promotes the service delivery also on an international level, the variable takes the value of 1, otherwise 0.

- The variable *origin* serves as an important indicator of the internationality of the consulting firms in the sample. This variable captures whether a firm's headquarters is located in Germany or outside of Germany. As mentioned before, all sample firms are active in the German market. This variable helps to identify the origin of consulting firms. If a firm's headquarters is located in Germany the variable takes the value 1, otherwise 0.

- Furthermore, the variable *international offices* (outside of Germany) completes the list of internationality indicators. This variable is a count measure as it counts the number of offices a sample firm has outside of Germany.

In addition, six additional control variables evaluate the recruiting focus of the examined consulting firms as well as their job descriptions. The analyses of the hiring policy add to the understanding of the consulting firms' market position. The knowledge and the experience of the staff of a consulting firm are the main assets of this knowledge intensive profession.

- The variable *career* serves as a control variable to whether specific career websites of the respective firm exist. In case specific websites for this matter exist, the value is 1, otherwise 0.

- The variables *busiskills*, *techskills* and *scienceskills* evaluate the study background the consulting firms expect from potential candidates. In case a firm regards business studies (business administration, economics, etc.) as mandatory the variable busiskills is set to 1, otherwise 0. In case a firm considers technological studies (computer science, information systems, etc.) as mandatory the variable techskills is 1, otherwise 0. In case a firm explicitly addresses students with a background in science (e.g. medicine, physics, biologie) the variable scienceskills is set to 1, otherwise 0.

- In order to gain further insights on the skill set a consulting firm is expecting from potential candidates the variables *spirit* and *experience* are introduced. The variable *spirit* takes the value of 1, if a firm is explicitly naming entrepreneurial spirit, management skills, self-responsibility or commitment as mandatory requirements for potential candidates; otherwise 0. The variable *experience* takes the value 1 if a firm is hiring only consultants with explicit work experience, otherwise 0.

Usability variables

In order to control for the usability of the analyzed websites I define a set of five variables. The usability serves as an indicator as to how much effort firms put into the design and content of this positioning measure. The usability of a website is defined as a quality attribute that assesses how easy the user interface is. I follow the recommendations of Cappel & Zhenyu (2007) as to what measures a website usability study should consist of. These variables are not included in the cluster analysis. They support to assess the overall quality of the data sources.

- The variable *searchbox* contains whether a firm's website is offering a box to enter specific terms to search for within the websites. In case the firm offers a searchbox the value is set to 1, otherwise 0.
- The variable *breadcrumb* analyzes whether the websites contain a breadcrumb trail that helps to structure the websites. This structuring element increases the usability of the websites as it supports the user in his efforts to obtain the information he seeks. If a firm's websites contain a breadcrumb trail the variable is set to 1, otherwise 0.
- The variable *homebutton* reflects whether a firm's websites consist of a possibility for the user to return to the starting website at any time within the website tree. In case all individual websites of a firm contain a homebutton the value is 1, otherwise 0.
- To assess the general impression and usability of the websites of a firm I defined a rank-ordered measure *homequality*. The raters are asked to assess the overall structure, user-friendliness and graphical appearance of the websites. The websites are rated on a scale from 1 (lowest usability) to 5 (highest usability).
- The variable *homecontent* evaluates the general quality and accessibility of the content of the websites of a sample firm. This variable serves as an indicator to whether potential clients are able to find the relevant information they are looking for. The rating scale ranks from 1 (lowest content quality) to 5 (highest content quality).

Additional variables

As a means of further analyzing the level differentiation between the sample firms I derived three additional, calculated variables. With regard to the service portfolios and as a measure of additional differentiation within a strategic group I defined the variable *number of functions* as the sum of functions (*strategy, organization, process, IT, Human resources, marketing, logistics and finance)* offered by an individual firm. Therefore, this variable counts the consulting services a firm is offering with a minimum of 1 and a maximum of 8. This variable serves as a means of identifying the degree of differentiation a company is seeking within the respective strategic group. In strategy research this notion is referred to as the level of horizontal differentiation (Fiss 2011, Pugh et al. 1968). In addition the variable *age* was derived from the variable *year of foundation* on the base of 2006. In addition to this, I calculated the variable *rarefunctions*. A rare function is defined as a consulting service that is offered by less than one third of the sample firms. Marlin et. al. (2007) used a similar differentiation measure, they defined rare services more moderately being offered by less than 50% of the sample firms. The idea is to identify the services that permit firms to differentiate from each other.

3.3 Analytical Methods

In the following chapter, the applied analytical methods are presented. First, the empirical methods for the strategic group analysis are presented. Second, the regression models for the analyses of performance differences across and within strategic groups are introduced.

3.3.1 Strategic Group Analysis

3.3.1.1 Relevance of Cluster Analysis

The preferred and widely accepted method to empirically analyze the existence of strategic groups is to apply cluster analysis to key variables of the subjects of interest (e.g. DeSarbo & Grewal, 2008; Ketchen & Shook, 1996; Short, et al., 2007). Cluster analysis is defined as a technique for "describing patterns of similarity and differences among objects under investigation by means of their class labels" (Everitt, 1993, p. 2). It uses distance or similarity measures to assign observations to distinguished groups based on clustering variables. The observations within the defined groups, i.e. clusters should be as homogenous as possible in their set of variable values and as heterogeneous as possible from those observations within other groups.

Despite certain challenges associated with its use in the past, the methodology of cluster analysis provides a valuable and important tool for discerning strategic groups of firms (Ennen, 2011; Fiss, 2011; Ketchen & Shook, 1996). A clear advantage of cluster analysis is that it enables the examination of firm groups both deductively (i.e. expectations exist a priori about the specific nature of groups) and inductively (i.e. no such expectations exist). This method allows the incorporation of the group constructs from a number of theoretical positions (Ketchen, et al., 1993). Today's common sense among strategy researchers is that cluster analysis is "valuable to future strategy research due to the technique's unparalleled ability to classify a large number of observations along multiple variables" (DeSarbo & Grewal, 2008; Ennen, 2011; Fiss, 2011; Short, et al., 2007).

There exist three main reasons for choosing cluster analysis as one central element of the methodology within this research. First, it does not discard information that is contained within the data and does not impose stochastic restrictions upfront (Everitt, 1993). Second, cluster analysis can significantly reduce the amount of data and point to the relevant issues to be interpreted. Third, it provides information that is not intuitive and obvious (Gordon, 1993). However, some challenges and common flaws have to be considered as well. Research on clustering techniques within strategy research found that only seven percent of studies followed a robust procedure (Ketchen, et al., 1997; Ketchen & Shook, 1996). This result stresses the importance of carefully choosing the right clustering procedure. Due to the fact that cluster analysis groups elements (e.g. firms) with the intend to maximize the distance between groups along all clustering variables, variables with large ranges are given more weight in defining a cluster solution than those with small ranges (Hair, Anderson, Tatham, & Black, 1998). In other terms, the relative scale of the applied variables may skew the results (Leask & Parker, 2007). Therefore, strong emphasis has to be put on the choice of the right variables to include in the analysis.

3.3.1.2 Three Choices within Cluster Analysis

There are three choices related to the application of cluster analysis methodology: first the choice of variables to be included, second the choice of the similarity measure and clustering algorithm and third after applying the algorithm the choice of the number of clusters. Choosing the variables along which to group the observations is the most influential and critical step in the application of cluster analysis. However, the choice of the right procedure is crucial to the validity and reliability of the statistical results of the analyses. The third statistically supported choice of the number of clusters clearly sets the basis for further interpretation of the clustering results.

The first choice concerns the set of variables included in the clustering analysis. In the previous chapter I have introduced the set of variables included in this empirical research. In the cluster analysis I include 25 variables of the three key dimensions *type of service model*, *intended relationship with the client* and *degree of functional & sectoral specialization*. These dimensions represent the strategic positioning of the consulting firms and their service exposition. The remaining variables are used after the clustering to determine further differences between the examined firms of the defined clusters.

The second choice relates to the similarity measure and clustering algorithm. There are numerous similarity measures and clustering algorithms to choose from, many of which were already applied within strategic management research (Ketchen & Shook, 1996). As the developed data set consists to large extent of binary variables and some rank-ordered variables the choice of similarity measures is limited. Generally, when measuring the similarity of two observations, the two observations are compared based on their values (Backhaus, Erichson, Plinke, & Weiber, 2003). This comparison is based on the definitions shown in the following (Everitt, Landau, & Leese, 2001):

		Observation j	
		1	0
Observation i	1	*a*	*b*
	0	*c*	*d*

Figure 7: Definition of Similarity Measures for Binary Data

In this table, *a* is the number of variables where observations *i* and *j* both have the value 1, *c* and *b* are the numbers of variables where the two observations do not have the same values and *d* is the number of variables where both observations have the value 0.

The choice of the *similarity measure* should be based on the specific properties of the data set and on the aspects one aspires to investigate. Within the data set used in this study, the similarity between single variables of objects is with respect to the interpretation is worth the same as the dissimilarity between variables. This aspect holds for both, the binary as well as the rank-ordered variables. Therefore, I choose the matching measure as the similarity measure for the clustering procedure (Everitt, 1993; Everitt, et al., 2001). The matching measure relates to the proportion of matches between observations or variables without prioritizing. In line with this the similarity of two firms can be determined on the basis of comparing each variable of the respective firms and summarizing it in a distance measure.

There are two basic types of *clustering algorithms*: hierarchical and nonhierarchical. Hierarchical algorithms progress through a series of steps that build a tree-like structure by either adding individual elements to (i.e., agglomerative) or deleting them from (i.e., divisive) clusters (Ketchen & Shook, 1996). The five most popular agglomerative algorithms are single linkage, average linkage, complete linkage, Ward's method, and centroid method (Hair, et al., 1998). The differences among them lie in the arithmetic procedures that are used to determine the distance between clusters. Nonhierarchical algorithms (also referred to as K-means or iterative methods) partition a data set into a prespecified number of clusters. After initial cluster centroids (the 'center points' of clusters along input variables) are selected, each observation is assigned to the group with the nearest centroid (Everitt, et al., 2001). In an iterative process, as each new observation is allocated, the cluster centroids are recomputed. There is a tendency to use nonhierarchical algorithms when theoretical assumptions on the data set can be drawn in advance. The prerequisite for these kinds of clustering approaches is to have the number of clusters as well as the centroids predefined.

For this research, I chose the within-groups average linkage algorithm. The average linkage algorithm is a hierarchical, agglomerative method. This algorithm uses the average similarity of observations between two clusters as the measure for similarity between two clusters. In general, the average linkage algorithm has no tendency to clumping or chaining of clusters. There exist two alternative variations of the average linkage algorithm: the within-groups average linkage and the between-groups average linkage (Everitt, et al., 2001). The latter considers only pairs of observations with one observation in each of the two clusters. The within-groups average linkage additionally considers pairs of observations within the same clusters. This algorithm has the effect that a cluster with more similar observations tends to be merged more easily with another cluster than a cluster with lower similarity among its observations. In other words, the procedure tends to merge clusters that exhibit a high degree of similarity within the cluster more easily than clusters with lower degrees of similarity. Therefore, the chosen procedure fits best the targeted study outcome.

The third choice relates to the appropriate number of clusters. A variety of techniques exists to determine the number of clusters in a data set. When using hierarchical methods, a basic but well-accepted procedure is the visual inspection of dendrograms (i.e. tree-plots) (Marlin, et al., 2007). In addition, many statistical indicators that support to identify the right number of clusters exist. Nevertheless, the appropriate number of clusters is always dependent on the context and aim of the research. Still, using a single method to determine the number of clusters is questionable as each method has its limitations (Everitt, 1980).

Therefore, I use a combination of visual inspection of dendrograms and the Caliński and Harabasz (1974) pseudo F index to determine the appropriate number of clusters (Ketchen & Shook, 1996). A local peak in the pseudo F statistic serves as a clear indicator of the appropriate number of clusters. These decision criteria are consistent with those used in prior strategy research (e.g. Ketchen, et al., 1993; Marlin, et al., 2007).

Finally, I named the resulting clusters on the basis of the variables taken into account in the clustering procedure. Following Lewis & Thomas (1990), I conducted an average analysis with respect to the individual strategic dimensions of each cluster in order to further structure the clustering results. This helps to clearly identify and interpret the differences in positioning efforts across strategic groups. Many strategy researchers find the industry or strategic group average useful to analyzing strategic positioning (e.g. Cool & Dierickx, 1993; Fiegenbaum & Thomas, 1995; Mintzberg, 1978). Each cluster mean variable is rated with respect to the overall sample mean for each variable:

- "+" if cluster(x) variable value (y) - 0.1 $\geq$ sample average M(y)
- "–" if cluster(x) variable value (y) + 0.1 $\leq$ sample average M(y)
- "0" if cluster(x) variable value (y) is not "+/-"

Following the identification of the clusters, I compared them in terms of their strategic positioning efforts and additional firm characteristics (e.g. average firm size, age, number of offices, etc.), using the non-parametric Mann-Whitney U test (Higgins, 2004). In addition, in order to compare the heterogeneity of the characteristics of the firms in the identified clusters,

I used Levene's (1960) test statistic for the equality of variance which produces robust results for samples that are not normally distributed.

3.3.1.3 Multinomial Logistic Regression and Additional Analyses

Building on the clustering results additional analyses are conducted. The intention is to use the clustering outcome to further deepen the insights on the resulting strategic group structure.

In order to identify the variables that have significant influence on the allocation of single firms to different clusters, multinomial logistic regression is applied. Multinomial logistic regression is a sub form of logistic regression. It is used when the dependent variable is of rank-ordered nature. Therefore, it serves as an extension of the binomial choice model as it covers analyses with more than two alternatives (Agresti, 2007). It simultaneously estimates binary logits for all comparisons among the dependent categories, with each binary logit based on a different sample (Long & Freese, 2001). As the clustering analysis is likely to result in a solution with more than two clusters, multinomial logistic regression is the right statistical choice for this study. All clustering variables are analyzed individually with respect to the significance of the contribution of allocating firms to different clusters. Consistently, I use *maximum-likelihood estimation* methods to test the significance of the applied cluster variables in dependency of the resulting rank-ordered cluster variable *Clustvar* in multinominal logistic (mlogit) regression models.

In a second step, an analysis of *cluster centroids* was carried out. The specific strategic group positioning strategy is mirrored by the set of key dimensions used within the clustering and it differs across individual strategic groups. The centroid of a cluster is reflected in a calculated, idealized center company that follows the group strategy most closely. All firms within the sample are described by an array of cluster variables. The array of the calculated center company is defined with the cluster means for each variable. In consequence, for each strategic group a centroid firm was calculated. This calculated centroid firm serves as a benchmark with regard to positioning efforts to each individual strategic group member. Each company within a cluster can hereafter be analyzed in terms of its positioning distance to the cluster centroid. This procedure allows insights on how closely a company identifies with a certain strategic group strategy and additional analyses on what are the effects of different positioning within a strategic group has. After determining the cluster centroids, the *distance* for each individual firm within the strategic group is calculated as the sum of differences for each variable within the array of strategic dimensions to the respective cluster centroid:

- Center *CompanyX*: centroid X [Mean for each variable]

- Distance: $D(CompanyX) = \sum_{1}^{X} |VarX - MeanVarX|$

Using the calculated distance for each company to the center company of a strategic group sets the base for the definition of core and secondary companies. In dependence of the distance of a firm to the center, each company is assigned to one of the two substructures. As defined above core firms associate tightly with group strategy and key dimensions and as a consequence have a smaller distance to the strategic group center than sample average. However, secondary firms follow the group's strategic recipe less closely and establish a distance to the center on group average level. According to established distance analyses, firms are defined as core or secondary within each individual cluster on the base of the following rules:

- Core firm: Firm(x): <u>distance</u> ≤ M (distance) – (SD (distance)/2)

- Secondary Firm: Firm(x): <u>distance</u> > M (distance) – (SD (distance)/2)

3.3.2 Analysis of Performance Differences

In order to determine performance differences across and within strategic groups I use mean comparison tests as well as hierarchical regression models within this study.

3.3.2.1 Analysis of Performance Differences across Strategic Groups

This analysis aims at verifying the hypotheses that performance differences exist across strategic groups. The assumption is that strategic positioning in a certain strategic group and following the strategy of that group has an impact on firm performance. In order to test the hypotheses, I use hierarchical regression models and mean comparison tests.

Dependent variable

The dependent variable within the regression models is firm *performance.* As described, firm *performance* is defined as revenue per employee.

Independent variables

I use *Clustvar* as the independent variable in the regression model. *Clustvar* serves as a rank-ordered measure of the resulting membership within a strategic group.

Control variables

As control variables I use *age, size,* and *origin.* The variable firm *age* was calculated on the base of the variable year of foundation. For *size,* I use the number of *employees* per firm. Firm *origin* contains whether the consulting company has its headquarters in Germany or outside of Germany (0=outside of Germany; 1=in Germany).

Methodology

Two models are used to provide answers to the hypothesis. Model 1 tests the control variables *age*, *size* and *origin*. Model 2 adds the independent variable *Clustvar*. The hierarchical regression points out, which model obtains a better fit. Model 2 is described by the equation:

$$\textbf{Performance} = \textbf{b0} + \textbf{b1} * \textbf{Clustvar} + \textbf{b2} * \textbf{Age} + \textbf{b3} * \textbf{Size} + \textbf{b4} * \textbf{Origin} + \varepsilon$$

3.3.2.2 Analysis of Performance Differences within Strategic Groups

The following analysis aims to prove that individual positioning efforts within strategic groups as core or secondary firms result in significant performance differences. The prediction is that secondary firms that find the right balance between positioning near to and far from competitors achieve superior performance as compared to competitors that position as core members of a strategic group.

Dependent variable

The dependent variable within the regression models is firm *performance*.

Independent variables

As independent variables I use *core* and *number of functions.* The variable *core* defines which positioning effort a firm is following within its strategic group (core or secondary). The variable number of functions serves as an indicator of differentiation measures within strategic positioning efforts.

Control variables

As control variables I use the variables *age, size,* and *origin*.

Methodology

Prior to the regression models, a correlation analysis is conducted among the dependent variable, the independent variables and the control variables in order to outline relationships between all variables.

The main analyses are conducted using hierarchical regression. Three models are developed to test the hypotheses. Model 1 tests the control variables age, size and origin. Model 2 adds the first independent variable core. Model 3 adds the independent variable number of functions. The hierarchical regression indicates which model achieves a better fit and outmatches the other hypotheses. Model 3 is described by the equation

$$\text{Performance} = b0 + b1 \cdot \text{Core} + b2 \cdot \text{Number of Functions} + b3 \cdot \text{Age} + b4 \cdot \text{Size} + b5 \cdot \text{Origin} + \varepsilon$$

3.3.3 Excursion: Structural Alignment view of similarity

I include the following excursion as it delivers an additional perspective on how differences between objects can be analyzed. Markman and Gentner's (1993) structural alignment view of similarity was developed within psychology research and offers a structure that helps to determine the degree of similarity between pairs. More specific, the approach offers a method to detect correspondences between representations. Furthermore, the approach helps to structure the analysis of complex comparisons, e.g. between firms in the same industry that are similar to a certain degree. In short, the idea is to not simply to distinguish firms dichotomously on the basis of similar and different items, but to differentiate more fine-grained between commonalities, alignable differences, and non-alignable differences.

Commonalities and non-alignable differences mirror to a certain extent commonly accepted concepts of similarities and differences between compared item pairs. However, alignable differences introduce an intermediary level in-between non-alignable differences and commonalities and allow for a more finely-grained analysis of the degree of similarity between pairs. Markman and Gentner (1993) use a structural alignment account of similarity in which the commonalities and differences of a pair are determined via the comparison of structured representations. In theory the structural alignment process suggests to take a pair of structured representations (e.g. comparison of firms on the basis of a structured list of characteristics) and compute the correspondences between them by seeking the maximal structural consistent match. A structural consistent match is defined as having one-to-one correspondences. One-to-one correspondence means that each element (e.g. attribute, characteristic) in one representation (e.g. firm) is placed in correspondence with exactly one element in the other representation. In other words, firms are compared on the base of a defined list of characteristics and only structural consistent firm characteristic values are considered as commonalities between firms.

An alignable difference exists when an object possesses a different value than another object along a shared characteristic dimension. To provide an example, comparing two red cars and one blue car, the color serves as a characteristic with one-to-one correspondence (each car has one color). The two red cars share the commonality of the same color, while the color blue as a characteristic value for the third car is an alignable difference to the red cars. Alignable in this sense means all three cars share the fact that they have a color and therefore one-to-one correspondence exists. However, as the color of the third car is different, color serves not as a commonality between the three cars, but marks an alignable difference. If only one of the cars had an airbag system and the other two had no such electronic device at all, the existence of an airbag system would be a non-alignable difference between the cars. This is, because the airbag system in the one car does not match any other system within the other two cars and therefore no one-to-one correspondence exists.

Empirical analyses support the theoretical proposition that the similarity between pairs increases with a high number of commonalities, but decreases with both its alignable and its non-alignable differences (Markman & Gentner, 1993). Nevertheless, three empirical findings point to the significance of the concept of alignable differences and its conceptual proximity to commonalities. First, empirical evidence verifies that commonalities and alignable differences are conceptually related. Second, commonalities and alignable differences are numerically linked, implying that pairs (e.g. firms, objects) that share many commonalities are likely to also share many alignable differences. Third, usually alignable differences outnumber non-alignable differences. This is due to the fact that it is often a precondition of comparisons that the compared pair that has commonalities shares a higher number of alignable differences than non-alignable differences.

If a company pursues the strategy to positioning near to competitors the commonalities are expected to outweigh the differences of the compared firms. Nevertheless, it will be of specific interest to assess which role alignable differences play in such a context. Positioning strategies far from competitors are likely to result in a higher number of alignable and non-alignable differences and less commonalities between firms. Although in markets like the professional service industries, where differences between firms are less obvious due to the similarity of the services offered, it is likely that many alignable differences between firms in general occur.

The high number of expected alignable differences could serve as an explanation to why service offerings of consulting firms are perceived as difficult to differentiate for clients. The concept of alignable differences provides a possible answer to this dilemma as it makes clear that significant differences exist between consulting firms, although they might seem less obvious. Finally, this approach could help with a more fine-grained assessment of the degree of similarity between consulting firms as these firms seem to be highly similar compared to other industries at first glance.

However, I will not apply the structural alignment view of similarity within this research. As introduced, I focus within my research on the supply side of the consulting market on the communicated strategic positioning. I will not take the perceptions of buyers and competitors into account. However, the research approach concentrates on perception-based empirical analyses. Especially, the important differentiation between alignable and non-alignable differences between individual firms is based on perceptions. Therefore, the procedure does not fit with the analyses that will be addressed in this research. Nevertheless, the view serves as a promising option for future research especially from a perception-based point of view.

4 Results

The following chapter describes the results of the empirical study. First, the results of the strategic group analyses are presented in-depth. Second, the results of the performance difference analyses on the base of the identified strategic group structure are illustrated.

4.1 Strategic Group Results

4.1.1 Clustering Results

As described above 233 consulting companies were included in the sample. The within-groups average linkage cluster algorithm using the matching similarity measure is conducted with 25 variables representing three key positioning dimensions: type of service model, intended relationship with the client and degree of functional & sectoral specialization. In order to determine the appropriate number of clusters, a combination of visual inspection of dendrograms and the Caliński and Harabasz (1974) pseudo F index (Ketchen & Shook, 1996) is used. As stated before a local peak in the pseudo F statistic serves as a clear indicator of the appropriate number of clusters. Inspection of the correlation coefficients provided in Table1 indicates limited correlations among the three strategic key dimensions taken into account in the clustering approach. This finding supports the notion that the constructs represented by these variables used for the clustering are clearly distinct from one another. However, there are some statistically significant and interesting correlations between the variables representing key dimensions and between some of the service characteristic variables. For example, the *Schein roles* variables *docpatient and process moderator* are negatively and significantly correlated with the Schein role *expert* in line with my definition. Also, in line with my expectations, firms that offer *implementation* services are likely to offer highly standardized services with *products*, *service methods* and *service solutions.* Firms offering *standard solutions* and *products* are likely to openly advertise their *partners* and *clients*. The variables *generalist* and *process moderator* are positively and significantly correlated, while *generalist* is negatively and significantly correlated with *standard solutions* and *products*. Results show, in line with my expectations, a strong correlation between the variables describing the service model of standardized consulting services (*standardized solutions, methods, implementation, and products*) and the offering of *IT* consulting service. The variables *benchmarks* and *generalist* are positively and significantly correlated with *performance*. Overall, the correlations between the variables are at low to moderate levels.

Table 1: Descriptive Statistics

Variables	M	SD	1	2	3	4	5	6	7	8	9	10	11	12	13	14
1. Cooperation	1.04	0.83														
2. Expert	0.62	0.48	-0.34***													
3. Docpatient	0.57	0.49	0.206†	-0.49***												
4. Process moderator	0.22	0.42	-0.24***	-0.194**	-0.108†											
5. Detail description	0.34	0.47	0.132*	-0.256***	0.123†	0.076										
6. Implement	1.21	0.71	0.184**	-0.197**	0.180**	0.034	0.166*									
7. Standard methods	0.74	0.70	0.028	-0.043	0.040	-0.092	0.242***	0.120								
8. Standard solutions	0.55	0.72	-0.122†	0.129*	-0.050	-0.192	-0.089	0.162	0.241***							
9. Products	0.36	0.48	-0.022	0.020	0.070	-0.160	-0.128*	0.299***	0.204**	0.603***						
10. Tailormade	0.88	0.82	0.410***	-0.205**	0.088	0.101	0.113†	0.261***	-0.081	-0.194*	-0.043					
11. Benchmarks	0.18	0.39	0.091	-0.171**	0.086	0.052	0.108†	0.082	0.036	-0.145	-0.096	0.187				
12. Advertise clients	0.57	0.49	0.028	-0.035	-0.026	0.052	-0.065	0.129	0.154*	0.159*	0.207**	-0.005	-0.006			
13. Partner	0.46	0.50	0.102	-0.94	0.013	0.004	0.020	0.157*	0.209**	0.347***	0.352***	0.100	0.009	0.283***		
14. Generalist	0.20	0.40	0.111	-0.089	0.012	0.229***	0.118†	0.051	-0.070	-0.276***	-0.191**	0.084	0.350***	-0.098	-0.052	

Variables	M	SD	1	2	3	4	5	6	7	8	9	10	11	12	13	14
15. Sectoral specialist	0.27	0.44	-0.081	0.025	0.036	-0.154†	-0.092	-0.016	0.051	-0.003	-0.059	-0.156*	0.042	-0.007	-0.046	0.038**
16. Functional expert	0.87	0.32	0.148†	-0.094	0.106	-0.019	0.103	0.296***	0.127†	0.084	0.091	0.172**	0.009	0.109†	0.082	-0.105
17. Sectoral expert	0.49	0.50	-0.192*	-0.249***	0.127†	-0.044	0.054	-0.141*	0.032	-0.168**	-0.025	0.222***	0.247***	-0.089	-0.030	0.240***
18. Strategy	0.38	0.48	0.104	-0.068	0.057	0.226***	0.093	0.006	-0.202**	-0.375***	-0.290***	0.110†	0.230***	-0.110†	-0.135*	0.538***
19. Organi-sation	0.41	0.49	0.182**	-0.176**	0.116†	0.247***	0.151*	0.045	-0.099	-0.339***	-0.231***	0.171**	0.193**	-0.084	-0.024	0.495***
20. Process	0.42	0.49	0.222***	-0.316***	0.261***	0.129*	0.077	0.170**	0.058	-0.069	0.001	0.153*	0.202**	0.148*	0.073	0.437***
21. IT	0.51	0.50	-0.006	-0.056	0.112†	-0.108†	0.005	0.284***	0.170**	0.476***	0.564***	-0.032	0.117†	0.173**	0.359***	0.260***
22. Human resources	0.41	0.49	0.068	0.051*	-0.049	0.211**	0.139*	-0.182**	-0.028	-0.381***	-0.423***	0.033	0.064	-0.233***	-0.155*	0.263***
23. Marketing	0.29	0.45	-0.036	0.007	-0.034	0.147*	0.027	-0.103	-0.168*	-0.299***	-0.275***	0.033	0.220***	-0.040	-0.223***	0.420***
24. Logistics	0.23	0.42	0.079	-0.164**	0.106	0.041	0.068	0.201**	-0.159*	-0.015	0.106	0.052	0.228***	0.040	0.076	0.499***
25. Finance	0.32	0.46	0.015	-0.049	0.048	0.081	-0.046	-0.046	-0.227***	-0.271***	-0.171**	0.020	0.2725***	-0.068	-0. 120†	0.483***
26. Perfor-mance	192,5	155,1	-0.034	0.025	-0.733	-0.015	0.043	-0.053	-0.050	-0.071	-0.114	-0.023	0.184*	0.032	-0.105	0.176†

Variables	M	SD	15	16	17	18	19	20	21	22	23	24	25	26
15. Sectoral specialist	0.27	0.44												
16. Functional expert	0.87	0.32	-0.093											
17. Sectoral expert	0.49	0.50	0.400***	0.127†										
18. Strategy	0.38	0.48	0.082	-0.062	0.195**									
19. Organi-sation	0.41	0.49	0.076	-0.062	0.176**	0.554***								
20. Process	0.42	0.49	0.176**	0.027	0.271***	0.299***	0.463***							
21. IT	0.51	0.50	0.010	0.090	0.150*	-0.103	-0.016	0.234***						
22. Human resources	0.41	0.49	-0.054	-0.173**	0.010	0.149*	0.230****	0.014	-0.321***					
23. Marketing	0.29	0.45	0.000	-0.140*	0.027	0.330***	0.166*	0.091	-0.057	0.076				
24. Logistics	0.23	0.42	0.066	0.015	0.210**	0.196**	0.237***	0.427***	0.288***	0.046	0.072			
25. Finance	0.32	0.46	0.036	-0.137*	0.137*	0.432***	0.285***	0.192**	-0.002	0.012	0.217***	0.268		
26. Perfor-mance	192,5	155,1	-0.098	-0.001	0.029	0.049	0.034	-0.056	-0.014	0.024	0.166	0.084	0.132	

† $p \leq 0.10$ * $p \leq 0.05$ ** $p \leq 0.01$ *** $p \leq 0.001$

Conducting cluster analysis and visually inspecting the dendrograms results in a plausible solution of six clusters. Inspection of the Caliński and Harabasz (1974) pseudo *F* index with a local peak at six clusters (Calinski/Harabasz pseudo-F index of 11.24) confirms that a reasonable cut-off is achieved with a clustering solution of six clusters (see Table 2).

Overall, several statistical approaches were used to investigate the sensitivity of the clustering results with variations of the similarity measure, clustering algorithm or different composition of the sample. Varying the similarity measure, using the Gower measure and even varying the linkage measure e.g. single linkage holds for similar clustering results. The results indicate that sensitivity to these variations is relatively low, so reliability of the clustering solutions is considered to be high. This result serves as an indicator of the robustness of the clustering results as the firms fall clearly into strategic groups, which are well differentiated along the chosen strategic dimensions.

Table 2: Calinski/Harabasz pseudo-F Index

Number of clusters	Calinski/ Harabasz pseudo-F
2	1.36
3	10.98
4	7.66
5	6.40
6	**11.24**
7	10.87
8	9.54
9	9.92
10	9.52
11	9.04
12	8.34
13	7.93
14	7.63

The six resulting clusters differ significantly in size. The first cluster consists of 78 firms (34 percent of the sample), the second of 108 (46 percent), the third of 42 (18 percent), and the remaining three clusters sum up to five firms (2 percent). As solitary firms are defined to exist when single clusters of firms emerge (DeSarbo, et al., 2008), I classify the remaining five firms distributed to three clusters as solitary firms. Further inspection of the five solitary firms confirms this definition. The services of these firms are highly specialized services with strong focus on special client groups, e.g. hotels, export firms. Therefore, I exclude these firms from further research due to the limited comparability of services to the essential research focus of management consulting services. As a consequence the sample size reduces from n = 233 to n = 228 firms clustered into three clusters. Due to its size, cluster 2 is delineated to a limited extent and the represented firms' service characteristics are not sufficiently distinguishable from one another to identify additional subgroups.

The results of the cluster analysis are summarized in Table 3 and Table 4 with respect to the cluster variables and additional control variables examined. Following this, I name the three clusters on the basis of their service characteristics described by the three key dimensions.

The results of the average analysis with respect to the individual strategic dimensions of each cluster are summarized in Table 5 and Table 6. This summary helps to further identify and interpret positioning differences across strategic groups. Derived from these analyses three strategic groups can be described as follows:

1. *Standardized solution providers*: This strategic group consists of 78 firms that provide highly standardized consulting services across client industries, with a strong focus on IT consulting. The degree of interaction between these firms and their clients tends to be low; the average values for both the *cooperation* level and the *process moderator role* variables are respectively medium high and almost zero. Ninety percent of the firms in this strategic group offer predefined *products* that can be bought 'off the shelf', use *standard methods* within the provision of consulting services and *implement standard solutions* on a high level. Especially the high degree of *implementation* orientation serves as a clear distinction in the strategic positioning of these companies within the market. Results suggest that firms providing standardized services tend to work together with *partner* companies that offer complementary services (e.g. software solutions) that are implemented within the consulting provision. As standardized solution providers often deal with recurring client

problems and solutions are comparable across client companies, consulting firms in this strategic group *advertise client* projects in order to attract new clients. Inspection of the Levene's robust test statistic indicates that in terms of *size* (measured by *revenues* and *number of employees* in Germany), the group is more varied than the firms in other strategic groups. This fact, in combination with a workforce average above industry average and an absolute revenue level within industry average, indicates that standardized solution providers follow a specific business model with a leverage ratio above industry average. This model implies the need to sell more consultants per client project in order to achieve revenues on industry average. In summary, leverage ratio for standardized solution providers shows evidences to be higher than industry average.

2. *Functional specialists*: As indicated above, this strategic group of consulting service providers (n=108) does not have a great number of outstanding characteristics that differ strongly from the other two strategic groups. Yet, it is not heterogeneous enough in order to justify dividing it into further sub-clusters. Most of the firms in this group are focused on few single consulting services out of the full spectrum of consulting services (except for IT consulting). The *number of services* offered is 2-3 services per firm and herewith at a low level. In line with a variable value for *generalist* of almost zero, this low level of differentiation indicates that firms within this cluster are dedicated functional specialists. In addition, functional specialists offer *rare services* at a significantly higher frequency than industry average. The *implementation* orientation is below industry average and only few firms use *standardized solutions* or offer "off-the-shelf"-*products*. Similarly, the proportion of firms that advertise their consulting services as standardized approaches is comparatively low. With regard to client relationship a medium degree of *client interaction* in the core consulting process is indicated while all three consulting roles are on average level. With respect to the other examined variables firms in this cluster represent industry average in many regards. Firms in this strategic group include mainly small and medium-sized firms (*employees*, *revenues* and *number of offices* significantly below industry average) providing various consulting advice to their clients. The degree of internationality is below sample average as only some firms within this strategic group operate *international offices* outside of Germany. The limited business scope of the companies is also shown in the limited number of firms that state professional recruiting efforts. Less than 50% of the firms implement specific recruiting websites. However, 35% of

the firms request work experience from potential employment candidates which is above total sample average. The average number of sectors to which the consulting firms in this group provide their services is relatively high, suggesting that this group of firms includes few industry specialists.

3. *Functional generalists:* The strategic group of functional generalists (n=42) is considerably different from the other two strategic clusters. In terms of intended client relationship results indicate that firms within this group put a strong emphasis on a high degree of client interaction within the provision of tailor-made consulting services. These firms are characterized by a low standardization level in their consulting approach. Consistently, predefined *standardized solutions* or even *products* as part of the consulting service delivery are not included in the service model. Although results indicate a low level of standardization, many firms include *detailed descriptions* of their service provision and emphasize a high level of implementation orientation. Furthermore many firms highlight the provision of *benchmarks* as part of the service model. A strong and significant positive correlation between firm *age* and *benchmarks* is measurable. As firms within this strategic group are significantly longer established in the consulting market than sample average, compulsory experience to conduct industry benchmarks seems to be present. Consultants of generalist firms cover all three different client-consultant *roles*. A stronger focus than among the rest of the consulting firms is put on the consultants' role as *process moderator*, supporting client companies in mastering challenges to major extent with own capacities. In addition, an accentuation of a particular *functional specialization and great expertise in different client sectors* is observable. *Generalists* advertise to offer broad bundles of functional specialists. However, results show that no specific sector specialization exists; rather all sectors are covered with equal intensity. Firms within this cluster are significantly larger than industry average (in terms of *revenues*, *employees and number of offices*) and contain more industry experience than industry average (in terms of firm *age*). More than 25 percent of the firms in this cluster are not of German origin and highly international (in terms of *number of international offices*) positioned. With regard to the carrier websites, functional generalists expect *entrepreneurial spirit* from their employees, but *work experience* is not mandatory.

The overall *quality* and *usability* of the websites is indicated as high throughout the whole sample. All management consulting firms offer profound, up-to-date and in-depth information. This confirms the proposition that websites are considered by consulting firms as an important measure to position in the market. The high quality of the websites indicates that consulting firms put a lot of effort in the content and design of their websites.

Table 3: Cluster Analysis – Strategic Groups

		Strategic dimension (* Rank-ordered variables)	**Strategic Group 1** (n=78)	**Strategic Group 2** (n=108)	**Strategic Group 3** (n=42)	**Arithmetic Mean** (n=228)	**Standard Deviation** (n=228)
Intended relationship	**1**	*Cooperation**	1.04	0.97	1.31	1.05	0.82
	2	*Expert role*	0.60	0.68	0.55	0.62	0.48
	3	*Docpatient role*	0.67	0.51	0.57	0.57	0.49
	4	*Process moderator role*	0.10	0.22	0.43	0.21	0.41
Type of service model	**5**	*Detail description*	0.27	0.37	0.40	0.34	0.47
	6	*Implement**	1.51	1.00	1.29	1.22	0.71
	7	*Standard methods**	0.94	0.64	0.57	0.72	0.69
	8	*Standard solutions**	1.24	0.23	0.14	0.56	0.72
	9	*Products*	0.90	0.06	0.19	0.36	0.48
	10	*Tailormade**	0.76	0.91	1.14	0.89	0.82
	11	*Benchmarks*	0.12	0.12	0.45	0.18	0.38
	12	*Advertise clients*	0.77	0.49	0.40	0.56	0.49
	13	*Partner*	0.71	0.31	0.38	0.46	0.49
Functional and sectoral specialization	**14**	*Generalist*	0.03	0.03	0.95	0.19	0.39
	15	*Sectoral specialist*	0.26	0.28	0.33	0.28	0.45
	16	*Functional expert*	0.95	0.86	0.86	0.89	0.31
	17	*Sectoral expert*	0.41	0.46	0.76	0.50	0.50
	18	*Strategy*	0.05	0.36	1.00	0.37	0.48
	19	*Organisation*	0.19	0.37	0.93	0.41	0.49
	20	*Process*	0.44	0.26	0.86	0.43	0.49
	21	*IT*	0.92	0.12	0.81	0.52	0.50
	22	*Human resources*	0.05	0.59	0.60	0.40	0.49
	23	*Marketing*	0.09	0.26	0.69	0.28	0.45
	24	*Logistics*	0.26	0.06	0.60	0.22	0.41
	25	*Finance*	0.12	0.31	0.74	0.32	0.46

Table 4: Cluster Analysis – Control Variables

		Control variables	Strategic Group 1 (n=78)	Strategic Group 2 (n=108)	Strategic Group 3 (n=42)	Arithmetic Mean (n=228)	Standard Deviation (n=228)
Firm characteristics	1	*Revenues (in EURO)*	36,750	10,683	106,409	37,234	102,983
	2	*Number of employees*	255.6	63.2	521.3	213.4	608.4
	3	*Number of offices in Germany*	3.47	2.18	5.16	3.17	4.13
	4	*Year of foundation*	1991.6	1989.1	1978.0	1987.9	16.0
Branches	5	*Healthcare & social services*	0.44	0.61	0.68	0.57	0.49
	6	*Trade & distribution*	0.62	0.69	0.60	0.64	0.48
	7	*Tourism*	0.50	0.55	0.71	0.57	0.49
	8	*Energy*	0.44	0.56	0.76	0.56	0.49
	9	*TIME*	0.59	0.64	0.74	0.64	0.48
	10	*Public sector*	0.60	0.55	0.56	0.57	0.49
	11	*Manufacturing*	0.90	0.87	0.91	0.89	0.31
	12	*Financial services*	0.68	0.63	0.74	0.67	0.47
	13	*Others*	0.81	0.90	0.92	0.87	0.33
Internationality	14	*Publications*	0.26	0.27	0.57	0.32	0.46
	15	*Home page language*	0.46	0.51	0.64	0.52	0.50
	16	*Service international*	0.55	0.50	0.67	0.55	0.49
	17	*Origin*	0.95	0.94	0.74	0.91	0.28
	18	*Number of international offices*	0.85	0.56	1.88	0.90	1.44
Career	19	*Career*	0.73	0.43	0.69	0.58	0.49
	20	*Business skills*	0.09	0.13	0.17	0.12	0.32
	21	*Technical skills*	0.61	0.10	0.28	0.37	0.48
	22	*Science skills*	0.61	0.80	0.83	0.72	0.44
	23	*Entrepreneurial spirit*	0.57	0.68	0.83	0.67	0.47
	24	*Work experience*	0.17	0.35	0.07	0.20	0.40

Table 5: Average Analysis – Strategic Groups

		Strategic dimension (* Rank-ordered variables)	Strategic Group 1 (n=78)	Strategic Group 2 (n=108)	Strategic Group 3 (n=42)	Arithmetic Mean (n=228)
Intended relationship	1	*Cooperation**	0	0	+	1.05
	2	*Expert role*	0	0	0	0.62
	3	*Docpatient role*	+	0	+	0.57
	4	*Process moderator role*	-	0	+	0.21
Type of service model	5	*Detail description*	0	0	0	0.34
	6	*Implement**	+	-	0	1.22
	7	*Standard methods**	+	-	-	0.72
	8	*Standard solutions**	+	-	-	0.56
	9	*Products*	+	-	-	0.36
	10	*Tailormade**	-	0	+	0.89
	11	*Benchmarks*	0	0	+	0.18
	12	*Advertise clients*	+	0	-	0.56
	13	*Partner*	+	-	0	0.46
Functional and sectoral specialization	14	*Generalist*	-	-	+	0.19
	15	*Sectoral specialist*	0	0	0	0.28
	16	*Functional expert*	0	0	0	0.89
	17	*Sectoral expert*	0	0	+	0.50
	18	*Strategy*	-	0	+	0.37
	19	*Organisation*	-	0	+	0.41
	20	*Process*	0	-	+	0.43
	21	*IT*	+	-	+	0.52
	22	*Human resources*	-	+	+	0.40
	23	*Marketing*	-	0	+	0.28
	24	*Logistics*	0	-	+	0.22
	25	*Finance*	-	0	+	0.32

Table 6: Average Analysis – Control Variables

		Control variables	Strategic Group 1 (n=78)	Strategic Group 2 (n=108)	Strategic Group 3 (n=42)	Arithmetic Mean (n=228)
Firm characteristics	1	*Revenues (in KEURO)*	0	-	+	37.234
	2	*Number of employees*	+	-	+	213.4
	3	*Number of offices in Germany*	+	-	+	3.19
	4	*Year of foundation*	+	0	-	1987.9
Branches	5	*Healthcare & social services*	-	0	+	0.57
	6	*Trade & distribution*	0	0	0	0.64
	7	*Tourism*	0	0	+	0.57
	8	*Energy*	-	0	+	0.56
	9	*TIME*	0	0	+	0.64
	10	*Public sector*	0	0	0	0.57
	11	*Manufacturing*	0	0	0	0.89
	12	*Financial services*	0	0	0	0.67
	13	*Others*	0	0	0	0.87
Internationality	14	*Publications*	0	0	+	0.32
	15	*Home page language*	0	0	+	0.52
	16	*Service international*	0	0	+	0.55
	17	*Origin*	0	0	-	0.91
	18	*Number of international offices*	0	-	+	0.90
Career	19	*Career*	+	-	+	0.58
	20	*Business skills*	0	0	0	0.12
	21	*Technical skills*	+	-	0	0.37
	22	*Science skills*	-	0	+	0.72
	23	*Entrepreneurial spirit*	0	0	+	0.67
	24	*Work experience*	0	+	-	0.20

"+" if variable (y-0.1) ≥ M(y) / "-" if variable (y+0.1) ≥ M(y) / "0" else

4.1.2 Results of Additional Analyses

As described above, I used additional analyses to deepen the insights on the strategic positioning efforts of the sample firms. In order to verify the interpretation of the clustering results, I used maximum-likelihood estimation methods to test the significance of the strategic positioning measures used in the clustering in dependency of the rank-ordered cluster variable *Clustvar (1-3)*, i.e. multinominal logistic (mlogit) regression models. Herewith, I tested the significance of the coefficients using Likelihood ratio tests. Table 7 contains the results of the mlogit regressions with *Clustvar* as the dependent variable and the results of Likelihood ratio (LR) tests.

The LR tests in Table 7 show that almost all measures are significant strategic positioning indicators and contribute to the allocation of individual firms to strategic groups. With the exception of the variables *expert role, detail description, sector specialist and functional expert* all variables show significance. The variable values across all sample firms are similar for the four identified insignificant variables.

Among the set of significant variables were some with major impact in explaining the strategic positioning of firms within the strategic group environment. More specifically, the variables *process moderator role, implement, standard solutions, products, generalist* as well as the functional variables *(strategy, organization, process, IT, human resources, marketing, logistics and finance)* were highly significant across all regressions. In particular, being a generalist or offering standardized consulting services (*products, standardized solutions*) serves as a clear and significant positioning distinction. The variables *expert role, detail description, sector specialist and functional expert* showed limited significance across the strategic groups.

Table 7: Multinominal Logistic Regression – Impact of Variables

Dependent variable: Strategic Group membership (default: Clustvar=2, n=110)

	Strategic dimension (* Rank-ordered variables)	**Strategic Group 1** (n=78)	**Strategic Group 3** (n=42)	**Likelihood ratio test** χ^2
1	*Cooperation**	0.09	0.51*	5.18
2	*Expert role*	0.31	0.54	2.43
3	*Docpatient role*	0.65*	0.25	4.64†
4	*Process moderator role*	-0.91*	0.96*	16.50***
5	*Detail description*	0.46	0.14	3.01
6	*Implement**	1.11***	0.57*	24.89***
7	*Standard methods**	0.60**	-0.15	10.80**
8	*Standard solutions**	2.51***	-0.59	116.36***
9	*Products*	5.00***	1.38*	161.27***
10	*Tailormade**	-0.22	0.34*	6.06*
11	*Benchmarks*	-0.04	1.79***.	21.79***
12	*Advertise clients*	1.24***	-0.34	20.92***
13	*Partner*	1.64***	0.29	29.68***
14	*Generalist*	-0.08	6.55***	164.41***
15	*Sectoral specialist*	-0.10	0.26	0.79
16	*Functional expert*	1.09	-0.03	4.64†
17	*Sectoral expert*	-0.21	1.31***	15.24***
18	*Strategy*	-2.34***	22.18***	128.33***
19	*Organisation*	-0.90**	3.09***	68.66***
20	*Process*	0.79*	2.84***	46.66***
21	*IT*	4.47***	3.43***	153.02***
22	*Human resources*	-3.29***	0.01	74.05***
23	*Marketing*	-1.26**	1.85***	48.00***
24	*Logistics*	1.76***	3.21***	50.54***
25	*Finance*	-1.21**	1.85***	48.87***

† $p \leq 0.10$ * $p \leq 0.05$ ** $p \leq 0.01$ *** $p \leq 0.001$

4.2 Results of Performance Differences Analyses

Inspection of the descriptive statistics in Table 8 shows that the variables carry sufficient variation. Firm performance varies between €4,166 and €1.05 million in revenues per employees. Furthermore, Table 8 lists correlations of the variables included in the performance analyses. Significant correlation exists between the variables distance and number of functions indicating that the greater the distance of a firm to the strategic group center, the higher the number of services offered. This result is in line with expectations that the number of services offered serves as a means of differentiation between consulting firms. Furthermore, age and size are also positively and significantly correlated with number of services. This finding indicates that the older and larger a firm is, the more consulting services are offered. This result is in line with expectations that generalist firms (per definition offering more services) tend to be longer established and comparably larger firms. Correlation between number of functions and performance is not established. With respect to firm origin and age, significant correlations show that German firms tend to be smaller and younger compared to foreign firms active in the German market. Overall, the correlations between the relevant independent variables of the performance analyses are at low to moderate levels. This suggests no multicollinearity problems and was confirmed by the calculation of variance inflation factors of the independent variables. The variance inflation factors revealed a maximum of 1.63 which is well below the multicollinearity indicating threshold of 2.5 - 4 (Allison, 1999; O'Brien, 2007).

With respect to performance rates strategic group means indicate that significant differences across strategic groups exist (Table 9). There is empirical support that being a member of a specific strategic group influences firm performance. The group of functional generalists has the highest average performance rate (242,586 EURO) in comparison to the two specialist groups. Standardized solution providers achieve the lowest performance rates (169,199 EURO) on average. This finding supports the proposed notion that standardized solution providers follow different service models as they use higher numbers of consultants within the provision of a standardized consulting process. The fact that performance is measured by revenue per employee underlines this finding.

As described, I measured the distance for each firm within its strategic group to the calculated cluster centroid firm. The distance range within strategic group 1 was between 4.91 and 11.50 (M 7.31; SD 1.28), within strategic group 2 between 5.12 and 11.72 (M 8.30; SD 1.25) and within group 3 between 6.71 and 11.19 (M 8.52; SD 1.18). Following this analyses,

I used the defined methodology to identify core and secondary firms within each strategic group.

The comparison of core and secondary firms with respect to performance, number of functions, age, size and origin shows significant differences as expected (in Table 9). Secondary firms reach on average higher performance rates than core firms within the specialist strategic groups 1 and 2. Results indicate that this is the contrary regarding the generalist strategic group 3. There is evidence that core firms in strategic group 2 reach lower performance rates that both core and secondary firms in strategic group 1. Results point out that the spread in performance between core and secondary firms in strategic group 3 is large. Mean comparison tests of the described performance differences within the respective strategic groups were all significant. With regard to age, core firms within cluster 3 seem to be significantly longer established in the market than the peer group, which is in line with expectations. Secondary firms in the two specialist groups are significantly larger in terms of employees and revenue than core firms. The opposite is found among functional generalists as core firms are significantly larger. Furthermore, the level of internationality among core functional generalists is significantly higher than industry average.

Preliminary results for performance differences within specialist strategic groups 1and 2 are similar as in both groups differentiation and positioning as secondary firms seems to increase performance. Therefore, I will concentrate on determining the positioning and performance differences between specialist strategic groups 1 & 2 (n=186) and generalist strategic group 3 (n=42). Mean comparison tests indicate that within both firm clusters significant performance differences exist.

Table 8: Performance Analyses – Correlation Table

Variables	M	SD	Min	Max	1	2	3	4	5	6
1. Performance	192,580	155,165	4,166	1,052,941						
2. Distance	8.06	1.36	4.9	11.7	0.04216					
3. Number of functions	2.96	1.97	1	8	0.077	0.320***				
4. Age	18.14	16.02	2	120	0.025	-0.015	0.286***			
5. Size	213.40	608.42	1	3996	-0.041	0.059	0.298***	0.200***		
6. Origin	0.90	0.28	0	1	-0.178**	0.022	-0.251***	-0.486***	-0.201***	

† $p \leq 0.10$ * $p \leq 0.05$ ** $p \leq 0.01$ *** $p \leq 0.001$

Table 9: Performance Analyses – Descriptive Statistics

	Additional variables		Strategic Group 1 (n=78)		Strategic Group 2 (n=108)		Strategic Group 3 (n=42)		Arithmetic Mean (n=228)	
			core (n=57)	secon-dary (n=21)	core (n=43)	secon-dary (n=65)	core (n=13)	secon-dary (n=29)	core (n=113)	secon-dary (n=115)
1	*Performance (in EURO)*	M	164,807	181,120	156,909	211,925	340,581	198,658	182,024	202,954
		SD	149,996	111,514	93,785	188,236	132,143	157,993	140,447	168,345
		M	169,199		190,020		242,586		192,580	
		SD	140,140		159,305		162,996		155,165	
2	*Distance*		6.7	8.9	7.2	9.1	7.2	9.2	6.9	9.1
			7.3		8.3		8.5		8.0	
3	*Number of functions*		1.80	2.95	1.95	2.56	7.0	5.8	2.15	3.39
			2.11		2.32		6.21		2.96	
4	*Age*		14.84	13.23	15.86	17.52	41.07	22.10	18.24	18.05
			14.41		16.86		27.97		18.14	
5	*Size*		235.03	311.33	23.65	89.35	442.38	556.72	178.45	247.74
			255.57		63.19		521.33		213.40	
6	*Origin*		0.94	0.95	0.97	0.92	0.61	0.79	0.92	0.89
			0.94		0.94		0.73		0.90	

Core firm: Firm(x): distance ≤ M (distance) – (SD (distance)/2)

Secondary firm: Firm(x): distance > M (distance) – (SD (distance)/2)

4.2.1 Results of Performance Differences across Strategic Groups

The empirical analysis of performance differences across strategic groups shows that - as descriptive statistics suggest - significant differences exist. The regression model follows a hierarchical structure. First, the influence of the control variables (*age*, *size*, *origin*) on performance is analyzed (Model 1). Second, I regress performance on the full model including the independent variable *clustvar*. The results of the regression can be found in Table 10.

Table 10: Regression - Performance Differences across Strategic Groups

Independent Variables	Model 1	Model 2
1. Age	-0.070 (730.2)	-0.103 (738.9)
2. Size	-0.073 (17.1)	-0.090 (17.5)
3. Origin	-0.227* (40,381.6)	-0.204** (40,515.6)
4. Clustvar = 2		0.059 (22,908.3)
5. Clustvar = 3		0.175* (30,821.5)
R^2	**0.0416***	**0.0635****
Adjusted R^2	**0.0287***	**0.0424****

Notes: $N = 228$
Standardized beta coefficients,
standard errors in parentheses
* $p<0.05$, ** $p<0.01$, *** $p<0.001$

Model 1 shows that origin has a significant impact on performance differences between consulting firms. It seems that being an international player in the consulting market holds for higher performance rates. This finding is in line with existing research (Uhlenbruck, Hitt, & Semadeni, 2006) In contrast, age and firm size do not significantly affect performance. My results in model 2 show that being a member of a specific strategic group has a significant impact on firm performance. In more detail, being part of the strategic group functional generalist (clustvar = 3) increases probability for significant above-average performance rates. The overall model is highly significant. Therefore, hypotheses 2 can be supported.

4.2.2 Results of Performance Differences within Strategic Groups

The following twofold results show that there exists evidence that different positioning efforts within strategic groups as core or secondary firms hold for significant performance differences. The calculation of core and secondary firms was based on the outcome of the maximum-likelihood estimation methods testing the significance of strategic positioning measures.

Both regression models follow a hierarchical structure. The first regression analyzes performance differences within the specialist strategic groups 1 & 2. The second regression analyzes performance differences within the strategic group of functional generalists. First, the influence of the control variables (*age*, *size*, *origin*) on performance is analyzed (model 1). Second, I include the independent variable *core* indicating if firms position as core or as secondary firms. Finally, I regress performance to the full model including the control variables as well as both independent variables *core* and *number of functions*. The results of the regression on performance differences within the specialist groups are described in Table 11 and the results of the analysis of functional generalists in Table 12.

Table 11: Regression - Performance Differences within Standardized Solutions Providers and Functional Specialists

Independent Variables	Model 1	Model 2	Model 3
1. Age	0.193** (951.5)	0.198** (945.1)	0.188* (933.2)
2. Size	-0.037 (17.1)	-0.036 (22.1)	-0.005 (22.2)
3. Origin	-0.267** (50,493.9)	-0.259** (40,515.6)	-0.251** (40,515.6)
4. Core		0.134* (21,475.8)	0.195** (22,413.5)
5. Number of functions			-0.186* (9,245.2)
R^2	**0.078****	**0.096****	**0.125*****
Adjusted R^2	**0.062****	**0.0760****	**0.101*****
Dependent Variable: Performance (revenue per employee)			

Notes: $N = 186$
Standardized beta coefficients,
standard errors in parentheses
* $p<0.05$, ** $p<0.01$, *** $p<0.001$

Model 1 of the specialist groups' regression indicates that the control variables *age* and *origin* have a high significant impact on firm performance within the two strategic groups. In contrast, size does not significantly impact performance rates. Model 2 includes the independent variable whether consulting firms position near to or far from competitors within a strategic group. The results show that positioning as a secondary firm has a significant positive impact on firm performance within the specialist strategic groups. Finally, model 3 shows that number of functions has a significant negative impact on firm performance among specialists. This finding implies that secondary firms profit from positioning on the competitive cusp while maintaining a specialized level of offered services. These results support hypothesis 3.

Table 12: Regression - Performance Differences within Functional Generalists

Independent Variables	Model 1	Model 2	Model 3
1. Age	0.200 (1,239.3)	0.062 (1224.2)	0.072 (1,237.9)
2. Size	-0.155 (29.3)	-0.109 (27.8)	-0.137 (28.9)
3. Origin	-0.035 (73,067.3)	0.042 (68,816.2)	0.054 (69,622.1)
4. Core		-0.387* (55,760.2)	-0.336* (62,414.5)
5. Number of functions			0.113 (22,389.3)
R^2	**0.051**	**0.181**	**0.190**
Adjusted R^2	**-0.023**	**0.092**	**0.078**

Dependent Variable: Performance (revenue per employee)

Notes: $N = 42$
Standardized beta coefficients,
standard errors in parentheses
* $p<0.05$, ** $p<0.01$, *** $p<0.001$

Model 1 of the functional generalist's regression indicates that the control variables *age, size* and *origin* do not significantly impact performance. Model 2 includes the independent variable *core* indicating if firms position as core or as secondary firms. The results show that positioning as a core firm has a significant positive impact on firm performance within this strategic group. Finally, model 3 shows that *number of functions* has a significant positive impact on firm performance among generalists. The results indicate that functional generalists profit from positioning close to the groups' center while offering a wide range of services. These results are not in line with hypothesis 3.

These findings indicate that among generalists neither size, nor age, nor origin seem to have significant influence on firm performance. The fact that the control variables show no significant influence on firm performance among functional generalist indicates that any consulting firm who manages to position among the functional generalists and close to the groups center profits in terms of performance. In the consulting market being a functional generalist per se holds for above-average performance rates.

In the following, I conduct a moderator analysis using the variable *age* to analyze the impact of firm age on *performance* within the specific strategic groups more in-depth (Baron & Kenny, 1986). I expect *age* to serve as a moderator between the independent positioning variables *core* and *number of functions* and the dependent variable *performance*. I exclude the control variables *size* and *origin* from this analysis as they are correlated to *age*. In order to determine the effect of *age*, I split the specialist strategic groups 1 & 2 and the functional generalist groups into two sub-samples on the basis of the individual group median of firm ite>(median age (group 1&2) = 13; median age (group 3) = 20) (Holmbeck, 1997). The first regressions analyze the influence of the variables *core* and *number of functions* on firm performance within the specialist subgroups. The second regressions analyze the influence of the variables *core* and *number of functions* on firm performance within the functional generalist subgroup.

The results of the regression on performance differences within the specialist subgroups using age as a moderator can be found in Table 13 and Table 14. The results of the moderator analysis of functional generalist subgroups are described in Table 15 and Table 16. The results indicate that among old specialist firms it is beneficial to position as secondary firms to achieve above average performance rates. Furthermore, the results show that among young generalist firms it is significantly beneficial to position as core firms in order to achieve above average performance rates.

The evidence from the regression results in combination with the moderator analyses lends support to the hypotheses 4 that young firms that manage to position alike old, established generalist firms achieve similar above-average performance rates.

Table 13: Moderator analysis – Performance differences between young Standardized Solutions Providers and Functional Specialists

Independent Variables	Model 1
1. Core	0.146 (38,546.5)
2. Number of functions	-0.180 (15,923.9)
R^2	**0.040**
Adjusted R^2	**0.020**
Dependent Variable: Performance (revenue per employee)	

Notes: N = 98 (only firms with age ≤ 13)
M(age) = 8.0 SD(age) = 2.7
Standardized beta coefficients,
standard errors in parentheses
* p<0.05, ** p<0.01, *** p<0.001

Table 14: Moderator analysis – Performance differences between old Standardized Solutions Providers and Functional Specialists

Independent Variables	Model 1
1. Core	0.344** (21,551.8)
2. Number of functions	-0.306** (8,566.6)
R^2	**0.131****
Adjusted R^2	**0.110****
Dependent Variable: Performance (revenue per employee)	

Notes: N = 88 (only firms with age > 13)
M(age) = 24.5 SD(age) = 12.5
Standardized beta coefficients,
standard errors in parentheses
* p<0.05, ** p<0.01, *** p<0.001

Table 15: Moderator analyses – Performance differences between young Functional Generalist

Independent Variables	Model 1
1. Core	-0.468* (67,520.4)
2. Number of functions	0.373 (20,895.8)
R^2	**0.538*** **
Adjusted R^2	**0.486*** **
Dependent Variable: Performance (revenue per employee)	

Notes: $N = 21$ (only firms with age ≤ 20)
M(age) = 11.9 SD(age) = 5.3
Standardized beta coefficients,
standard errors in parentheses
* $p<0.05$, ** $p<0.01$, *** $p<0.001$

Table 16: Moderator analyses – Performance differences between old Functional Generalist

Independent Variables	Model 1
1. Core	-0.280 (80,578.3)
2. Number of functions	-0.267 (35,013.2)
R^2	**0.108**
Adjusted R^2	**0.009**
Dependent Variable: Performance (revenue per employee)	

Notes: $N = 21$ (only firms with age > 20)
M(age) = 44.0 SD(age) = 27.1
Standardized beta coefficients,
standard errors in parentheses
* $p<0.05$, ** $p<0.01$, *** $p<0.001$

5 Discussion

In the following chapter, I will reflect on the theoretical and practical implications of my study. I discuss the theoretically derived hypotheses in the light of the empirical results of my study. Furthermore, practical implications for consulting firms as to how strategic positioning positively influences performance are illustrated.

5.1 Reflection on theory

Strategic balance theory states that firm strategists need to optimize company positioning along multiple dimensions and decide along which dimensions to differentiate relative to competition. Furthermore, it argues that positioning on the competitive cusp – balancing proximity and differentiation - is generally beneficial for all market participants. Within my research I tested the theoretical propositions of strategic balance theory. My results imply that competitive positioning theory in general and strategic balance theory in particular should take moderating factors into account, which reflect the structure of the "local" competitive environment. My results indicate that it depends on the prevailing market structure, dominant industry specifics and the pursued service model of a firm to define the right balance between positioning near to or far from competition. These results stand in conflict with existing literature on strategic balance theory. Strategic group theory argues that in every industry different groups of firms are following similar strategic recipes closely and hereby build strategic groups. My research shows the existence of a strong interrelation between the principles of strategic group and strategic balance theory.

So far, only a limited number of studies applied strategic balance theory to professional service industries. However, most of the existing research was limited to single elements of this multidimensional theoretical system and did not take boundary conditions into account. Semadeni (2006) applied strategic balance theory study in his study on management consulting firms with the limitation of an undifferentiated sample. He focused on the 50 largest management consulting firms in the U.S. Furthermore, Semadeni concentrated, in his positioning analyses, on the two-dimensional differentiation between expertise- and experience-based firms. Hence, he measured positioning efforts according to Maister's (1993) dimensions of innovation and specialization. Hereby, he did not take multidimensional constructs for firm positioning and efficiency-focused consulting firms into account. As a result, the study outcome is of limited validity and generalizability for the multi-facetted consulting industry. Reflecting on legitimacy in a study with a limited sample composition lacks significance as it seems plausible that the largest consulting firms are already well established in this outnumbered industry. These firms have established their service offering in the market, mastered firm growth and gained market experience. Thus, these firms have less need to establish legitimacy to succeed in the market than medium- or small-sized market entrants that were not included in the study. McNamara et al. (2003) applied strategic balance theory to a highly regulated sector of the banking industry with limited competitive forces and high barriers to entry and exit. They used a small sample of locally delineated firms (n=30). The question remained how strategic balance theory alters the understanding of firm positioning behavior in unregulated, outnumbered markets with low mobility barriers. The discussion on positioning near to or far from competitors in such a market environment lacks in depth and generalizability. Consistently, the empirical proof for the applicability of strategic balance theory to professional service firms and possible limitations of its generalizability have not been sufficiently tested and validated, yet.

Different to McNamara et al.'s and Semadeni's studies with rather small samples of locally delineated banks or homogeneous large management consulting firms, my well-balanced sample (n=228) covers a broad picture of the consulting service industry. The consulting market is highly competitive, has comparably low barriers of entry/exit and differentiation in market positioning is comparably easy to achieve. These specific characteristics hold for promising analyses. I include small, medium and large consulting providers in relation to the existing market segmentation. Hereby, my sample mirrors the large diversity of company settings within the consulting industry and allows testing strategic balance theory in a realistic market setting. This ensures a greater generalizability and validity of results. Furthermore, my research helps to advance strategic group research methodologically by using a multi-dimensional, non-perception based, and supply oriented measure of strategic positions based on content analysis of the service offerings communicated on the consulting firms' websites.

In the following, I am going to discuss my empirical findings in the light of the defined theoretical framework and the derived hypotheses.

H_1: *The consulting industry is characterized by the existence of a small number of strategic groups.*

I find support for the general assumption that barriers to imitation within the consulting industry are low compared to regulative or asset specific industries. There is evidence that the consulting market is characterized by low barriers to entry and exit. This steadily evolving market is mirrored by the fact that one third of firms active in the consulting market leave the market just after 5 years (Keeble & Schwalbach, 1995). My empirical results show that firm age and size have limited impact on firm performance. In line with this, the derived key positioning dimensions are comparably easy to imitate among existing competitors and consulting market entrees. Market entry is achieved relatively easy due to three reasons. First, institutional protection of consulting as a profession is missing. Second, most service models are easy to imitate with only little investments required due to a low capital intensity of the service models. Third, limited persistence of specific market positions is obvious in dynamic industries with business models that are easy to imitate. In line with this, it is challenging to defend market positions and prevent potential new market players from entry into the consulting market.

Established research considers strategic groups as highly stable as they reflect decisions and behaviors that are long-term, costly and difficult to change (McGee & Thomas, 1986). The argument is that firms are unable to move easily from one strategic group to another (Caves & Porter, 1977). Mobility barriers such as switching costs, brand name, and reputation impede firms from entering other strategic groups. However, these theoretical propositions are based on industries with high mobility barriers. I propose that the level of stability in strategic groups correlates with the size of the mobility barriers. In addition, I find support for my theoretical proposition that intra-industry mobility barriers still exist within markets with low barriers to entry and exit. When analyzing the stability of strategic group structures the concept of intra-industry mobility barriers has to be considered. Even in industries with low barriers to entry and exit, asymmetric high intra-industry mobility barriers exit. Herewith, I support the notion that intra-industry mobility barriers are structural forces impending companies from freely changing their competitive position and alter their strategic group membership. Nevertheless, as intra-industry mobility barriers are dynamic - especially within industries like consulting - their development over time offers companies the possibility to change market positions. My results show that some strategic groups share interest in maintaining high intra-industry mobility barriers. This preserves exclusive conditions (e.g. price per consultant, reputation, legitimacy) and above-average performance rates. In my empirical study I find evidence that functional generalists have interest in maintaining high intra-industry barriers. They have established competitive advantages over the competing strategic groups and achieve, by being member of a specific strategic group, above-average performance rates. However, I do not fully support the notion that consulting firms directly collude within a certain strategic group in order to sustain high barriers. I agree with Shapiro (Shapiro, 1989) that it is more an informal/tacit collusion in that sense that firms recognize mutual dependence and act accordingly e.g. in the way companies promote their services and align their positioning. However, I have not included the analysis of evidence for efforts among consulting companies in order to artificially raise intra-industry mobility barriers within this study.

Deephouse (1999) has introduced the range of acceptability of strategic similarity in which firms maintain legitimacy. I find support that the strategic similarity level among strategic groups is significantly higher than that across strategic groups. Firms that follow a similar strategy build a strategic group. The extent to how close competitors follow a similar strategy varies and is equivalent to the range of acceptability. Therefore, I propose that the range of acceptability among firms within a strategic group is consistent with the barriers of a strategic group. My results show that different industry recipes, acceptable and legitimate strategies evolved and naturally build different strategic groups in the German consulting market.

In consequence, I find support for the hypotheses that different strategic positioning efforts are observable in the consulting market and that the consulting market is characterized by the existence of a small number of strategic groups. The German market is segmented into three significantly different strategic groups: Standardized solution providers (n= 78), functional specialists (n= 108), and functional generalists (n= 42). Consulting firms within the identified three strategic groups follow different positioning strategies, base their service offerings on different service models and coexist within the defined market environment. The proposition is that firms position in strategic groups to establish legitimacy, reduce uncertainty and to profit from spill-over effects. At the same time, competition for resources and clients increases among firms that position similar in a strategic group. There is evidence that consulting firms are increasing the perceived legitimacy by being part of a strategic group. For example, among the functional generalists young, small consulting providers manage successfully to be perceived as legitimate as old, established providers (e.g. McKinsey, BCG or Roland Berger). They profit from positioning as functional generalists resulting in above-average performance rates. Clients who face numerous and difficult to compare consulting companies in a limited regulated market have to rely on perceived strategic market positioning, on perceived legitimacy as well as on reputation in choosing a consulting provider. Strategic groups serve in this regard as a sub-regulation of market participants.

I support the argument that strategic groups build a shared strategic identity. Strategic identity is a set of mutual understandings among members of a strategic group regarding the central, enduring, and distinctive characteristics of the group. This shared identity facilitates group members' alignment of their positioning with those of other strategic group members. In summary, strategic identity can be described as the shared understanding of the key dimensions of each strategic group. Reflecting on my empirical results, this can be illustrated by common understandings among functional generalists e.g. to offer the full range of management consulting services, provide services on a low standardization level and implement a high level of client interaction. Common understanding among standardized solution providers is to focus on a highly standardized service provision, mainly in IT and provide services with limited client interaction as well as a high degree of implementation orientation. Functional specialists differ from the other two strategic groups, but are rather heterogeneous within the group. Companies within this strategic group specialize on 2-3 services and try to build reputation as specialized providers of expert knowledge in the market.

However, within each strategic group additional differences between members occur. Some consulting firms align strongly with the key positioning similarities of the respective group (core firms) and some firms align just close enough to be considered as a member of the strategic group (secondary firms). In other words, secondary firms align as part of a strategic group and at the same time differentiate from other group members. I found significant evidence for this proposition within all three resulting strategic groups. However, I found evidence that it is not always advantageous to position as a secondary firm on the competitive cusp of a strategic group in terms of performance. This finding contradicts strategic group theory that states that firms should strive for a positioning on the competitive cusp to balance the advantages of positioning next to and far from competition. Therefore, I claim to extend strategic balance theory. I propose that the right balance between positioning near to or far from competition always depends on moderating factors e.g. the structure of the "local competitive environment. This limits the generalizability and general validity of the strategic balance theory. These insights extend the context of intra-group positioning and have implications for strategic balance theory and its application to competitive positioning in general.

My findings have further implications for theory as they cast doubt on existing typologies of consulting services. Existing typologies of consulting firms focus primarily on few dimensions in differentiating consulting firms (e.g. Ketchen, et al., 1993; Maister, 1993; Semadeni, 2006). So far, researchers focussed e.g. on types of services mainly provided or types of knowledge required for problem solving, but little on the comprehensive service model and further dimensions of the consulting industry. In line with existing strategy research (e.g. Armbrüster, 2006), I have argued that consulting service models and derived service expositions are multidimensional in nature. Consistently, my study adds a multidimensional perspective on the strategic positioning of consulting firms to consulting research. My results suggest that consulting services differ along a combination of more key dimensions than the extant typologies of consulting services imply. This research adds to existing typologies by differentiating consulting firms on the base of three key dimensions: the type of service model, intended relationship with the client, and degree of functional and sectoral specialization. Within my analysis 21 of the 25 applied variables significantly contributed to segmenting German consulting providers. Hereby, my typology of consulting firms shows validity and serves as a sound means to test my theoretical propositions.

Nevertheless, I find general support for the applicability of Maister's (1993) three professional service firm classes: expertise-based firms, experience-based firms and efficiency-based firms. He suggests that expertise- and experience-based firms essentially focus on differentiation strategies while efficiency-based firms strive for cost leadership. The three strategic groups identified in my research fit to a certain extent into this classification. Standardized solution providers follow a service model that is primarily focused on efficiency in providing standardized consulting services. Their service model is based on an above-average leverage ratio and efficient service provision. This service model implies the need to "sell more consultants per client project" in order to achieve revenues on industry average. The large number of consultants involved in the provision of standardized solution e.g. the implementation of an IT system ensures the success of the consulting companies. As a consequence, the suggestion is that successful companies are able to offer their off-the-shelf services at smaller prices than the competition. However, I have neither analyzed the cost structure nor the profitability of consulting firms to undoubtedly prove the sustainable success of different service models.

Functional as well as general specialists fall into Maister's expertise-based classification of consulting firms. Their service models are based on offering their clients highest expertise and tailor-made solutions at above-average prices per consultant. However, my results indicate that functional generalists also fit to some extent into Maister's classification of experience-based consulting providers. Old, established generalists profit from their experience in the market and therefore, are able to achieve above-average performance rates. My empirical results present evidence that experience-based companies achieve relatively higher performance rates. However, additional performance indicators and efficiency indicators could add additional empirical insights on the typology of consulting firms and the profitability of existing service models.

Despite the multidimensional efforts on typologizing consulting services and firms, I still find evidence for the proposition that overall a "lack of differentiation" prevails in the consulting market (Galal & Richter, 2007). Although some firms differ in terms of how they position and describe their service offering, overall differentiation efforts are still comparably limited. This is in line with the argument that some firms seek successfully to position alike their competitors. In addition, organizational characteristics such as age and size seem to have only limited influence on differentiation in this specific market. Especially in the specialist strategic groups, the positioning efforts of consulting company are more similar than expected. This reflects the reaction of consulting clients who focus increasingly on professionalization of the selection process due to the similarity of consulting offerings. It also raises the proposition that consulting firms are on a similarly high professional level in promoting their individual service offering.

To summarize, I find strong support for my hypothesis that the consulting industry is characterized by the existence of a small number of strategic groups. At this point, it is necessary to reiterate that examined communicated strategic positioning has not been matched to the perceived positioning of potential buyers' of consulting services or the intended strategic positioning of consulting firms. This could be addressed in future research to cross-validate and complement the picture on intended strategic positioning, communicated positioning and perceived positioning.

H_2: There are performance differences between the strategic groups in the consulting industry.

My results present evidence that the identified strategic groups achieve significantly deviating performance rates. Analyses show that functional generalist achieve significantly higher performance rates than the two specialist strategic groups. This implies that being positioned as a member of the functional generalists contributes to an above-average performance rate. Functional specialists achieve on average performance rates that are in line with overall industry average. Standardized solution providers achieve performance rates that are significantly below industry average. These results illustrate that different strategic positioning efforts and different service models lead to deviating performance rates across strategic groups.

I find substantial empirical evidence in my research for the underlying basic assumptions of strategic balance theory that different firm positioning efforts result in different firm performances. Strategic balance theory argues that firms need to maximize the advantages and disadvantages of proximity and distance. Strategic balance serves as a response to the pressure of both to conform and to differentiate from competitors. This research contains moderate support that the right balance between conformity and differentiation is a sound means to establish potential for above-average performance. My results support the notion that strategic positioning does not necessarily follow a bipolar dichotomy between conformity and differentiation across and within strategic groups. All three strategies – positioning near to, far from or on the competitive cusp - seem prosperous under certain circumstances. Secondary firms balancing on the competitive cusp follow a strategic recipe less closely than core firms that try to imitate each other's strategic positioning closely. Establishment of a certain level of proximity to ensure legitimacy of the service offering, but not so close as to engage in direct competition seems advantageous. At the same time, I find evidence that positioning close to competitors can also be a valid strategic option to achieve above-average performance rates.

Strategic balance theorists propose that it is always beneficial to position on the competitive cusp and that this is not dependent on industry or firm specifics. In summary, I find limited support for the general applicability and validity of strategic balance theory within the context of my strategic group research. My results rather show that in relation to the specific strategic positioning efforts that align market participants, empirical evidence within the consulting market does not fully support strategic balance theory. Results show that the right positioning option depends on the specific market situation, strategic group structure and firm characteristics.

In consequence, my research results show that it is necessary to sharpen theoretical propositions and analyze more in-depth the temporal and contextual factors that set the boundaries of generalizability of the strategic balance theory. I propose to extend the propositions of strategic balance theory as well as these of strategic group theory in dependence of specific industry and firm settings. As explained, the highly dynamic consulting industry is marked by low barriers to entry and exit. However, I found evidence that consulting firms share interest in establishing intra-industry mobility barriers to compensate for evolving high dynamics and ensure individual long term success. In this regard, I follow Mascarenhas & Aaker (1989) who argue that size of the mobility barriers is positively related to performance of strategic groups. They state that mobility barriers refer more to "who we are" than to "what we do". This definition suits the consulting industry as service models are comparably easy to imitate, but reputation and brand are not.

In this argumentation, the functional generalist group manages it best to sustain high intra-industry mobility barriers like e.g. reputation, brand name, customer loyalty, and skilled employees. These barriers help to preserve above-average performance. Consistently, functional generalists should have interest in hindering the entrance of new members to their strategic group as they profit from positioning exclusively. As the strategic group of functional specialist lacks in differentiation and includes a broad scale of consulting firms, intra-industry mobility barriers are comparably low. For members of this group additional differentiation seems to be valid to attract potential clients. As standardized solution providers follow a different service model and try to establish efficient service provision, they distinguish themselves from other consulting firms. By establishing efficient provision of standardized consulting services that is challenging to imitate, they establish intra-industry mobility barriers that help to protect them from direct competition. These findings indicate that intra-industry mobility barriers are asymmetrical as size of the barriers varies in dependency of the strategic group structure.

Furthermore, my results show that firms within different strategic groups are not posing equal threats to each other. Functional generalists are more threatened by group members than by members of other strategic groups. On the other hand, functional specialists are posing equally high threats to each other as functional generalists. Herewith, I answer Semadeni's criticism that competitive asymmetry has been largely absent from research on strategic positioning.

In summary, my results indicate that there are significant performance differences between the strategic groups in the consulting industry. Significant variance differences across strategic groups were detected.

H_3: *Within a particular strategic group in the consulting industry secondary firms show superior performance as compared to core firms.*

Overall, the results lend partial support for my third hypothesis. I find significant evidence that standardized solution providers and functional specialists profit from positioning on the competitive cusp between proximity and differentiation relative to competition. On the one side, they align their positioning to be members of a specific strategic group. On the other side, results show that establishing a certain degree of differentiation and positioning as a secondary firm has significant positive impact on performance in relation to the core members. I find empirical support within the specialist strategic groups for Deephouse's (1999) argument that firms achieve maximum performance at the level of strategic similarity, where the gains of reduced competition are equal to the costs of balanced legitimacy, uncertainty and spillover effects. There is evidence that a marginal level of strategic similarity establishes legitimacy and at the same time leaves room for organizational uniqueness to attract potential clients. Secondary specialist firms differentiate from core specialists on the base of how closely they align their positioning efforts to the strategic group center. Comparison of the control variables of core and secondary firms shows that secondary firms offer on average one additional functional service and are on average larger than the core firms of the specialist strategic groups. In addition, average firm age among core firms and secondary firms is at the same level. However, my results indicate that firm size as well as age does not significantly impact firm performance. Consulting firms that follow efficiency based service models with a high degree of standardization try to differentiate by efficient service provision, high leverage ratio, price and aim to establish high economies of scale with a limited level of interaction.

One of my key findings - contrary to McNamara et al.'s results (2003) - is that, depending on the strategic group, it seems to be more or less advantageous to position as core or secondary firms. In contrast to the specialist strategic groups, for functional generalists this relationship is reversed: Here, secondary firms show significantly lower performance than core firms. Among functional generalists no significant evidence was detected that secondary firms outperform core firms. The argument that increased competition among core firms reduces high performance rates was not observed in that specific strategic group. On the contrary, functional generalists profit from positioning as close as possible to the most reputable firms. Increasing legitimacy and potential for spillover effects compensate for the disadvantages. Certainly the fact that the consulting industry is still growing and not a mature market supports this finding. It would be interesting to observe how this relation develops over time with an increasing market consolidation and maturity. However, my results do not necessary serve as contradictions to previous research. It serves more as an extension of existing research as my research scope covers a broader scale of them examined management consulting industry.

In line with density dependence theory, positioning near to established competitors increases perceived legitimacy and decreases uncertainty at a declining rate, while competition grows at an increasing rate. Consulting companies imitating their established competitors follow certain obligatory action, which correlates with the common understanding within a group. Hereby, a certain way e.g. in delivering consulting services becomes taken for granted among consulting companies and clients.

My results indicate that members of the functional generalist group show significantly higher performance rates when they follow the strategic recipe of the group as closely as possible. In other terms, core firms achieve significantly higher performance rates as compared to secondary firms. There is evidence that among the high performing core firms, age and size do not significantly impact performance. High-reputable, large and established firms (e.g. McKinsey, BCG, and Bain) achieve similar performance rates like young, small generalist firms. This proves that it is a valid and successful positioning strategy to position as close as possible to reputable, established consulting firms.

In line with my proposed argumentation and contrary to proposals by previous research (Baum & Haveman, 1997; Haveman, 1993) increased concentration among generalists does not necessarily lead to failure among large generalists. Functional generalists establish a self-reifying community in the consulting market and profit from positioning similar to each other. Hereby, they manage to achieve high levels of legitimacy and reputation. As a result, high strategic similarity proves to be the best positioning effort in this specific market segment to achieve above-average performance rates. As core firms outperform secondary firms, established generalist seem not to profit from additional differentiation. However, it would be interesting to analyze the dynamics of market development and test whether this observation holds over time.

In summary, my results lend partial support for the hypotheses that professional service firms gain from additional differentiation in their positioning strategy. They manage successfully to balance the advantages and disadvantages of positioning like direct competitors within a strategic group. By ensuring a limited amount of differentiation they reduce similarity and gain client attendance. My results show that in the identified specialist strategic groups secondary firms achieve superior performance as compared to core firms. In this market segment, firms profit from positioning on the competitive cusp.

Each strategic group has a beneficial positioning strategy that holds for above-average performance rates. The competitive behavior of functional generalists offers potential for specialist firms to differentiate their market positioning and raise client attention. Companies that follow a strategy of offering selected consulting services position within the specialist strategic groups. In order to highlight their specific expertise and focused service provision, differentiation proves to be the preferable positioning option. Small specialists position far from strong established generalists to exploit market niches. They benefit from being different from functional generalists. However, to maintain a necessary level of legitimacy they align their positioning in different strategic groups and position as secondary firms.

However, the hypotheses that secondary firms that find the right balance between positioning near to and far from competitors show superior performance as compared to competitors that position as core members of a strategic group cannot be fully supported. Depending on the specific strategic group, different positioning strategies hold for above-average performance rates. Support for this hypothesis was confirmed among the strategic group of the standardized solution providers and among the functional specialists. In summary, this hypothesis can only be supported with limitations.

The opposing findings on the optimum intra-group competitive position between functional generalist on the one side and standardized solutions providers/functional specialists on the other are in conflict with the generalizability of strategic balance theory, which states that a position on the competitive "cusp" should always result in superior performance. My findings suggest that moderating factors e.g., the structure of the "local" competitive environment, matter for the optimum intra-group competitive position. These insights extend the context of intra-group strategic positioning and have implications for strategic balance theory and its application to competitive positioning in general.

H_4: *Young firms that manage to position near to old, established firms achieve above-average performance in the consulting industry.*

My research shows that young and small firms position their services similar to large, established and reputable management consulting firms. I find evidence that in the consulting market firm age does not directly impact performance. In consequence, results in this context suggest that age and size do not play a decisive role in positioning differences in the consulting market. This outcome challenges existing theory and empirical findings of previous strategy research (e.g. McNamara, et al., 2003; Semadeni, 2006). The described specific market characteristics of the consulting market like low barriers to entry and exit, high dynamics and competitiveness support this outcome. Potential for spill-over effects from established to young competitors should be higher in immature markets with low entry barriers. Young firms that manage to position near to established firms profit from existing reputation for quality and reliability. They achieve this by e.g. openly advertising the fact that their consultants are using the same methodology and processes as established market players. This alignment of positioning efforts makes it challenging for potential buyers to differentiate the service offering from those of its established competitors. However, reputation in combination with firm size as a contributor to firm performance has not been examined within this study. The positive correlation between age, size and reputation has been discussed within existing research (Harste, 2008; Lange, et al., 2011).

My results from the moderator analyses show that firm age serves as a moderator. Furthermore, the analyses indicate that depending on the specific strategic group different positioning strategies are beneficial to young and old firms. Among the specialist strategic groups especially old, established firms ($age > 13$) benefit from positioning on the competitive cusp and herewith differentiate from other members of that strategic group. In line with strategic balance theory they seem to have less need to establish legitimacy, reduce ambiguity and achieve spill-over effects. They rather gain from additional differentiation and from establishing a more distinct market position to raise the attention of potential clients. Consequently, they gain from promoting their specialization to potential clients and expertise in certain service area.

Contrary to this, my findings indicate that especially young generalist firms ($age \leq 20$) that manage to position as close as possible to old established players show superior performance. Successful young generalists follow established service models, intend the same level of client interaction and offer the full spectrum of services as established generalist firms. Hereby, they show potential clients that they are capable of delivering the same services at the same quality level as the well-established generalist players in the market.

Consistently, young and old generalist firms achieve equal performance rates above-industry-average. In summary, my research shows that firm age serves as a moderator as to which positioning strategy within the different strategic groups holds for superior performance.

Therefore, my findings are partly in line with existing research (Semadeni, 2006; Singh, et al., 1986) arguing that legitimacy is important for young consulting firm, especially as it increases the probability of organizational survival of young firms. But contrary to Semadeni's findings that young firms position near to old firms and old firms try to position differently from young firms, I find that the positioning variance is generally less dependent on firm age than on the service model a firm follows. I expect that with increasing buyer professionalization the influence of age as a selection criteria is further diminishing. To summarize, I find support for the hypothesis that young firms that manage to position near to old, established firms achieve above-average performance.

In summary, it has become obvious that it is not always advantageous to position on the competitive cusp as suggested by strategic balance theory. Depending on the actual market position all three positioning strategies - near to competitors, far from competitors or on the competitive cusp - serve as valid and suitable options. My results indicate that there exist temporal and contextual factors that set the boundaries of the generalizability of the strategic balance theory.

5.2 Implications for consulting firms and clients

The consulting market is a highly dynamic and competitive market that is constantly evolving. In addition, the consulting market is marked by an internal and external unboundedness e.g. by limited institutional protection and low barriers to entry and exit. This combination offers large potentials for new market entrants and imposes threads to existing market players. Consulting firms profit from shaping their market position carefully as different market positions hold for deviating performance potentials. With my results, I respond to the claim that there is a need to establish better methods and tools in order to differentiate effectively in the consulting market (Ou & Chai, 2007). I find that consulting firms differentiate along the three identified key dimensions: the type of service model, intended relation with the client, and degree of functional and sectoral specialization. My results on relative positioning and its impact on performance have multiple implications for practitioners.

First, market entrants as well as established firms should analyze the competitive environment closely and decide which market position they favor to establish or maintain. Second, the key competitors in the respective market segment have to be identified and the right balance between positioning near to and far from them has to be pursued. Third, they have to shape their market positioning along the critical positioning dimensions. Strategic positioning within a strategic group is generally advisable to establish a basic level of legitimacy and reduce uncertainty. Depending on the targeted position in the identified three strategic groups, the balance between conformity and differentiation has to be implemented in the service model, the intended relation with the client and the service offering. In summary, firms have to decide which strategic group they target and analyze which inner-group positioning is preferable in order to shape their own firm positioning along the key dimensions accordingly.

For instance, challenger firms that aim at offering the full range of consulting services should conform their positioning to established functional generalists as close as possible. My empirical results show that generalist firms profit from positioning near to each other. Challenger firms should signal to potential clients that they are capable of providing the same services at the same quality levels as established, reputable competitors. Herewith, they increase the possibility to achieve spill-over effects from established providers. On the other hand, my results indicate that specialist providers should differentiate their market position from existing providers. This market segment still lacks in differentiation. Consistently, clients often make use of consulting providers that they have already had good experiences with. Therefore, in order to acquire new clients and to convince them to switch their preferred supplier of consulting services, companies have to offer similar services, but at the same time, differentiate to a certain extent from their competitors. They profit from highlighting their unique service propositions and those service characteristics that are different from competitors. A clear description of how their consulting services add value for clients should be provided to respond to increasing buyer professionalization. However, greater buyer professionalization offers opportunities to young challenger firms as the importance of age and size as selection criteria is expected to diminish. Firms concentrate further on the competencies of potential consulting providers.

Being perceived as an international service provider has a significantly positive impact on performance. The reason is that clients perceive internationally positioned providers as more reliable, experienced, capable and trustworthy. As a consequence, it is advisable for consulting providers to institute an international brand appearance and shape their market position accordingly. My research shows that international experience and company identity have a significant positive impact on firm performance.

An interview-based survey on the buying behavior of consulting clients (Galal & Richter, 2009) indicates that the perceived competence of a consulting firm, general reputation of the firm and existing relationships between consultants and clients are the most important factors that determine clients' buying decisions. All three factors were far more important than price levels, age and size. This is in line with previous research that proves that price pays a subordinate role in client decisions whether and which consulting firms to engage in experienced expertise (Clark, 1993, 1995; Dawes, et al., 1992; Harste, 2008). Responding to the intransparent consulting market, many clients trust established relationships and rely on subsequent repurchasing of consulting services. In addition, clients increasingly seek for competent consulting providers that offer the full range of consulting services from concept development to implementation.

It becomes obvious that the consulting industry has turned from a seller- into a buyer market as the times of high fees, limited competition and limited success measurement of the consulting provision are over. I propose three future challenges for consulting providers. First, I expect an enduring market consolidation. The market is going to develop towards a mature market and consolidation efforts among existing market players will increase. This development has often been encountered in professional service industries e.g. auditing industry; testing, inspection and certification (TIC) industry. Functional specialists will increasingly try to enter the strategic group of functional generalists to establish above-average performance rates. Functional generalists are likely to further concentrate and maintain intra-industry mobility barriers in order to preserve their unique market positions. Existing intra-industry mobility barriers will encumber this, but general barrier level is still comparably low. As a consequence, established generalist providers will encounter the danger of increasing loss of uniqueness in the market. Second, the consulting market will still be growing but at a declining growth rate. Clients are increasingly building internal consulting know-how and it is unlikely that market enlarging innovative consulting service will compensate for the increased buying professionalization and competition. In line with this, current economic market developments deem for reduced external clients' expansions e.g. in consulting services in order to increase profitability levels. Third, consulting firms will increasingly encounter recruiting problems. Consulting firms compete with their clients for the same talent pool. Consistently, it will be more costly to hire top talents and preserve the key asset for consulting firms.

Recommendations for clients comprise three aspects that improve client buying professionalization. First, potential clients need to analyze existing consulting providers closely on a regular basis. Second, in case a consulting provider should be engaged, it is advisable to have a full picture of what specific service and which competencies are needed. Client strategists should carefully define along the three outlined key positioning dimensions what specific consulting provider is needed and derive their specific selection criteria. Third, it is advisable to build up internal knowledge e.g. hire staff that is experienced in working together with consultants. Hereby, clients improve client expertise and efficiency in cooperating with consultants.

However, I am convinced that for all three strategic groups sufficient market potential is still available. Dependent on the specific clients' needs, different providers will be engaged to carry out a consulting service. Small, specialized consulting providers with specific know-how, large providers with high capabilities in standardized solutions as well as full-service providers with high expertise and tailor-made services will coexist in the market.

6 Conclusion

6.1 Overall summary

Within the introduction I referred to Porter's statement that in competitive markets firms need to develop competitive positioning strategies carefully vis-à-vis their competitors to achieve enduring competitive success. The intention of this research is to address Porter's fundamental principle and discuss its applicability for the management consulting services. As outlined, the market for management consulting services underwent far reaching changes over the last years that impose three major challenges to consulting providers. First, competition is constantly increasing on the market that is characterized by limited barriers to entry e.g. low capital intensity. Second, in line with increased competition demand is still growing at a significant pace. However, the demand curve has become more elastic. This indicates greater professionalization of buyers of consulting services and a shifting of the balance of power between consultant-client towards the client side. Third, with the expansion of both supply and demand side an even higher intransparency of the market and increasing uncertainty arose. In an attempt to master theses challenges, consulting firms need to position their service offering carefully in the market to compete with sustainable success.

In my research I have examined the market for management consulting firms and different types of strategic positioning closely. More specifically, I analyzed consulting firms active in the German market with respect to the existence of strategic groups and the influence of strategic positioning on performance. The following three research questions were addressed:

1. **Given the economic characteristics of consulting services, into which strategic groups is the German consulting market segmented?**

2. **What is the effect of strategic positioning on the performance of consulting firms in Germany?**

3. **What do we learn from this for strategic positioning theory in general?**

To address these research questions I followed a straightforward research structure. In general, I introduced the concepts, existing research and empirical findings on strategic balance theory and strategic group theory. After outlining the objectives of this research and the research approach I set the theoretical groundings of my study. The theoretical foundation of my work followed a seven step process.

First, I defined the notion of strategic positioning and derived three key positioning dimensions relevant for the consulting market: the type of service model, intended relationship with the client, and degree of functional and sectoral specialization. I introduced the three complementing levels of strategic positioning: the notion of 'intended positioning', 'communicated positioning' and 'perceived strategic positioning'. The three positioning elements constitute the strategic positioning of a firm. Second, I outlined three positioning strategies (near to competitors, far from competitors, on the competitive cusp) and discussed them in light of the characteristics of the consulting market. In addition, the concept of core, secondary and solitary firms was introduced.

Third, I discussed the concept of strategic groups as an intermediary level between industry- and firm-level. Herewith, strategic group theory efficiently fills an existing research gap by borrowing ideas and concepts from IO research as well as from strategic management research. In addition, I expanded the concept of mobility barriers and introduced intra-industry mobility barriers to strategic group theory. Forth, I discussed theoretical approaches and concepts within strategic group research. Besides referring to the concepts of rivalry and spatial competition, I elaborated on the concept of strategic identity.

Fifth, I analyzed empirical research on the existence of strategic groups. I found that the amount and quality of empirical research within strategic group literature on professional service firms is still limited. Many researchers concentrate their empirical studies on industries with high barriers to entry and exit and on locally delineated markets. Sixth, I examined existing empirical evidence on the strategic groups-performance relationship. It became obvious that the relationship between strategic group membership and performance remains ambiguous. Meta-analyses show that the variance between firm performance differences is higher within strategic groups than across. However, empirical research on within performance differences is still limited and research calls for more elaborate empirical analyses. Seventh, I derived four hypotheses from strategic balance theory and strategic group research that where empirically addressed in my study. In applying my theoretical propositions to the German consulting market I answer the claim for more dedicated empirical research on professional service firms (e.g. Ou & Chai, 2007; Semadeni, 2006; von Nordenflycht, 2010).

Within the empirical part of this thesis, I presented the empirical approach and my data sample. My well-balanced sample is composed of 233 management consulting firms active in the German market and is representative for the existing market structure. I defined variables and operationalized measures to test against my sample. I used different clustering methods and additional analyses to test for strategic group structures. Furthermore, I applied multidimensional logistic regression to test for differences between strategic groups. I used the resulting strategic group structure for regressions and additional test statistics on performance differences across and within strategic groups.

My results show the existence of strategic groups within the German consulting market. I found three significantly different strategic groups: standardized solution providers, functional specialists and functional generalists. In general, empirical results support the theoretically derived hypotheses. First, strong support is found on the existence of a small number of strategic groups in markets with low barriers to entry and exit e.g. the German consulting market. Second, significant support is found for the hypotheses that performance differences between strategic groups in the consulting industry exist. Third, partial support is established for the hypotheses that within a particular strategic group in the consulting industry secondary firms show superior performance as compared to core firms. I found that it strongly depends on the individual strategic group whether positioning on the competitive cusp or positioning near to core companies positively impacts firm performance. Forth, I found evidence that it is beneficial for young generalist firms to position close to established, functional generalist firms. However, my results indicate that age serves as a moderating element of beneficial firm positioning. It depends on the specific strategic group and the firm age whether it is beneficial to position as a core or a secondary firm.

Overall, my findings show that strategic group theory is a valid approach to analyze and structure market environments. I found evidence for three different strategic groups that follow significantly different positioning strategies. In addition, significant performance differences across and within strategic groups were detected. In combination, the application of strategic balance theory in this specific setting holds for interesting results. My results do not fully support the generalizability of strategic balance theory as positioning on the competitive cusp is not always superior to achieve above-average performance rates. There is evidence that industry specifics such as low barriers to entry and to exit, missing institutional protection in combination with firm specifics such as age, size and type of service model serve as contextual factors that set the boundaries of generalizability of strategic balance theory. In line with this contribution, my results provide evidence that adapting positioning strategies to strategic group structures is necessary to realize superior performance rates.

Overall, my study shows that it is worthwhile for consulting firms to carefully position in the market relative to competitors. However, my results indicate that it significantly depends on the service model and the strategic group structure which positioning strategy is favorable in terms of performance. Furthermore, my results imply that competitive positioning theory in general and strategic balance theory in particular should take moderating factors into account which reflect the structure of the "local" competitive environment.

6.2 Outlook and Future Research

My study is subject to several limitations that should be addressed in future research. Therefore, I address five aspects that might be rewarding for future research on strategic positioning and strategic groups in the management consulting market.

First, strategic researchers have paid little attention to the influence of intra-organizational factors of consulting service firms on strategic positioning and performance. Moreover, clear descriptions of what the consulting firm does and how it concretely adds value for clients should be provided, as a further tool to differentiate strategic firm positioning of firms. Building on this, I have not analyzed the cost structure or the resulting profitability of consulting firms to prove the sustainable success of different established service models.

Second, there is still limited insight on the persistence of strategic positioning and strategic group structures over time. A longitudinal research would help to understand the relative importance of the dynamics of strategic positioning along different stages of the market saturation cycle. This thesis does not aim at investigating the longitudinal effects and the particular changes in the strategic group structure over time. This addresses one significant limitation of the study as the dynamics of strategic positioning over time and their impact on firm performance were not included in this study. Building on this research, the necessity to follow positioning efforts over time and its impact on performance seems promising for future theory building. Especially, to analyze the dynamic interplay of low entry barriers with high intra-industry mobility barriers over time, offers potential for promising insights.

Third, the primary geographical focus of my study was Germany. I suspect that to conduct this study in a non-Western context yields different results. In consequence, I suggest future research to investigate the effects of culture and institutional setting on the development of strategic positioning and strategic group structures in a more systematic fashion.

Fourth, as the emphasis of this thesis was put on the objective to examine the communicated positioning of firm and not on perceived positioning by market participants, future research potential arises. In order to cross-validate my findings complementing research on the perspectives of clients as the buyers of consulting services and on the subjective view of consultants is necessary. In other words, within this research, examined strategic positioning has not been matched to the perceived firm positioning of potential buyers' of consulting services and consultants' view on competition. This could be addressed in future research to complement the picture on strategic positioning, intended positioning, communicated positioning and perceived positioning.

Fifth, additional empirical methods and complementing performance indicators of consulting firms could further increase the significance of the derived results. As information on the profitability of consulting firms is rare, this limitation should be addressed in future research.

LIST OF REFERENCES

Aaker, D., & Shansby, J. (1982). Positioning Your Product. *Business Horizons, 25*(3), 56-62.

Abrahamson, E., & Hegeman, R. (1994). *Strategic Conformity: An Institutional Theory Explanation*. Paper presented at the Academy of Management Conference.

Agresti, A. (2007). *An Introduction to Categorical Data Analysis*. Chichester: Wiley & Sons.

Albert, S., & Whetten, D. A. (1985). Organizational Identity. In L. L. Cummings & B. M. Staw (Eds.), *Research in Organizational Behavior* (Vol. 7, pp. 263-295). Greenwich: JAI Press.

Allison, P. D. (1999). *Logistic Regression using the SAS System - Theory and Application*. Cary, NC.

Armbrüster, T. (2004). Rationality and Its Symbols: Signaling Effects and Subjectification in Management Consulting. *Journal of Management Studies, 41*, 1247-1269.

Armbrüster, T. (2006). *The Economics and Sociology of Management Consulting*. Cambridge: University Press.

Arnott, D. C. (1992). *Bases of Financial Services Positioning in the Personal Pension, Life Assurance and Personal Equity Plan Sectors*. Unpublished Doctoral Thesis, Manchester Business School, University of Manchester, UK.

Asker, J. (1995). *Strategic Market Management*. New York: John Wiley & Sons, Inc.

Backhaus, K., Erichson, B., Plinke, W., & Weiber, R. (2003). *Multivariate Analysemethoden. Eine anwendungsorientierte Einführung (10th ed.)*. Berlin: Springer.

Bain, J. S. (1959). *Industrial Organization*. New York: John Wiley & Sons, Inc.

Barney, J. B. (1991). Firm Resources and Sustained Competitve Advantage. *Journal of Management, 17*(1), 99-120.

Barney, J. B. (2002). *Gaining and Sustaining Competitive Advantage*. Upper Saddle River, NJ: Prentice-Hall.

Barney, J. B., & Hoskisson, R. E. (1990). Strategic Groups: Untested Assertions and Research Proposals. *Managerial & Decision Economics, 11*(3), 187-198.

Baron, R. M., & Kenny, D. A. (1986). The Moderator-Mediator Variable Distinction in Social Psychological Research: Conceptual, Strategic and Statistical Considerations. *Journal of Personality and Social Psychology, 51*, 1173-1182.

Baum, J., & Haveman, H. (1997). Love Thy Neighbor: Differentiation and Agglomeration in the Manhatten Hotel Industry, 1898-1990. *Administrative Science Quarterly, 42*, 304-338.

Baum, J., & Mezias, S. (1992). Localized Competition and Organizational Failure in the Manhattan Hotel Industry, 1898-1990. *Administrative Science Quarterly, 37*, 580-604.

Baum, J., & Singh, J. V. (1994). Organizational Niche Overlap and the Dynamics of Organizational Mortality. *American Journal of Sociology, 100*, 346-380.

BDU (2006). *Facts & Figures zum Beratermarkt 2006/2007*, Berlin, Bonn.

Besanko, D., Dranove, D., & Shanley, M. (2000). *Economics of Strategy*. New York: John Wiley & Sons.

Blankson, C., & Kalafatis, S. P. (1999). Issues and Challenges in the Positioning of Service Brands: A Review. *Journal of Product and Brand Management, 8*(2), 106-118.

Blankson, C., & Kalafatis, S. P. (2004). The Development and Validation of a Scale Measuring Consumer/ Customer-Derived Generic Typology of Positioning Strategies. [Article]. *Journal of Marketing Management, 20*, 5-43.

Blankson, C., & Kalafatis, S. P. (2007). Positioning strategies of international and multicultural-oriented service brands. [Article]. *Journal of Services Marketing, 21*, 435-450.

Blankson, C., Kalafatis, S. P., Cheng, J. M.-S., & Hadjicharalambous, C. (2008). Impact of Positioning Strategies on Corporate Performance. [Article]. *Journal of Advertising Research, 48*, 106-122.

Böcklund, J., & Werr, A. (2005). Breaking the Personal Tie. In S. Furusten & A. Werr (Eds.), *Dealing with Confidence. The Construction of Need and Trust in Management Advisory Services*. Copenhagen: Business school press.

Bogner, W. C. (1991). *Patterns of Intra-Industry Competition: A Dynamic Analysis of Theoretical Foundations of Strategic Groups*. Urbana Champaign: University of Illinois.

Bogner, W. C., Thomas, H., & McGee, J. (1999). Competence and Competitive Advantage: Towards a Dynamic Model. *British Journal of Management, 10*, 275-290.

Boulding, K. (1966). *Economic Analysis* (Vol. 1). New York: Harpers.

Boxall, P., & Steeneveld, M. (1999). Human Resource Strategy and Competitive Advantage: A Longitudinal Study of Engineering Consultancies. *Journal of Management Studies, 36*(4), 443-463.

Brown, J. S., & Duguid, P. (1991). Organizational Learning and Communities-of-Practice: Toward a Unified View of Working, Learning, and Innovation. *Organization Science, 2*(1), 40-57.

Brown, S. P., Jones, E., & Leigh, T. W. (2005). The Attenuating Effect of Role Overload on Relationships Linking Self-Efficacy and Goal Level to Work Performance. *Journal of Applied Psychology, 90*(5), 972-979.

Brunsson, N., Rasche, A., & Seidl, D. (2012). The Dynamics of Standardization: Three Perspectives on Standards in Organization Studies. *Organization Studies, 33*(5), 613-632.

Caliński, T., & Harabasz (1974). A Dendrite Method for Cluster Analysis. *Communications in Statistics, 3*, 1-27.

Campbell, D. (2003). Intra- and Intersectoral Effects in
Environmental Disclosures: Evidence for Legitimacy
Theory? *Business Strategy and the Environment, 12*(6), 357-371.

Cappel, J. J., & Zhenyu, H. (2007). A Usability Analysis of Company Websites. *Journal of Computer Information Systems, 48*(1), 117-123.

Carmeli, A., & Tishler, A. (2004). Resources, Capabilities, and the Performance of Industrial Firms: A Multivariate Analysis. *Managerial & Decision Economics, 25*(6), 299-315.

Carroll, G. R. (1985). Concentration and Specialization: Dynamics of Niche Width in Populations of Organizations. *American Journal of Sociology, 90*, 1262-1283.

Caves, R. E., & Porter, M. E. (1977). From Entry Barriers to Mobility Barriers: Conjectural Decisions and Contrived Deterrence to New Competition. *Quarterly Journal of Economics, 91*(2), 241-261.

Chang, W.-L., Chang, K., & Hsin, J. (2006). Analysis of Financial Performance by Strategic Groups of Digital Learning Industry in Taiwan. [Article]. *Journal of American Academy of Business, 10*(1), 298-304.

Chapman, A. D. (2005). Principles and Methods of Data Cleaning - Primary Species and Species-Occurrence Data. Global Biodiversity Information Facility Copenhagen.

Chen, M. J. (1996). Competitor Analysis and Interfirm Rivalry: Toward a Theoretical Integration. *Academy of Management Review, 21*(1), 100-134.

Clark, T. (1993). The Market Provision of Management Services, Information Asymmetries and Service Quality - Some Market Solutions: an Empirical Example. *British Journal of Management, 4*, 235.

Clark, T. (1995). *Managing Consultants. Consultancy as the Management of Impressions.* Buckingham: Open University Press.

Collier, D., & Meyer, S. (1998). A Service Positioning Matrix. *International Journal of Operations and Production Management, 18*(12), 1223-1244.

Cool, K., & Dierickx, I. (1993). Rivalry, Strategic Groups and Firm Profitability. *Strategic Management Journal, 14*(1), 47-59.

Cool, K., & Schendel, D. (1987). Strategic Group Formation and Performance: The Case of the U.S. Pharmaceutical Industry, 1963-1982. *Management Science, 33*(9), 1102-1124.

Cool, K., & Schendel, D. (1988). Performance Differences among Strategic Group Members. *Strategic Management Journal, 9*(3), 207-223.

Cowell, D. (1989). *The Marketing of Services*. London: Heinemann.

Cyert, R. A., & March, J. G. (1963). *A Behavioral Theory of the Firm*. Englewood Cliffs, NJ: Prentice-Hall.

Dawes, P., Dowling, G., & Patterson, P. (1992). Criteria Used to Select Management Consultants. *Industrial Marketing Management, 21*, 187-193.

Deephouse, D. L. (1996). Does Isomorphism Legitimate? *Academy of Management Journal, 39*(4), 1024.

Deephouse, D. L. (1999). To be different, or to be the same? It's a Question (and Theory) of Strategic Balance. [Article]. *Strategic Management Journal, 20*, 147.

Demsetz, H. (1973). Industry Structure, Market Rivalry, and Public Policy. *Journal of Law and Economics, 16*(1), 1-9.

DeSarbo, W., & Grewal, R. (2008). Hybrid Strategic Groups. *Strategic Management Journal, 29*(3), 293-317.

DeSarbo, W., Grewal, R., & Scott, C. J. (2008). A Clusterwise Bilinear Multidimensional Scaling Methodology for Simultaneous Segmentation and Positioning Analyses. *Journal of Marketing Research, 45*, 280-292.

Dess, G. G., & Davis, P. S. (1984). Porter's (1980) Generic Strategies as Determinants of Strategic Group Membership and Organizational Performance. *Academy of Management Journal, 27*, 467-488.

Devlin, J., Ennew, C., & Mirza, M. (1995). Organisational Positioning in Retail Financial Services. *Journal of Marketing Management, 11*, 119-132.

DiMaggio, P., & Powell, W. (1983). The Iron Cage Revisited: Institutional Isomorphism and Collective Rationality in Organizational Fields. *American Sociological Review, 48*(2), 147-160.

Dranove, D., Peteraf, M., & Shanley, M. (1998). Do Strategic Groups Exist? An Economic Framework for Analysis. [Article]. *Strategic Management Journal, 19*, 1029-1044.

Easingwood, C. J., & Mahajan, V. (1989). Positioning of Financial Services for Competitive Advantage. *Journal of Product Innovation Management, 6*, 207-219.

Eaton, B. C., & Lipsey, R. G. (1975). The Principle of Minimum Differentiation Reconsidered: Some New Developments in the Theory of Spatial Competition. *Review of Economic Studies, 42*, 27-49.

Ebrahimchel, M., Mohe, M., & Sternzeld, R. (2006). Evaluation of Consulting Projects - the Consultants' View. In T. Deelmann & M. Mohe (Eds.), *Selection and Evaluation of Consultants. Management Consulting Research* (Vol. 1, pp. 159-177). München: Rainer Hampp Verlag.

Eisenhardt, K. M. (1989). Agency Theory: An Assessment and Review. *Academy of Management Review, 14*(1), 57-74.

Eisenhardt, K. M., & Bourgeois, L. J. (1988). Politics of Strategic Decision Making in High-velocity Environments: Toward a Midrange Theory. *Academy of Management Journal, 31*(4), 737-770.

Ennen, E. (2011). *The Impact of Complementarities on the Performance of Law Firms.* Unpublished Doctoral Thesis, European Business School, Oestrich-Winkel.

Ernst, B., & Kieser, A. (2002). The Expansion of Management Knowledge. Carriers, Flows, and Sources. In K. Sahlin-Andersson & L. Engwall (Eds.), *In Search of Explanations for the Consulting Explosion.* (pp. 47-73). Stanford, CA: Stanford University Press.

Esper, F. S., Mas, C. V., & Murillo, C. (2008). Competitive Analysis with Strategic Groups: Application to the Spanish Insurance Sector, 2000-2005. *Academia, Revista Latinoamericana de Administración, 40*, 32-53.

Everitt, B. S. (1993). *Cluster analysis.* London: Arnold.

Everitt, B. S., Landau, S., & Leese, M. (2001). *Cluster analysis (4th ed.).* London: Arnold.

Feka, V., Xouris, D., & Tsiotras, G. (1997). Mapping Strategic Groups: An international Example. *Journal of Business & Industrial Marketing, 12*(1), 66-75.

Ferguson, T. D., Deephouse, D. L., & Ferguson, W. L. (2000). Do Strategic Groups Differ in Reputation? [Article]. *Strategic Management Journal, 21*, 1195-1214.

Fiegenbaum, A., McGee, J., & Thomas, H. (1988). Exploring the Linkage between Strategic Groups and Competitive Strategy. *International Studies of Management & Organization, 18*(1), 6-25.

Fiegenbaum, A., & Primeaux, W. J., Jr. (1987). Strategic Groups and Mobility Barriers: The Level of Struggle in an Industry. *Journal of Behavioral Economics, 16*(3), 67-92.

Fiegenbaum, A., Sudharshan, D., & Thomas, H. (1987). The Concept of Stable Strategic Time Periods in Strategic Group Research. *Managerial & Decision Economics, 8*(2), 139-148.

Fiegenbaum, A., Sudharshan, D., & Thomas, H. (1990). Strategic Time Periods and Strategic Groups Research: Concepts and an Empirical Example. *Journal of Management Studies, 27*(2), 133-148.

Fiegenbaum, A., & Thomas, H. (1990). Strategic Groups and Performance: The U.S. Insurance Industry, 1970-84. *Strategic Management Journal, 11*(3), 197-215.

Fiegenbaum, A., & Thomas, H. (1993). Industry and Strategic Group Dynamics: Competitive Strategy in the Insurance Industry, 1970-84. *Journal of Management Studies, 30*(1), 69-105.

Fiegenbaum, A., & Thomas, H. (1995). Strategic Groups as Reference Groups: Theory, Modeling and Empirical Examination of Industry and Competitive Strategy. *Strategic Management Journal, 16*(6), 461-476.

Fiegenbaum, A., Thomas, H., & Ming-Je, T. (2001). Linking Hypercompetition and Strategic Group Theories: Strategic Maneuvering in the US Insurance Industry. *Managerial & Decision Economics, 22*(4/5), 265-279.

Fincham, R. (1999). The Consultant-Client Relationship: Critical Perspectives on the Management of Organizational Change. *Journal of Management Studies, 36*(3), 335-351.

Finkelstein, S., & Hambrick, D. C. (1990). Top Management-Team Tenure and Organizational Outcomes: The Moderating Role of Managerial Discretion. *Administrative Science Quarterly, 35*, 484-503.

Fiol, C. M. (1994). Consensus, Diversity, and Learning in Organizations. *Organization Science, 5*, 403-420.

Fisher, R. J. (1991). The Durable Differentiation Strategies for Services. *Journal of Services Marketing, 5*(1), 19-28.

Fiss, P. C. (2011). Building Better Causal Theories: A Fuzzy Set Approach to Typologies in Organization Research. *Academy of Management Journal, 54*.

Fleiss, J. L., Levin, B., & Paik, M. C. (2003). *Statistical Methods for Rates and Proportions*. New York: Wiley.

Frey, L. R., Botan, C. H., & Kreps, G. L. (2000). *Investigating Communication: An Introduction to Research Methods*. Boston: Allyn & Bacon.

Galal, K., & Richter, A. (2007). *Positioning of Consulting Firms: A Segmentation Study of the German Market for Management Consulting Services.* Paper presented at the 3rd Conference of the Management Consulting Division of the Academy of Management, Copenhagen.

Galal, K., Richter, A., & Wendlandt, V. (2012). IT Consulting and Outsourcing Firms: Evolution, Business Models and Future Prospects. In M. Kipping & T. Clark (Eds.), *The Oxford Handbook of Management Consulting*. Oxford: Oxford University Press.

George, W. R., & Berry, L. L. (1981). Guidelines for the Advertising of Services. *Business Horizons, 24*, 52-56.

Ghazanfar, A., McGee, J., & Thomas, H. (1987). The Impact of Technological Change on Industry Structure and Corporate Strategy. In A. Pettigrew (Ed.), *The Management of Strategic Change*. Oxford: Basil Blackwell.

Gimeno, J., & Woo, C. (1996). Hypercompetition in a Multimarket Environment: The Role of Strategic Similarity and Multimarket Contact in Competitive De-escalation. *Organization Science, 7*(3).

Gordon, A. D. (1993). *Classification: Methods for the exploratory analysis of multivariate data*. London: Chapman&Hall.

Gray, R., Kouhy, R., & Lavers, S. (1995). Corporate Social and Environmental Reporting: A Review of the Literature and a Longitudinal Study of UK Disclosure. *Accounting, Auditing & Accountability Journal, 8*(2), 47-77.

Greenwood, R., Deephouse, D. L., & Li, S. X. (2007). Ownership and Performance of Professional Service Firms. *Organization Studies, 28*, 219-238.

Greenwood, R., Li, S. X., Prakash, R., & Deephouse, D. L. (2005). Reputation, Diversification, and Organizational Explanations of Performance in Professional Service Firms. *Organization Science, 16*, 661-673.

Greiner, L. E., & Metzger, R. O. (1983). *Consulting to Management*. Englewood Cliffs: Prentice Hall.

Greve, H. R. (1998). Managerial Cognition and the Mimetic Adoption of Market Positions: What You See is What You Do *Strategic Management Journal, 19*(10), 967-988.

Grewal, R., & Dharwadkar, R. (2002). The Role of the Institutional Environment in Marketing Channels. [Article]. *Journal of Marketing, 66*, 82-97.

Guedri, Z. (1998). *Performance Variations among Strategic Group Members in the Pharmaceutical Industry: An Examination of Individual Sustainable Growth Capabilities, 1995 - 1997.* Montreal: Concordia University.

Haferkamp, S., & Drescher, S. (2006). Client Professionalization: Proposed Approach for the Knowledge-centered Management of Consulting Projects. In T. Deelmann & M. Mohe (Eds.), *Selection and Evaluation of Consultants. Management Consulting Research, Vol. 1* (pp. 121-137). München, Mering: Rainer Hampp Verlag.

Hair, J., Anderson, R., Tatham, R., & Black, W. (1998). *Multivariate Data Analysis*. Upper Saddle River, NJ: Prentice-Hall.

Hambrick, D. C., & D'Aveni, R. A. (1992). Top Management Team Deterioration as Part of the Downward Spiral of Large Bankruptcies. *Management Science, 38*, 1445-1466.

Hannan, M. T., & Carroll, G. R. (1992). *Dynamics of Organizational Populations: Density, Legitimation and Competition*. New York: Oxford University Press.

Hannan, M. T., & Freeman, J. H. (1977). The population Ecology of Organizations. *American Joumal of Sociology, 82*, 929-964.

Hannan, M. T., & Freeman, J. H. (1989). *Organization Ecology*. Cambridge, MA: Harvard University Press.

Harste, R. (2008). *The Interaction Between Managers and Consultants in Strategy Projects: Three Essays.* Unpublished Doctoral Thesis, European Business School, Oestrich-Winkel.

Hatten, K. J., & Hatten, M. L. (1987). Strategic Groups, Asymmetrical Mobility Barriers, and Contestability. [Article]. *Strategic Management Journal, 8*, 329-342.

Hatten, K. J., & Schendel, D. (1977). Heterogeneity within an Industry: Firm Conduct in the U.S. Brewing Industry, 1952-71. *Journal of Industrial Economics, 26*(2), 97-113.

Hatten, K. J., Schendel, D., & Cooper, A. C. (1978). A Strategic Model of the US. Brewing Industry: 1952-1971. *Academy of Management Journal, 21*, 592-610.

Haveman, H. A. (1993). Follow the Leader: Mimetic Isomorphism and Entry into New Markets. *Administrative Science Quarterly, 38*, 593-627.

Heldal, F., Sjøvold, E., & Heldal, A. (2004). Success on the Internet - Optimizing Relationships through the Corporate Site. *International Journal of Information Management, 24*(2), 115-129.

Henderson, A. D. (1996). *Uniqueness vs. Conformance: The Role of Technology Strategy in Coping with Highly Disruptive Episodes*. Paper presented at the Academy of Management Conference.

Higgins, J. J. (2004). *Introduction to modern nonparametric statistics*. Pacific Grove, CA: Thomson.

Hinterhuber, H., & Kirchebner, M. (1986). The Analysis of Strategic Groups of Firms. *European Management Journal, 4*(2), 95-103.

Holder-Webb, L., Cohen, J., Nath, L., & Wood, D. (2009). The Supply of Corporate Social Responsibility Disclosures among U.S. Firms. *Journal of Business Ethics, 84*, 497–527.

Holmbeck, G. N. (1997). Toward terminological, conceptual, and statistical clarity in the Study of Mediators and Moderators: Examples from the Child-Clinical and Pediatric Psychology Literatures. *Journal of Consulting and Clinical Psychology, 65*, 599-610.

Hooley, G., Broderick, A., & Moller, K. (1998). Competitive Positioning and the Resource-based View of the Firm. *Journal of Strategic Marketing, 6*, 97-115.

Hooley, G., & Greenley, G. (2005). The Resource Underpinnings of Competitive Positions. *Journal of Strategic Marketing, 13*, 93-116.

Hooley, G., Greenley, G., Fahy, J., & Cadogan, J. (2001). Market Focused Revenues, Competitive Positioning and Firm Performance. *Journal of Marketing Management, 17*, 503-552.

Hotelling, H. (1929). Stability in Competition. *Economic Journal, 39*, 41-57.

Houthoofd, N., & Heene, A. (2002). The Quest for Strategic Groups: Overview, and Suggestions for the Future Research. Unpublished Working Paper. Universiteit Gent.

Hunt, M. S. (1972). *Competition in the Major Home Appliance Industry, 1960-1970.* Unpublished Doctoral Thesis, Harvard University, Boston.

Itami, H. (1987). *Mobilizing Invisible Assets*. Cambridge, MA: Harvard University Press.

Jones, E., Chonko, L., Rangarajan, D., & Roberts, J. (2007). The Role of Overload on Job Attitudes, Turnover Intentions, and Salesperson Performance. *Journal of Business Research, 60*(7), 663-671.

Kalafatis, S. P., Tsogas, M., & Blankson, C. (2000). Positioning Strategies in Business Markets. *Journal of Business and Industrial Marketing, 15*(6), 416-437.

Kalra, A., & Goodstein, R. (1998). The Impact of Advertising Positioning Strategies on Consumer Price Sensitivity. *Journal of Marketing Research, 35*(2), 210-224.

Keats, B., & Hitt, M. A. (1988). Diversification and Business Economic Performance Revisited: Issues of Measurement and Causality. *Journal of Management, 16*, 61-72.

Keeble, D., & Schwalbach, J. (1995). *Management Consultancy in Europe*: ESRC Centre for Business Research.

Ketchen, D., Combs, J. G., Russel, C. J., Shook, C., Dean, M. A., Runge, J., et al. (1997). Organizational Configurations and Performance: A Meta-Analysis. *Academy of Management Journal, 40*, 223-240.

Ketchen, D., & Shook, C. (1996). The Application of Cluster Analysis in Strategic Management Research: An Analysis and Critique. *Strategic Management Journal, 17*, 441-458.

Ketchen, D., Snow, C., & Hoover, V. (2004). Research on Competitive Dynamics: Recent Accomplishments and Future Challenges. *Journal of Management, 30*, 779-804.

Ketchen, D., Snow, C., & Street, V. (2004). Improving Firm Performance by Matching Strategic Decision-Making Processes to Competitive Dynamics. *Academy of Management Executive, 18*, 29-43.

Ketchen, D., Thomas, J., & Snow, C. (1993). Organizational Configurations and Performance: A Comparison of Theoretical Approaches. *Academy of Management Journal, 36*, 1278-1313.

Kling, J., & Smith, K. A. (1995). Identifying Strategic Groups in the US Airline industry: An Application ofthe Porter Model. *Transportation Journal, 135*(2), 26-34.

Kotha, S., & Nair, A. (1995). Strategy and Environment as Determinants of Performance: Evidence from the Japanese Machine Tool Industry. [Article]. *Strategic Management Journal, 16*, 497-518.

Lacity, M. C., & Janson, M. A. (1994). Understanding Qualitative Data. *Journal of Management Information Systems, 11*(2), 137-155.

Lal, D., Pitt, D., & Strachan, P. (2004). Strategic Change in UK Telecommunications: Empirical Evidence. *European Management Journal, 22*, 99-109.

Lange, D., Lee, P. M., & Dai, Y. (2011). Organizational Reputation: A Review. *Journal of Management, 37*, 153-184.

Langerak, F. (2003). The Effect of Market Orientation on Positional Advantage and Organizational Performance. *Journal of Strategic Marketing, 11*(2), 93-115.

Leask, G. (2007). Marketing Strategy Making Sense of Industry Dynamics: Is there still Value in Strategic Group Research? *Journal of Medical Marketing, 7*(3), 189-202.

Leask, G., & Parker, D. (2007). Strategic Groups, Competitive Groups and Performance within the U.K. Pharmaceutical Industry: Improving our Understanding of the Competitive Process. *Strategic Management Journal, 28*(7), 723-745.

Lee, J. (2003). Innovation and Strategic Divergence: an Empirical Study of the U.S. Pharmaceutical Industry from 1920 to 1960. *Management Science, 49*, 143-159.

Levine, S., & White, P. E. (1961). Exchange as a Conceptual Framework for the Study of Interorganizational Relationships. *Administrative Science Quarterly, 5*, 583-601.

Levinthal, D., & March, J. (1993). The Myopia of Learning. *Strategic Management Journal, Winter Special Issue, 14*, 95-112.

Levitt, T. (1981). Marketing intangible products and product intangibles. *Harvard Business Review, May-June.*

Lewis, P., & Thomas, H. (1990). The Linkage between Strategy, Strategic Groups, and Performance in the U.K. Retail Grocery Industry. [Article]. *Strategic Management Journal, 11*, 385 397.

Long, J. S., & Freese, J. (2001). *Regression Models for Categorical Dependent Variables Using STATA*. Texas: STATA Press.

Maister, D. H. (1993). *Managing the Professional Service Firm*. New York et. al.: Free Press.

Makadok, R. (1998). Can First-Mover and Early-Mover Advantages Be Sustained in an Industry with Low Barriers to Entry/Imitation. [Article]. *Strategic Management Journal, 19*, 683-696.

March, J. G. (1981). Decisions in Organizations and Theories of Choice. In A. H. Van de Ven & W. F. Joyce (Eds.), *Perspectives on Organization Design and Behavior* (pp. 205-244). New York: Wiley.

Markman, A., & Gentner, D. (1993). Splitting the Differences: A Structural Alignment View of Similarity. *Journal of Memory and Language, 32*, 517-535.

Marlin, D., Ketchen, D., & Lamont, B. (2007). Equifinality and the Strategic Groups - Performance Relationship. *Journal of Managerial Issues, 19*(2), 208-232.

Martens, R. (1988). *Strategic Group Formation and Performance. The Case of the Pharmaceutical Industry in Five EC Countries 1978-1985.* Unpublished PhD Thesis, Antwerp University.

Mas-Ruiz, F. J., Nicolau, J. L., & Ruiz-Moreno, F. (2005). Asymmetric Rivalry between Strategic Groups: Response, Speed of Response and ex ante vs. ex post Competitive Interaction in the Spanish Deposit Market. [Article]. *Strategic Management Journal, 26*, 713-745.

Mascarenhas, B., & Aaker, D. (1989). Mobility Barriers and Strategic Groups. [Article]. *Strategic Management Journal, 10*, 475-485.

Massarik, F., & Pei-Carpenter, M. (2002). *Organization Development and Consulting. Perspectives and Foundations.* San Francisco, CA: Jossey-Bass, Pfeiffer.

McAlexander, J., Becker, B., & Kaldenberg, D. (1993). Positioning Health Care Services: Yellow Pages Advertising and Dental Practice Performance. *Journal of Health Care Marketing, 13*, 54-57.

McGee, J., & Segal-Horn, S. (1990). Strategic Space and Industry Dynamics: The Implications for International Marketing Strategy. *Journal of Marketing Management, 6*, 175-193.

McGee, J., & Thomas, H. (1986). Strategic Groups: Theory, Research and Taxonomy. *Strategic Management Journal, 7*, 141-160.

McGee, J., Thomas, H., & Pruett, M. (1995). Strategic Groups and the Analysis of Market Structure and Industry Dynamics. *British Journal of Management, 6*, 257.

McKelvey, B. (1975). Guidelines for empirical classification of organizations. *Administrative Science Quarterly, 20*, 509-525.

McKenna, R. (1986). The Regis Touch: New Marketing Strategies for Uncertain Times. Addison-Wesley Publishing Company.

McLachlin, R. D. (2000). Service Quality in Consulting: What is Engagement Success? *Managing Service Quality, 10*, 239-247.

McNamara, G. M., Deephouse, D. L., & Luce, R. A. (2003). Competitive Positioning within and across a Strategic Group Structure: The Performance of Core, Secondary and Solitary Firms. *Strategic Management Journal, 24*(2), 161-181.

McNamara, G. M., Luce, R. A., & Tompson, G. H. (2002). Examining the Effect of Complexity in Strategic Group Knowledge Structures on Firm Performance. *Strategic Management Journal, 23*(2), 153.

Mehra, A. (1996). Resource and Market based Determinants in the U.S. Banking Industry. *Strategic Management Journal, 17*, 307-322.

Mehra, A., & Floyd, S. W. (1998). Product Market Heterogeneity, Resource Imitability and Strategic Group Formation. *Journal of Management, 24*(4), 511-531.

Meyer, A. D., Tsui, A. S., & Hinings, C. R. (1993). Configurational Approaches to Organizational Analysis. *Academy of Management Journal*(36), 1175-1195.

Michael, S. (2003). Two Faces of Strategic Group Theory. *Multi-Level Issues in Organizational Behavior and Strategy - Research in Multi-Level Issues, 2*, 199-209.

Middleton, V. T. (1983). Product Marketing - Goods and Services Compared. *The Quarterly Review of Marketing, Summer*, 1-10.

Miles, S. J., & Mangold, W. G. (2005). Positioning Southwest Airlines through Employee Branding. *Business Horizons, 48*(6), 535-545.

Mills, P., & Moberg, D. (1982). Perspectives on the Technology of Service Operations. *Academy of Management Review, 7*, 467-478.

Mintzberg, H. (1975). The Manager's Job: Folklore and Fact. *Harvard Business Review, 53*(4), 49-61.

Mintzberg, H. (1978). Patterns in Strategy Formation. *Management Science, 24*(9), 934-948.

Mintzberg, H. (1987). The Strategy Concept I: Five Ps for Strategy. *California Management Review, 30*(1), 11-24.

Mitchell, V.-W. (1994). Problems and Risks in the Purchasing of Consultancy Services. *The Service Industries Journal, 14*(3), 315–339.

Morris, M., Schindehutte, M., & Allen, J. (2005). The Entrepreneur's Business Model: Toward a Unified Perspective. *Journal of Business Research, 58*, 726-735.

Nachum, L. (1999). Measurement of Productivity of Professional Services. *International Journal of Operations & Production Management, 19*(9), 922-949.

Nair, A., & Kotha, S. (2001). Does Group Membership Matter? Evidence from the Japanese Steel Industry. *Strategic Management Journal, 22*, 221–235.

Nath, D., & Gruca, T. S. (1997). Convergence across alternative Methods for forming Strategic Groups. [Article]. *Strategic Management Journal, 18*, 745-760.

Neuendorf, K. A. (2002). *The Content Analysis Guidebook*: Sage Publications, Inc.

Neuman, W. L. (2005). *Social Research Methods: Quantitative and Qualitative Approaches* (6th Edition ed.): Allyn & Bacon, Boston.

Newman, H. H. (1978). Strategic Groups and the Structure-Performance Relationship. *Review of Economics & Statistics, 60*(3), 417.

Niewiem, S. (2005). *The Contractual Relationship Between Clients and Management Consultants.* Deutscher Universitäts-Verlag/GWV Fachverlage GmbH, Wiesbaden.

Nissen, V. (2007). Consulting Research - Eine Einführung. In V. Nissen (Ed.), *Consulting Research - Unternehmensberatung aus wissenschaftlicher Perspektive* (pp. 3-38). Wiesbaden: Deutscher Universitätsverlag.

Normann, R. (1984). *Service Managetnent: Strategy and Leadership in Service Businesses.* Chichester, U.K.: Wiley.

O'Brien, R. M. (2007). A Caution Regarding Rules of Thumb for Variance Inflation Factors. *Quality & Quantity, 41*, 673-690.

O'Shea, J., & Madigan, C. (1997). *Dangerous Company: The Consulting Powerhouses and the Businesses They Save and Ruin.* London: Nicholas Brealey.

Olusoga, S. A., Mokwa, M. P., & Noble, C. H. (1995). Strategic Groups, Mobility Barriers, and Competitive Advantage: An Empirical Investigation. [Article]. *Journal of Business Research, 33*, 153-164.

Osborne, D. J. (1996). *Strategic Group Antecedents: Thematic Groups in the Pharmaceutical Industry 1963-1982*. Carbondale: Department of Management, Graduate School, Southern Illinois University.

Oster, S. (1982). Intraindustry Structure and the Ease of Strategic Change. *Review of Economics and Statistics, 64*, 376-383.

Ou, W.-M., & Chai, K.-W. (2007). Use of Leadership and Differentiation Strategies by Professional Service Firms: A Case Study. *International Journal of Management, 24*(3), 477-488.

Page, C. (1998). How Clients Pick Management Consultants in Australia and New Zealand. *Journal of Management Consulting, 10*, 56-58.

Pandian, J. R., Thomas, H., Furrer, O., & Bogner, W. C. (2006). Performance Differences across Strategic Groups: an Examination of Financial Market-Based Performance Measures. *Strategic Change, 15*(7), 373-383.

Pegels, C. C., & Sekar, C. (1989). Determining Strategic Groups Using Multidimensional Scaling. [Article]. *Interfaces, 19*, 47-57.

Pegels, C. C., & Song, Y. (1997). Identification of Strategic Groups Based on Market Competition and Cooperation: A Network-Analytic Approach. *Academy of Management Proceedings*, 40-44.

Peteraf, M. (1993). The Cornerstone of Competitive Advantage: A Resource-based View. *Strategic Management Journal, 14*(3), 179-191.

Peteraf, M., & Shanley, M. (1997). Getting to Know You: A Theory of Strategic Group Identity. [Article]. *Strategic Management Journal, 18*, 165-186.

Platteau, J. P. (1994a). Behind the Market Stage Where Real Societies Exist. *Journal of Development Studies*, 753-817.

Platteau, J. P. (1994b). The Role of Public and Private Order Institutions. *Journal of Development Studies, 30*, 533-578.

Porac, J. F., Thomas, H., & Baden-Fuller, C. W. (1989). Competitive Groups as Cognitive Communities: The Case of Scottish Knitwear Manufacturers. *Journal of Management Studies, 26*, 397-416.

Porac, J. F., Thomas, H., Wilson, F., Paton, D., & Kanfer, A. (1995). Rivalry and the Industry Model of Scottish Knitwear Producers. *Administrative Science Quarterly, 40*, 203-227.

Porter, M. E. (1979). The Structure within Industries and Companies Performance. *Review of Economics & Statistics, 61*(2), 214-227.

Porter, M. E. (1980). *Competitive Strategy*. New York: Free Press.

Porter, M. E. (1991). Towards a Dynamic Theory of Strategy. *Strategic Management Journal, Winter Special Issue, 12*, 95-117.

Porter, M. E. (1996). What is Strategy? *Harvard Business Review*, 61-78.

Porter, M. E. (2008). *On Competition, Updated and Expanded Edition.* Boston: Harvard Business School Press Books.

Prahalad, C. K., & Hamel, G. (1990). The Core Competence of the Corporation. *Harvard Business Review, 68*(3), 79-91.

Primeaux, W. J. (1985). A Method for Determining Strategic Groups and Life Cycle Stages of an Industry. In H. Thomas & D. Gardner (Eds.), *Strategic Marketing and Management*. New York: John Wiley.

Rao, H. (1994). The Social Construction of Reputation: Certification Contests, Legitimation, and the Survival of Organizations in the American Automobile Industry: 1895-1912. *Strategic Management Journal, Winter Special Issue, 15*, 29-45.

Reger, R. K., & Huff, A. S. (1993). Strategic Groups: A Cognitive Perspective. *Strategic Management Journal, 14*, 103-124.

Richter, A., & Niewiem, S. (2004). The Changing Balance of Power in the Consulting Market. *Business Strategy Review, 15*, 8-13.

Richter, A., & Schmidt, S. (2006). Antecedents of the Performance of Management Consultants. *Schmalenbach Business Review, 58*, 365-391.

Richter, A., & Schroeder, K. (2008). The Determinants and Performance Effects of the Allocation of Ownership Rights in Consulting Firms. *Journal of Organizational Behavior, 29*, 1049-1074.

Ries, A., & Trout, J. (1986). *Positioning, the Battle for your Mind.* New York: McGraw-Hill.

Roberts, P. W., & Greenwood, R. (1997). Integrating Transaction Cost and Institutional Theories: Toward a Constrained-efficiency Framework for Understanding Organizational Design Adoption. *Academy of Management Review, 22*, 346-373.

Rockwood, G. F. (1993). Edgar Schein's Process versus Content Consultation Models. *Journal of Counseling & Development, 71*(6), 636-638.

Rumelt, R. P., Schendel, D., & Teece, D. J. (1991). Strategic Management and Economics. *Strategic Management Journal, 12*, 5-29.

Ryans, A. B., & Wittink, D. R. (1985). Security Returns as a Basis for Estimating the Competitive Structure in an Industry. In H. Thomas & D. M. Cardner (Eds.), *Strategic Marketing and Management* (pp. 329-346). New York: Wiley.

Scarbrough, H. (1996). Commodifying Professional Expertise: IT in Financial Services. In H. Scarbrough (Ed.), *The Management of Expertise* (pp. 217-237). Houndsmill, Basingstoke: Macmillan.

Schein, E. H. (1978). The Role of the Consultant: Content Expert or Process Facilitator? *Personnel & Guidance Journal, 56*(6), 339.

Schein, E. H. (1988). *Process Consultation. Its Role in Organization Development.* Massachusetts: Addison-Wesley.

Schein, E. H. (1998). *Process Consultation Revisited: Building the Helping Relationship.* Massachusetts: Addison-Wesley.

Scherer, F. M., & Ross, D. (1990). *Industrial Market Structure and Economic Performance.* Boston: Houghton Mifflin.

Schnell, R., Hill, P., & Esser, E. (1999). *Methoden der empirischen Sozialforschung* (6 ed.). München: Oldenburg.

Scott, W. (1995). *Institutions and Organizations*. Thousand Oaks, CA: Sage.

Scott, W. (2002). *Organizations: Rational, Natural, and Open Systems*. Upper Saddle River, NJ: Prentice-Hall.

Semadeni, M. (2001). *Competing in Concept Space: The Competitive Use of Service Marks by Management Consulting Firms.* Paper presented at the Academy of Management Proceedings.

Semadeni, M. (2006). Minding Your Distance: How Management Consulting Firms Use Service Marks to Position Competitively. *Strategic Management Journal, 27*, 169-187.

Shamsie, J. (2003). The Context of Dominance: An Industry-Driven Framework for Exploiting Reputation. *Strategic Management Journal, 24*, 199–215.

Shapiro, C. (1989). Theories of Oligopoly Behavior. In R. Schmalensee & R. D. Willig (Eds.), *The Handbook of Industrial Organization* (pp. 329-410). New York: Elsevier Science Publishers B.V.

Sharma, A. (1997). Professional as Agent: Knowledge Asymmetry in Agency Exchange. *Academy of Management Review, 22*(3), 758–799.

Sherer, P. D. Mapping the Competitive Space of Large US Law Firms: A Strategic Group Perspective. (pp. 162-185).

Short, J. C., Ketchen, D., Palmer, T. B., & Hult, G. T. M. (2007). Firm, Strategic Group and Industry Influences on Performance. *Strategic Management Journal, 28*(2), 147-167.

Short, J. C., Palmer, T. B., & Ketchen, D. (2002). Resource-Based and Strategic Group Influences on Hospital Performance. *Health Care Management Review, 27*(4), 7.

Silvestro, R. (1999). Positioning Services along the Volume-variety Diagonal: the Contingencies of Service Design, Control and Improvement. *International Journal of Operations and Production Management, 9*(4), 399-420.

Simon, H. A. (1983). *Reason in Human Affairs*. Stanford, CA: Stanford University Press.

Singh, J. V., Tucker, D. J., & House, R. J. (1986). Organizational Legitimacy and the Liability of Newness. *Administrative Science Quarterly, 31*(2), 171-193.

Skaggs, B. C., & Youndt, M. (2004). Strategic Positing, Human Capital, and Performance in Service Organizations: A Customer Interaction Approach. *Strategic Management Journal, 25*(1), 85-99.

Smith, K. G., Grimm, C. M., Wally, S., & Young, G. (1997). Strategic Groups and Rivalrous Firm Behavior: Towards a Reconciliation. [Article]. *Strategic Management Journal, 18*, 149-157.

Sommerlatte, T. (2004). Life Cycle Phenomena in the Consulting Sector - Driving Forces of Fundamental Value Changes. . In J.-P. Thommen & A. Richter (Eds.), *Management Consulting Today. Strategies for a Challenging Environment.* (pp. 133-140). Wiesbaden: Gabler.

Spender, J. C. (1989). *Industry Recipes: An Inquiry into the Nature and Sources of Managerial Judgment.* Oxford, U.K.: Basil Blackwell.

Streicher, H., & Lünendonk, T. (2007). *Die aktuelle Lünendonk-Liste 2006*. Bad Wörishofen.

Stuart, T. E. (1998). Network Positions and Propensities to Collaborate: An Investigation of Strategic Alliance Formation in a High-Technology Industry. *Administrative Science Quarterly, 43*(3), 668-698.

Stuart, T. E., & Podolny, J. M. (1996). Local Search and the Evolution of Technological Capabilities. *Strategic Management Journal, Summer Special Issue 17*, 21-38.

Suchman, M. C. (1995). Managing Legitimacy: Strategic and Institutional Approaches. *Academy of Management Review, 20*(3), 571-610.

Sudharshan, D., Thomas, H., & Fiegenbaum, A. (1991). Assessing Mobility Barriers in Dynamic Strategic Groups Analysis. *Journal of Management Studies, 28*(5), 429-438.

Suzuki, Y. (2000). The Effect of Airline Positioning on Profit. *Transportation Journal, 39*(3), 44-54.

Tang, M.-J., & Thomas, H. (1992). The Concept of Strategic Groups: Theoretical Construct or Analytical Convenience. *Managerial & Decision Economics, 13*(4), 323-329.

Teece, D. J. (2003). Expert Talent and the Design of (Professional Services) Firms. *Industrial and Corporate Change, 12*(4), 895-916.

Thomas, H., & Pollock, T. (1999). From I-O Economics' S-C-P Paradigm Through Strategic Groups to Competence-Based Competition: Reflections on the Puzzle of Competitive Strategy. *British Journal of Management, 10*, 127-140.

Thomas, H., & Venkatraman, N. (1988). Research on Strategic Groups: Progress and Prognosis. *Journal of Management Studies, 25*, 537-555.

Thomas, L., & Weigelt, K. (2000). Product Location Choice and Firm Capabilities: Evidence from the U.S. Automobile Industry. *Strategic Management Journal, 21*(9), 897-909.

Toppin, G., & Czerniawska, F. (2005). *Business Consulting: A Guide to How it Works and How to Make it Work*. London: Profile Books.

Trout, J. (1996). *The New Positioning, The Latest on the World's #1 Business Strategy*. New York: McGraw-Hill.

Tywoniak, S., Galvin, P., & Davies, J. (2007). New Institutional Economics' Contribution to Strategic Groups Analysis. *Managerial & Decision Economics, 28*(3), 213-228.

Uhlenbruck, K., Hitt, M. A., & Semadeni, M. (2006). Market Value Effects of Acquisitions Involving Internet Firms: A Resource-Based Analysis. *Strategic Management Journal, 27*(10), 899-913.

Van de Ven, A. H., & Poole, M. S. (1990). Methods for Studying Innovation Development in the Minnesota Innovation Research Program. *Organization Science, 1*, 313-335.

von Nordenflycht, A. (2010). What is a Professional Service Firm? Toward a Theory and Taxonomy of Knowledge-Intensive Firms. *Academy of Management Review, 35*(1), 155-174.

Voyer, J. J. (1993). *Pharmaceutical Industry Strategic Groups Based on Cognitive Maps.* Paper presented at the Academy of Management Conference.

Wernerfelt, B. (1984). A Resource-Based View of the Firm. *Strategic Management Journal, 5*, 171-180.

Werr, A., & Pemer, F. (2007). Purchasing Management Consulting Services-From Management Autonomy to Purchasing Involvement. *Journal of Purchasing & Supply Management, 13*, 98-112.

Weyrather, C. (2004). Marketing in der Beratung. Positionierung. Wie sich Top-Consultants positionieren und profilieren. In V. Lindemann (Ed.), *Consulting in Deutschland - Eine Branche unter Druck.* (pp. 17-32). Munich: Finanz Buch Verlag.

Whetten, D. A. (1989). What Constitutes a Theoretical Contribution? *Academy of Management Review, 14*, 490-495.

Williamson, O. (1998). Transaction Cost Economics: How it Works; Where it is Headed. *De Economist, 146*(1), 23-58.

Williamson, O. (2000). The New Institutional Economics: Taking stock, Looking ahead. *Journal of Economic Literature, 38*, 595-613.

Wind, Y. (1982). *Product Policy, Concepts, Methods, and Strategy*: Addison-Wesley Publishing.

Wright, M. (1997). When Strength Means Death. *Brand Strategy, 107*, 3-5.

Zook, C. (2007). Finding Your Next Core Business. *Harvard Business Review, 4*, 67-75.

APPENDIX

Appendix A: Rating Rules

Dimension	Variable name	Rating Rule	Variable=0	Variable=1	Comments/Examples
Intended relationship with the client	Cooperation*	Wie stark betont das Beratungsunternehmen eine partnerschaftliche Zusammenarbeit und eine Involvierung des Klienten in den Beratungsprozess? Suche nach Begriffen wie "wir arbeiten gemeinsam/ kooperieren/ unterstützen/ gemischte Teams/ Partnerschaftliche Zusammenarbeit" Wichtig, Augenmerk dabei auf: gemeinsame Projektarbeit und Lösungsfindung durch Berater und Klient!	nein	**1=schwach** (bspw. wir kooperieren, "Unterstützung der Berater durch Klienten", "gemischte Teams", "Zusammenarbeit mit dem Klienten"), **2=stark** (bspw. "frühzeitige" "permanente", "vertrauensvolle" Involvierung" "Partnerschaftlich") Dimensionen (**Häufigkeit:** nie, manchmal/gelegentlich, immer/häufig; **Zeit:** garnicht, im Laufe des Projekts/in Abständen, permanent/frühzeitig; **sachliche Dimension**: Keine Zusammenarbeit/keineTeams, Unterstützung/Kooperation/Zusammenarbeit, intensive partnerschaftliche Zusammenarbeit)	"Every step of every project is closely coordinated with the client's management." "Kunden von der innovativen Produktidee bis zum Erfolg im Markt zu unterstützen" "in enger Zusammenarbeit mit dem Klienten" "truly collaborative approach" "Durch die individuelle Betreuung ... unserer Klienten..."
	Expert role	Sieht sich das Beratungsunternehmen als externen Experten, den das Klientenunternehmen um Rat fragt und der aus einer Außenbetrachtung des Unternehmens heraus Lösungsanweisungen (bspw. Gutachten, Studie, etc.) erteilt?	nein	1= (Begriffe wie "Experte, Gutachten, Neutralität, Außenperspektive, Unabhängige Meinung, neutral, Studie, eher kurzfristige Beziehung/Kontakt mit Kunden, etc.)	"Manager brauchen Beratung von externen Experten, die objektiv und unvoreingenommen Vorschläge zur Verbesserung der Unternehmensprozesse liefern." "Wem fühlen wir uns verbunden? - Unternehmern, die [...] wissen, was kaufmännisch nötig wäre" "use our knowledge to win"
	Docpatient role	Sieht sich das Beratungsunternehmen in einer "Doktor-Patient-Rolle"? Diese kennzeichnet sich durch einen Berater der dem Klienten Handlungsempfehlungen verschreibt und das Klientenunternehmen durch eingehende Analysen untersucht. Der Klient beteiligt sich dabei auch an den Analysen, wird dabei aber vom Berater gelenkt.	nein	1= (Begriffe wie "Handlungsempfehlungen" "Analysen erstellen", Maßnahmenplan erstellen, mittelfristige Beziehung, etc.)	"wir analysieren ... und zeigen Wege und Maßnahmen..."
	Process moderator role	Sieht sich das Beratungsunternehmen in einer Prozess-Moderatorfunktion, das die Interaktionen der Klientenmitarbeiter begleitet und interne Entscheidungsprozesse unterstützt? (Begriffe wie "Moderator, Begleiten Sie, ")	nein	1= (Begriffe wie "Moderator, Begleiten Sie bei der Entscheidungsfindung, "Begleiten", Interaktion des Klienten begleiten, unterstützen, eher langfristige Beziehung, etc.)	"Wir helfen dem Topmanagement herauszufinden..." "Hilfe zur Selbsthilfe"

Type of service model	Detail description	Wird der Beratungsprozess des Anbieters umfassend beschrieben (mit Fokus auf den Ablauf eines Beratungsprojektes)?	nein	**1=** (Auflisten von Phasen, Ablauf eines Beratungsprojekt, Milestones, bestimmte Aufgaben/Tätigkeiten innerhalb des Projektes)	Case Studies
	Implement*	Wie stark betont das Beratungsunternehmen die Beteiligung bei/Durchführung der Implementierung bzw. der Umsetzung der konzipierten Lösungsvorschläge/ Ergebnisse des Beratungsprozesses?	nein	**1=schwach** ("Erwähnung der Implementierung""Hilfestellung bei der Implementierung" "Unterstützung der Umsetzung"), 2= **stark** (bspw. Beteiligung, Kontrolle, Projektmanagement der Implementierung, "Umfassende Begleitung/Durchführung der Implementierung") Dimensionen (**Häufigkeit**: nie, manchmal/gelegentlich, häufig/oft/immer/sehr häufig; ; **sachliche Dimension**: Keine Implementierung/Umsetzung/nur Konzeption, Unterstützung/Hilfestellung,Kontrolle/Beteiligung an/ Management der Implementierung/ intensive umfassende Durchführung der Umsetzung)	
	Standard methods*	Wie stark lassen sich Anzeichen für einen standardisierten Beratungsansatz festmachen? Beschreibt das Unternehmen die Verwendung einer stets ähnlichen Vorgehensweise, den Einsatz bestimmter Methoden und Tools?	nein	**1=schwach** (feste Vorgehensweise beschrieben, Phasenmodell, Nennen konkreter Methoden, Tools), **2=stark** (bspw. Stets Einsatz eines festes Vorgehensmodell mit Methoden ist beschrieben)	
	Standard solutions*	Wie stark lassen sich Anzeichen für den Einsatz von standardisierten, fertigen Lösungen/ etc. festmachen? Vorstrukturierte Beratungslösungen die eher auf das Kundenunternehmen angepasst werden als vollkommen neu konzipiert werden müssen?	nein	**1=schwach** (Einzelne Elemente von Beratungslösungen kommen zum Einsatz, Best practices/ konkrete erste Hinweise auf Standardlösungen), **2= stark** (bspw. Stark standardisierte Fertiglösungen, die nur geringfügig individuell auf den Kunden angepasst werden müssen)	

Products	Kooperationsverträge mit Softwareherstellern, Bücher, Studien, Grundstücke/Immobilien, Drucksachen) angeboten/verkauft, die unter Umständen nur auf das jeweilige Kundenunternehmen angepasst werden müssen? (kein Benchmark, keine Seminare, Workshops)	nein	ja
Tailormade*	Wie stark betont das Beratungunternehmen individuell auf den Kunden zugeschnittenen, neu konzipierte, an die Kundenbedürfnisse angepasste Beratungslösungen?	nein	**1=schwach** (Individuelle Beratungsleistungen werden erwähnt), **2= stark** (Individuelle Beratung wird hervorgehoben, " Individuell auf Sie zugeschnitten" Komplette, kreative Neu-Entwicklung wird ausdrücklich betont " Individuelle, komplette Neukonzipierung")
Benchmarks	Wirbt das Unternehmen mit der Erstellung von Benchmarks/Vergleichen mit anderen Marktteilnehmern die im Beratungsprozess zum Einsatz kommen?	nein	ja
Advertise clients	Wirbt das Unternehmen mit bereits beratenen Klientenunternehmen (namentliche Nennung)?	nein	ja
Partner	Wirbt das Unternehmen mit Partnerunternehmen? Firmen die in den Beratungsprozess mit eingebunden werden können (bspw. A-connect, SAP)	nein	ja

Functional specialization	Generalist	Positioniert und versteht sich das Unternehmen selbst als Generalist in funktionaler Hinsicht? Finden sich Begriffe wie Generalist, umfassender Beratungsansatz, etc. also keine reine Fokussierung auf einzelne funktionale Beratungsfelder?	nein	**1=** (Begriffe wie " Generalist, umfassender Beratungsansatz, Angebot vieler Funktionen, "Fullservice aus einer Hand" etc.)	5 oder mehr funktionale Bereiche
	Sectoral specialist	Positioniert sich das Unternehmen selbst als branchenspezifischer Spezialist, Fokussierung auf wenige, bestimmte Branchen (Handel, verarbeitendes Gewerbe, Energie, TIMES, etc.)?	nein	ja	
	Functional expert	Wirbt das Unternehmen mit funktionsspezifischem Expertenwissen, Expertise, spezifischem Knowhow? Experten-Berater, Spezialisten die langjährige Erfahrung in einer bestimmten Funktionsberatung haben? (bspw. Wir sind Experten in Marketingthemen)	nein	ja	
	Sectoral expert	Wirbt das Unternehmen mit branchemspezifischem Expertenwissen, Expertise, spezifischem Knowhow? Experten-Berater die langjährige Erfahrung in bestimmten Branchen aufweisen? (bspw. "branchenspezifisches Wissen" "Wir verfügen über jahrelanger Erfahrung in der Energiebranche")	nein	ja	"professionals each have deep, specialized knowledge of and experience in their marketplace"
	Strategy	Werden Strategieberatungsleistungen angeboten?	nein	ja	
	Organisation	Werden Organisationsberatungsleistungen angeboten?	nein	ja	Schließt auch Outsourcing mit ein, da tiefgreifende organisationale Veränderungen (wenn es auch Kernbereich der Consultingfirma ist)
	Process	Werden Operations-, Prozessberatungsleistungen angeboten?	nein	ja	"Prozessoptimierung in Finanzdiensleistungen" ist hier Prozessberatung Hier auch Facility Management und Project Management
	IT	Werden IT-Beratungsleistungen angeboten?	nein	ja	
	Human resources	Werden HR-Beratungsleistungen angeboten?	nein	ja	
	Marketing	Werden Marketing-Beratungsleistungen angeboten?	nein	ja	
	Logistics	Werden Logistik-, Supply-Chain-Beratungsleistungen angeboten?	nein	ja	
	Finance	Werden Finanz- und Controlling-Beratungsleistungen angeboten?	nein	ja	

Additional firm characteristics	Revenues	Erzielter Umsatz in 2006 in Deutschland (aus Hoppenstedt Datenbank)	0	in KEURO	
	Number of employees	Anzahl der in Deutschland beschäftigten Mitarbeiter (aus Hoppenstedt Datenbank)			
	Number of offices in Germany	Anzahl der Offices in Deutschland (aus Hoppenstedt Datenbank)	0=keine	Anzahl	
	Age	Gründungsjahr der Firma (aus Hoppenstedt Datenbank)	18xx	200x	
Branches	health	Berät das Unternehmen Kunden der Branche: Gesundheits-/ Sozialwesen?	nein	ja	
	trade	Berät das Unternehmen Kunden der Branche: Groß-/ Einzelhandel?	nein	ja	
	tourism	Berät das Unternehmen Kunden der Branche: Verkehr/ Gastgewerbe?	nein	ja	
	energy	Berät das Unternehmen Kunden der Branche: Energie-/ Wasserversorgung?	nein	ja	
	times	Berät das Unternehmen Kunden der Branche: TIMES?	nein	ja	
	public	Berät das Unternehmen Kunden der Branche: Öffentliche Verwaltung?	nein	ja	
	manufact	Berät das Unternehmen Kunden der Branche: Verarbeitendes Gewerbe/ Industrie?	nein	ja	
	financial	Berät das Unternehmen Kunden der Branche: Finanzdienstleister?	nein	ja	
	others	Berät das Unternehmen Kunden der Branche: Sonstige?	nein	ja	Verbände, Immobilienwirtschaft, Bau, "Dienstleistungen", Universitäten, Logistik, Messen, Beratungsindustrie / Professional Services, Privatpersonen, Rohstoffgewinnung, Eventmanagement, Erfinder, Kanzleien

Internationality	Publications	Veröffentlicht das Unternehmen Publikationen, Reports, Studien auf der Homepage? (im Sinne des Transfers von im Unternehmen generiertem Wissen, kein Infomaterial zum Unternehmen)	nein	ja
	Home page language	Ist die Seite in englischer und deutscher Sprache verfügbar?	nein	ja
	Service international	Werden die Services des Unternehmens auch im Ausland angeboten? Wirbt das Unternehmen damit, dass die angebotenen Beratungsleistungen auch international erbracht werden?	nein	ja
	Origin	Ist der Hauptsitz des Unternehmens in Deutschland? (aus Hoppenstedt Datenbank)	nein	ja
	international offices	Anzahl der Offices international (Klassen 0=keine, 1=1, 2=2-10, 3=10-25, 4=mehr als 25)	0=keine	1=1, 2=2-10,
Career	Career	Gibt es Unterseiten die sich vornehmlich mit Recruiting, Karriere, etc. befassen?	nein	ja
	Business skills	Wird explizit ein Studium mit wirtschaftswissenschaftlichem Hintergrund gefordert/erwünscht (BWL, VWL, Wirtschftsingenieur, - informatik)?	nein	ja
	Technical skills	Werden ausdrücklich Bewerber mit technischen, IT-lastige Studiengänge (Ingenieure, Maschinenbau, Informatik, etc.) angesprochen?	nein	ja
	Science skills	Werden Bewerber mit naturwissenschaftlichen Studiengängen (Biologie, Physik, Medizin, etc.) angesprochen/nicht ausgeschlossen?	nein	ja
	Entrepreneurial sp	Sind unternehmerischer Geist, Managementfähigkeiten, hohes Engagement, Eigenverantwortung bei potenziellen Mitarbeitern ausdrücklich gefordert?	nein	ja
	Work experience	Wird vorhandene Berufserfahrung ausdrücklich als Voraussetzung zum Einstieg (kein Praktikum) in das Beratungsunternehmn gefordert?	nein	ja

Usability/ Quality of the websites	searchbox	Stellt die Homepage eine "Search box" zur Verfügung? Diese hilft dabei Inhalte der Seite zu finden und ist von allen Unterseiten aus zugänglich!	nein	ja	
	breadcrumb	Verfügt die Homepage über einen sog. "breadcrumb trail" (Gliederungsebene der jeweiligen Unterseiten werden stets angezeigt)?	nein	ja	
	homebutton	Existiert ein Home-Button bzw. Verlinkung im Firmenlogo über die man jederzeit zur Startseite zurückkehren kann?	nein	ja	
	homequality	Wie ist insgesamt die Qualität der Homepage hinsichtlich Übersichtlichkeit, Struktur, Darstellung zu bewerten?	.	Skala 1=unübersichtlich, 5=sehr gut strukturiert, anspruchsvolle Darstellung	abwertend: Zu starke / schwache Aggregation der Menüpunkte; Navigationselemente verstreut; keine Gliederung; unübersichtliche Verschachtelung; Redundante Gliederungspunkte; Rechtschreibfehler / unprofessionelles Auftreten aufwertend: intuitive Navigation; konsistente Erscheinung; strukturierte Darstellung; gute Lesbarkeit; Gesamteindruck positiv auch: 1 = nicht navigierbar / unzumutbar; 5 = intuitiv und ansprechend
	homecontent	Wie reichhaltig ist der Infomationsgehalt der Homepage?	.	Skala 1=geringer Informationsgehalt, 5=sehr reichhaltige Informationen	abwertend: Buzzwords / wiederholt leere Phrasen, Unvollständigkeit, unnütze Informationen, etc. aufwertend: Publikationen; Hintergrundinformationen; Komplette Beschreibung von Firma, Beratungsansatz, Lösung; Stimmigkeit des Informationsgehaltes mit Seitenumfang (d.h., kleinere Firmen mit weniger Seiten überladen diese nicht mit Überflüssigem)